THE COMPLETE
VEGETARIAN
COOKBOOK

THE COMPLETE
VEGETARIAN
COOKBOOK

ANNE MARSHALL

Charles E. Tuttle Company, Inc.
Boston • Rutland, Vermont • Tokyo

= Egg   = Milk

This book is dedicated to my daughter Natasha,
so that she and her peers may inherit a world of love,
harmony and sustainable development.

First published in the United States in 1993 by
Charles E. Tuttle Company Inc., of Rutland, Vermont & Tokyo, Japan,
with editorial offices at 77 Central Street, Boston, Massachusetts 02109.

ISBN   0-8048-1974-2

Library of Congress Catalog Card Number available at the Library of Congress

Originated by Lansdowne
Level 5, 70 George Street, Sydney NSW 2000, Australia

Printed in Singapore

Page 2: Cauliflower and broccoli au gratin, p.96
Page 6: Tapenade stuffed squash (top), p.36; Samosas (front), p.44
Page 11: Five bean soup and cornbread, p.77
Page 14: Corn and egg soup, p.80; Chinese noodle soup, p.81
Page 18/19: Hummus tahina (left), p.264; Guacamole (top right), p.264;
Warm sunflower and caper dip (front), p.266

CONTENTS

INTRODUCTION

As the author of this vegetarian cookery book, I think it is both important and interesting for the reader to know 'where I am coming from'.

I was led into a vegetarian diet and vegetarian cookery by my teenage daughter who, for humanitarian reasons, first declined to eat red meat and a year later began declining chicken as well. Because of my long involvement with and love of good food, I was determined to take up the challenge of creating a nutritionally well-balanced, yet tasty and delicious, vegetarian diet for us, instead of passing off my responsibilities by directing her to help herself to the cheese in the refrigerator!

My daughter is a lacto-ovo-vegetarian, which means she enjoys dairy foods and eggs in her diet, as well as legumes, grains, nuts and seeds. While the lacto-ovo-vegetarian diet gave me a bigger repertoire of ingredients to work with than those available in a vegan diet, where all foods of animal origin are avoided, it still presented a challenge to include sufficient complete protein, iron, calcium, zinc and vitamins in the daily menu. All these nutrients are very important in a vegetarian diet, particularly in that of a growing teenager.

Another challenging factor was that the development of good taste in food is immensely important to me, for it adds greatly to the social side of sitting down to enjoy a meal with family and friends. This became an amusing issue during consultations with nutritionists and other friends on the contents of this book. While we agreed on most of the recipes, at times I've had to negotiate with my nutrition consultant in order to retain the delicious ingredients in some of the richer recipes, while she took care of nutritive value! I believe that food in a vegetarian cookbook must look good and taste good (just like any other cookbook), as well as be a vehicle for valuable nutrients.

As a working mother, it has always been necessary for me to be able to produce an evening meal very quickly, within a limit of half an hour whenever possible, in order to have some quality time with my family and valuable time for personal relaxation, professional commitments and social engagements. You will find that many of the recipes in this book can be prepared very quickly and with basic skills. Others can be prepared ahead of serving time. Leave the more complicated ones to prepare and enjoy at the weekend or during vacation time.

Finally, there sometimes are experiences in your life which make you stop and think, and they become a turning point. I had such an experience a few years ago. At the time it was disturbing and left me feeling disempowered, but this is now partly resolved by my involvement with and promotion of a vegetarian diet. As a delegate at an international conference in the United States, I listened to a speaker describe her personal experiences of the silent tragedy of the third world where helpless babies and infants are dying at the rate of six every minute. This silent tragedy continues even as I write and you read these words. It is due mainly to third world malnutrition, while the Western world luxuriates in overabundance in the nearest supermarket.

My eyes were opened further when, while researching for an article on legumes, I discovered the vast difference between protein production per acre (or hectare) from cattle and sheep and protein production per acre (or hectare) from nuts and legumes. I'll expand on this later when I discuss the food chain. At that time my thoughts raced to question why no one with political power and food production knowledge was doing anything about this totally imbalanced situation. Now I no longer feel powerless because I understand how I can assist in reducing this imbalance by changing my eating pattern.

In short, vegetarians eat low on the food chain, from the first level of plant protein and, in global terms, more people can be fed if more of us eat low on the food chain. If we are ever to attain sustainable farming and ecologically sustainable development on the planet earth, we must be more responsible at our own personal level. We can all consciously contribute to a better world in our own small way. Eating a vegetarian diet has therefore become preferable to me.

So I now say thank you to my daughter for leading me along this path and for helping to make it possible for me to enjoy creating this book, a collection of well-balanced, nourishing vegetarian recipes that look good and taste delicious.

VEGETARIANISM

Vegetarianism is on the increase in the Western world, especially among young adults according to the latest surveys. A vegetarian is 'one who abstains from the use of flesh, fish and fowl as food, with or without the addition of eggs and dairy produce, and whose diet includes roots, leafy vegetables, cereals, seeds, fruit and nuts' according to the dictionary.

Why become a vegetarian?

People choose to become vegetarian for a variety of reasons, ranging from humanitarian, ecological and health concerns to religious, social and economical reasons.

Many people who have a love and respect for life in all its forms, for anything that walks, flies, swims, breathes and has eyes, consciously avoid any product that has been obtained by suffering and pain to animals, fowl and fish or by killing another life form. This sometimes extends to eggs from battery hens, fertile eggs and to dairy products.

On ecological grounds, many people prefer to eat plant protein rather than animal protein as it is much more economical in land usage, water requirements and in the time and processing taken to produce it. The production of meat is expensive, and some say immoral in a global context, considering that precious legumes which could go towards feeding people are used to fatten beef cattle for human consumption in affluent countries. It takes seven pounds (three-and-a-half kilograms) of soy beans and grain and 352 fluid ounces (eleven litres) of water to yield one pound (half a kilo) of beef steak on a dinner plate. The ecological scales of planet earth are very lopsided. Four-fifths of the world's agricultural land is used for feeding animals, yet only one-fifth is used for feeding humans directly; and we must not forget that ecologically precious rainforests are cleared to create more land for raising more cattle. So vegetarians choose to eat low on the food chain. This term 'food chain' refers to the transfer of food energy from the source in plants through various organisms.

The first level of the food chain is closest to the primary production of plant protein and, by eating low on the food chain, more people can be fed in global terms.

The decision to become a vegetarian is now frequently made by people who are concerned about restoring or maintaining their good health and about the safety of the food they put into their bodies. A vegetarian diet is a healthy diet because it is lower, sometimes negligible, in animal fats and cholesterol and ensures an adequate intake of soluble and insoluble fiber and complex carbohydrates. Wholefoods form the basis of the vegetarian diet in preference to processed foods and this means you avoid the high levels of salt, sugar and 'hidden' fat often present in such foods. We now have many nutritional studies illustrating that vegetarians generally have better health, less coronary heart disease, less high blood pressure, cancer, diabetes, obesity, arthritis, rheumatism, constipation, and kidney disorders. Research also claims that vegetarianism can enrich the quality of our lives and helps us cope with stress.

It is interesting to note that the diet described in Genesis is the best possible diet. It consists of fruit, grains, nuts and vegetables. Similarly, the Hindus and Buddhists do not eat meat as it is in conflict with their belief in the perpetuation of life. It is not surprising therefore that India is well known among chefs and cooks as the home of vegetarian cooking.

Children born into a vegetarian family are brought up socially on a vegetarian diet. It becomes the diet they are familiar with and so they grow into it and the lifestyle that often goes with it.

Finally, there is a good economical reason to choose a vegetarian diet. Legumes, wholegrain cereals and nuts, which are the staple ingredients for a healthy vegetarian diet, are usually less expensive than meat, though some of them can take longer to prepare.

Whatever your reason for choosing vegetarian food, a well-balanced vegetarian diet that provides all the nutrients necessary for your health, development and well-being is very important.

Types of vegetarian diet

Vegetarians are categorized according to the kind of foods they eat.

• The vegan diet is a vegetarian diet which consists of food of plant origin only and no animal products whatsoever. It is based on a wide variety of legumes, grains and cereals, nuts and seeds with plenty of vegetables and fruit.

• The lacto-vegetarian diet supplements the vegan diet with dairy products, that is milk, yogurt, buttermilk, cheese, cream, butter and ghee.

• The lacto-ovo-vegetarian diet supplements the vegan diet with dairy products and eggs, usually free-range eggs.

It is easier to create nutritionally well-balanced meals in a lacto-ovo-vegetarian diet than in the more restrictive vegan diet, but vegetarians of each kind can create healthy meals if they plan their menu carefully and conscientiously.

It is very important that your vegetarian diet provide you with sufficient protein, iron, zinc and vitamins. Sufficient calcium, a nutrient found in milk and other dairy products, is also important in the vegetarian diet. An understanding of the correct combination of vegetarian foods can ensure a nutritious well-balanced diet for vegetarians of both sexes and all ages.

Protein in the vegetarian diet

'Where do I get my protein from?' and 'Am I getting enough protein?' are the main concerns when people first become vegetarians.

Proteins are made up of chains of basic units called amino acids. There are twenty different amino acids that the body uses to make the protein it needs. These amino acids can be combined in many different ways to make a complete protein. Nine of the amino acids are called essential amino acids because they must be provided by the food we eat, and the remaining eleven amino acids can be manufactured by the body.

Plant protein or vegetable protein foods do not contain all the nine essential amino acids, so they have to be eaten in appropriate combinations in order to make up the complete balance of essential amino acids. This process is called protein complementation and gives you a 'complete protein' dish or meal.

To make a complete protein dish, follow these formulas to ensure you are getting the right balance of essential amino acids.

• Legumes + Grains (e.g. Pea Soup with wholemeal rolls, Nachos, or baked beans on toast)

• Legumes + Dairy Products (e.g. Vegetable Minestrone with parmesan cheese, Curried Spinach and Lentil Tart)

• Grains + Dairy Products (e.g. Pasta Shells with Three Cheeses, Wild Rice Pilaf with Cheese or muesli with milk)

• Nuts and Seeds + Dairy Products (e.g. Broccoli and Cheese Strudel, Mandarin Muesli Cheesecake)

• Legumes + Nuts and Seeds + Green Vegetables (e.g. Chick Pea Dip with celery and cucumber sticks, Bean Sprout and Spinach Salad)

• Grains + Nuts and Seeds + Green Vegetables (e.g. Layered Vegetable and Nut Pie, Cannelloni with Spinach and Pine Nuts, Vegetarian Sandwiches or peanut butter and lettuce sandwich)

As you can see, complete protein meals and snacks can be quite simple and easy to prepare. When the protein sources are combined like this, or even eaten at adjacent meals, they provide the right balance of essential amino acids. Combining foods has become a natural part of many national food cultures, providing staple dishes such as dhal with rice in India and beans with tortillas in Mexico. Just refer to the formulas above when you work out your weekly vegetarian menu plan and shopping list and in no time it will become quite simple and easy to follow. Now let's look closer at the plant proteins available in the vegetarian diet.

LEGUMES

Legumes, also known as pulses, are identified commonly as dried peas, beans and lentils. They provide the staple food of millions throughout the world, along with grains, and are now emerging as a nutritious and versatile food in many delicious dishes. They have the useful capacity to be dried and stored easily for long periods of time. The season for fresh pulses is very short, when peas, broad beans and navy (haricot) beans can be enjoyed while fresh, sweet and tender.

Most legumes are left on the plant to dry out in the sun. Others have to be exposed to sunshine or put in a hopper and dried with blowing warm air.

Legumes are sometimes described as nutritional powerhouses, as they produce a much higher yield of protein per acre (or hectare) as a direct crop, on the first level of the food chain, than that produced by animal foods. Legumes are economical as they provide both nutritional value and quantity for money. They are best stored in air-tight containers such as glass jars.

To prepare them, soak them for 6–8 hours (or overnight) in cold water, drain off the water and boil them in fresh water until tender. This can take from 1–1½ hours according to the type of legume. To speed the process of preparation, soak them in boiling water for 1 hour, then cook them in fresh water in a pressure cooker for a third of the given cooking time. The cooked legumes may be frozen successfully for up to six months in 1 cup quantities, which are good to have on hand. Many legume varieties are available in cans. These are high quality, nutritious products due to the quality control exercised by the processors and they save a lot of time in the preparation of interesting and tasty recipes.

Nutritional value of legumes

All legumes are rich in high quality plant protein, low in fat, have no cholesterol and are a good source of fiber. They contain the important B vitamins, some contain vitamin C, and many minerals, iron, calcium, potassium and phosphorous in particular. The fiber in legumes is the soluble kind which helps reduce cholesterol levels. The protein is incomplete as it does not provide all the essential amino acids, but this is easily overcome, as explained earlier, by combining with another source of plant protein, such as grains, nuts or seeds, to make a complete protein. For example, beans are combined with pasta in a traditional minestrone soup.

What to look for in legumes

Adzuki Beans

Tiny, reddish-brown beans with a cream seam. They are cooked then mashed to a paste and used in Chinese and Japanese buns, sweets and jellies.

Black Beans

Small, almost round black beans with a white seam. Used in Chinese soups and stir-fries.

Black-Eyed Beans

An eye-catching creamy white, kidney shaped bean with a black 'eye' on the edge. Sometimes called black-eye peas and used in soups, casseroles and the 'soul food' of the southern states in the U.S.A.

Black Mexican Turtle Beans

Kidney shaped black beans with a short white seam on the edge. Popular in main course dishes and salads.

Borlotti Beans

Brown-beige, plump, kidney shaped beans with burgundy speckle markings. Used in Italian dishes, soups, casseroles and salads and mashed for a dip.

Broad Beans

Large, broad flat beans ranging from light olive green to brown. Used in casseroles, sauces and salads and chopped or ground in patties.

Butter Beans

Large, broad flat white beans, similar to broad beans. Can be pureed to make a sauce or soup, also used whole in casseroles and salads.

Cannellini Beans

Small white kidney beans, with square ends. Used in soups and salads or processed as baked beans as an alternative to haricot beans.

Chick Peas

Round, rough textured with a point at the top. The larger ones are yellow or white, the smaller ones are brown and dried. Also known as garbanzo beans or peas. Also used in soup, casseroles, patties and salads and ground into flour sometimes known as besan flour.

Lentils

Tiny, round, lens-shaped, split, orange legume and larger, round, lens-shaped, green-brown

legume. Used in soup, patties, pies, pasties and tarts or curried and served as dhal. Popular in Indian cuisine. Brown lentils used for lentil sprouts.

Lima Beans

Large, flat, kidney shaped white beans. Baby lima beans are smaller and light green or white. Used in casseroles and salads.

Mung Beans

Tiny, black and green round-oval beans with a cream stripe on the side. Used for sprouting mung bean sprouts which contain five times more vitamin C than the dry bean.

Navy (Haricot) Beans

Small, white oval beans used in processed baked beans. Also used in soup and casseroles and useful for filling greaseproof paper-lined pastry cases when 'baking blind'.

Pigeon Peas

Small, round cream or brown peas. Used in salad or ground for patties and vegetarian loaves.

Pinto Beans

Beige oval beans with brown speckles. Popular in vegetarian chili dishes and in other Mexican dishes.

Red Kidney Beans

Kidney shaped, shiny, dark red brown beans. Popular in Mexican dishes and dips. Also used in soup and salads.

Soy Bean (Soya Bean)

Small, very hard, beige, oval beans. Weight for weight, they are richer in protein than most other plant foods, containing approximately 40 percent protein, which is twice as much as other legumes. Used in soup and casseroles. Rolled beans become soy grits and ground beans become soy flour, both used in baked products. An ever increasing range of ingredients have been developed from soy beans, such as tofu, tempeh, okara, soy sauce, soy drinks, soy compound, and soy cheese.

Split Peas

Split whole yellow or green dried peas. Popular in soup or patties.

Whole Dried Peas

Round, dimpled brown or blue-green dried peas. The brown pea is split to produce the yellow split pea, the blue-green pea is split to produce the green split pea. Used in soup and sauces.

Soy Bean Products

Tofu, tempeh, okara, soy sauce, soy drinks and compound, soy cheese, and textured vegetable protein, or T.V.P., are all made from soy beans. Used as a protein staple in China and Japan, the soy bean is one of the oldest crops grown.

Tofu

Also known as bean curd. It is the white soy bean curd made from soy 'milk'. Soy beans are cooked, then mashed, then strained, producing a soy 'milk'. This liquid is curdled which causes the protein of the soy bean to coagulate and form a curd. It is lightly pressed to produce silken tofu, pressed to give soft tofu and firmly pressed to produce firm tofu. All types are usually found in the refrigerator cabinet in leading health food stores. Plastic wrapped and canned firm tofu is also now available in supermarkets. Firm tofu is good for tofu balls, kebabs and burgers. Soft tofu is good in loaves and stir-fries. Silken tofu is ideal for ice creams, chocolates, sauces and dressings.

Tempeh

Tempeh is fermented soy beans. It is good for marinating and adding to stir-fries, and it tastes good in curries. The black marks on it do not affect its quality. It is also found in the refrigerator cabinet in leading health food stores. It is a good source of vitamin B12.

Okara

Okara is the soy pulp left after the soy 'milk' is strained off for tofu. It is used in soup, casseroles, bread and stir-fries.

Soy Drink

Often called soy 'milk', this drink has been made in China for hundreds of years. The soy beans are soaked, then ground, water is added and brought to the boil and simmered for 10 minutes before straining off the soy drink. It has a pleasant nut-like taste, is free of sugar and cholesterol and is low in saturated fat, so is very useful in a vegetarian diet in both savory and sweet dishes.

Soy Compound

Soy compound is the dehydrated form of soy drink.

Soy Cheese

Soy cheese is one of the latest soy bean products to be developed. Low in fat and free of cholesterol and enhanced with the addition of some delicious seasonings, such as onion, garlic, herbs, black pepper and chili. It is a very tasty and useful vegetarian product. Look for it in your health food shop, in the refrigerator cabinet.

Textured Vegetable Protein

Also know as T.V.P. and is made from soy flour. It is a dried vegetable protein and in its character somewhat resembles meat. It can be reconstituted in hot water and used in casseroles, loaves and burgers. It is often used as a protein extender in commercially prepared non-vegetarian foods.

Soy Sauce

Soy sauce is a popular liquid condiment made from soy beans.

GRAINS

Grains, also known as cereals, are humanity's basic food supply. The global population is enormously dependent on grains. Cereal grains were first cultivated from wild grasses by ancient tribes and became known as the 'seeds of civilization'. Cereal grains later became the chief crop of agriculture as it developed and were soon the staple food of the healthy peasant diet.

Grains are 'the staff of life' for half the world's population and are produced in many forms. Most grains may be stored in air-tight glass jars, but in hot climates it is advisable to store grains, particularly when ground, in the refrigerator.

Nutritional value of Grains

Grains are rich in complex carbohydrate and are a good source of insoluble or dietary fiber, plant protein, vitamins of the B complex group and vitamin E which is found only in the germ, also the minerals iron with small amounts of potassium, calcium, zinc, magnesium, manganese and copper.

Wheat, rye, barley and oats are unique cereals because they are the only ones which contain sufficient gluten, the protein which is necessary for the rising of the dough when making leavened bread. Corn contains a small percentage of gluten.

Grains provide filling, sustaining food but their protein is incomplete. However, by combining grains with legumes, nuts and seeds and dairy products, you can have a complete protein meal. For example, serve wholewheat (wholemeal) bread rolls with lentil soup, combine rice with ground nuts and seeds in rice balls and serve pasta with a cheese sauce.

Grains are low in sugar, sodium and fat, which is mainly polyunsaturated, and do not contain cholesterol.

Wholegrain cereals are much more nutritious than refined cereals. A cereal grain consists of three parts. The inner part is the germ, the embryo or 'growing point', of the plant, from which the new shoots and roots emerge. The germ contains protein, oils, thiamin and vitamin E. The endosperm surrounds the germ and is made up of carbohydrate and protein. The outer layer of protective husk is rich in minerals, B vitamins, riboflavin, niacin and thiamin, important for energy release, and this is where bran is extracted from. Wholegrain cereal products, such as flour and bread, are made of the whole cereal grain and therefore contain all of its nutrients. Refined cereals, such as white flour and white bread, are made of the endosperm with only a small addition of the germ and the husk, so they contain less nutrients than wholegrain cereals.

What to look for in grains
Barley

A golden-hued grain, similar in appearance to a wheat grain. It had been superseded as a food for

many years because it takes a long time to cook and is used mainly in brewing. However, recent technology to pre-steam barley means it can now be cooked in twenty minutes, making it more convenient to use in recipes. Also rolled into flakes for muesli and ground into flour for baked products. Pearl barley is the polished grain obtained after removing the husk or bran and is popular in milk puddings and soup. The barley husk is used to produce barley bran which may assist in lowering blood cholesterol levels.

Buckwheat

A small grain, caramel in appearance, which is not a true grain but the fruit of a herbaceous plant. The grains are roasted before cooking then cooked like rice. Buckwheat can be used in soup, stuffings, porridge and baked products. Also ground into flour which is used to make pancakes called blini and Japanese noodles called soba.

Corn/Maize

An large dry orange grain. Fresh corn on the cob can be eaten as a vegetable. Popcorn is a variety of corn with a very hard endosperm which expands and pops when heated. Another variety is ground into meal to make well-known 'cornflakes' and is also used to make cornbread, tortillas and corn chips.

Millet

A tiny, round, fragile yellow grain, popular in Africa and Asia. It can be added to soup, casseroles, salads and used in main course dishes like rice. Also rolled into flakes for muesli and used in crumble toppings.

Oats

A golden grain which is known as a groat and takes a long time to cook. More commonly used as rolled oat flakes in porridge oats and oatmeal, muesli and cookies. Oats can be used for binding and coating. Steel cut oats are used in baked products. The oat husk is used to produce oat bran.

Rye

A dark brown grain or groat, similar in shape and size to brown rice, which is used in rye bread.

Rolled rye flakes are used in muesli. The whole rye grain is ground into dark rye flour, husked rye grains are ground into light rye flour. Both are used like wheat flour in bread and baked products and are popular in Russian pancakes, or 'blini'.

Rice

Rice comes in many varieties. Brown rice looks similar in size, shape and shading to wheat grains. Long-grain rice is longer, thinner and white as a lot of the rice grain, with important nutrients, is lost by milling. Long-grain rice remains separate when cooked. Short-grain rice is shorter, rounder and white, also due to the milling. Short-grain rice is sticky when cooked. Rice, brown and white, can be used in pilafs, risottos and many other main course dishes. Wild rice is not a grain but the seed of a wild grass. It is longer and thinner than brown rice, black, and sold unpolished. It is used as an accompaniment or in stuffing. Rice is also rolled to form flakes and puffed to make breakfast cereals and rice cakes. Brown and white rice is ground into flour which is used in desserts and cookies.

Triticale

A long, slim, dark brown grain, similar to a wheat grain. It is a wheat-rye hybrid. The durum wheat-rye cross is found in health food stores and can be used in baked goods. It can be rolled to make flakes for muesli. Triticale resembles rye flour as it has a lower gluten content than wheat flour.

Wheat

Wheat comes in many forms as it is the base of many foods, including flour, bread, pasta, noodles and breakfast cereals.

The wheat grain is hard and caramel in appearance. It is lightly rolled to make cracked wheat or kibbled wheat, which can be used like rice. It is hulled, steamed, baked then cracked to make bulghur wheat which is popular in tabbouleh. It is heavily rolled to make wheat flakes which are used in muesli.

The germ of the wheat grain is rolled to make wheatgerm and the outer husk of the grain is used to make wheat bran. Both can be added to muesli, crumble toppings and main course dishes.

The whole grain of wheat is ground to produce wholewheat (wholemeal) flour, whereas white flour is ground wheat (endosperm only) with most of the germ and bran removed.

Pasta is made from ground durum wheat which is a very hard grain.

Semolina is the meal ground from the endosperm of durum wheat and is used to make pasta, gnocchi and milk puddings.

Couscous, the basis of many North African dishes, is made from semolina grains coated with wheat flour.

NUTS AND SEEDS

Nuts are dry, hard shelled fruits with a single seed or kernel. They have been gathered from trees in the wild for centuries and are valued as a concentrated food which is easy to store in its own natural packaging. Most nuts today are cultivated but some, like the Brazil nut, remain native nuts, while others are emerging as native 'bush food', such as the Australian bunya bunya nut. Nuts are now being used to make delicious nut butters and pâtés, as well as oils, which adds enormously to their versatility of use in a vegetarian diet.

The peanut, sometimes called groundnut is, however, not a true nut but comes from a leguminous plant. It is covered by a soft pod which grows on long tendrils below ground.

Nuts provide a much higher yield of protein per acre (or hectare), as a direct plant crop on the first level of the food chain, than that produced by animal foods. They keep well stored in their shells. Once shelled, some have to be blanched to remove their skin and some are roasted to enhance their taste. Once shelled, nuts should be stored in the refrigerator to prevent their fat content from turning rancid.

Seeds are found in the fruits of plants. The seeds commonly eaten in a vegetarian diet are sunflower seeds (kernels), pumpkin seeds, often called pepitas, sesame seeds, mustard seeds, poppy seeds and linseeds. Seeds should be stored in air-tight glass jars.

Nuts and seeds feature in many traditional cuisines and add great variety as well as very good nutritional value to a vegetarian diet.

Nutritional value of nuts and seeds

Nuts and seeds are high plant protein foods. Peanuts have the highest protein content of any nut and, along with almonds and American black walnuts, they have a higher percentage of protein than lean beef. The protein does not provide all the essential amino acids, but when nuts (and seeds) are combined with legumes or grains the proteins complement each other giving a complete protein. Nuts have a high fat content, which is mainly monounsaturated and polyunsaturated, except for coconuts, where 80 percent of the fat is saturated. Macadamia nuts have the highest fat content of all nuts. Nuts and seeds are a good source of iron and zinc and are also a source of dietary fiber, vitamins, other minerals and carbohydrates. Seeds are also a good source of calcium.

What to look for in nuts

Almonds

A long, flat, oval, smooth, off-white nut with a pointed end, in a brown skin, in a pitted, light brown shell. The skin can be removed by blanching. Available in the shell, in the skin, blanched, slivered, flaked and ground. Ground almonds are used to make almond paste, marzipan and almond butter. Also used for almond oil.

Brazil Nuts

A large, three-sided long hard off-white nut with a dark brown skin, in a tough, angular, dull brown shell. The nuts cling together in a round, like the segments of an orange, in a very hard outer shell and grow wild in the Amazon jungle. The nut's skin can be removed by blanching. They are used whole in fruit cakes, and confectionery, chopped in savory dishes and ground in nut butter.

Bunya Nuts

Also known as the bunya bunya pine nut. A long, cone shaped, creamy white nut with a brown skin and a thin, woody brown shell. Can be eaten raw but usually boiled before use like the chestnut, and used in savory and sweet dishes.

Candle Nuts

A round, off-white nut, similar to a macadamia nut. One or two nuts are enclosed in a round, flattened, light black shell. Used mainly in Asian cuisine.

Cashew Nuts

A kidney shaped, creamy brown nut, usually sold pre-shelled as the shell contains a caustic oil. Popular as a snack, used in main courses and made into nut butter.

Chestnuts

A large, round, dark white nut with a point at the top and a smooth, thin, reddish brown shell. Must be shelled and cooked or toasted before use. Slit the shell before cooking by boiling or roasting in the oven. Popular roasted in red hot coals as a snack. Used in main course and sweet dishes and made into marrons glacé and crème de marrons.

Coconuts

A very large, heavy, brown fibrous covered, brown shelled nut with a thick lining of white soft flesh and liquid (thin coconut milk) inside. On ripening, the white flesh hardens and most of the liquid is absorbed leaving the nut hollow. The soft white flesh is used in main course and sweet dishes and drinks and processed to make coconut milk and coconut cream. The hard white flesh is grated and infused to make coconut milk. Hard coconut is also desiccated, flaked, shredded and compressed into blocks. Liquid coconut oil is made and is also solidified and is used for confectionery and Asian cuisine.

Hazelnuts

Also known as filberts. A small, round, white nut with a point at the top, with a brown skin in a hard, smooth brown shell with a caramel mark at the base. Hazelnuts are blanched and often roasted to enhance their taste. Popular in sweet dishes but can also be used in main courses.

Macadamia Nuts

A round, creamy white nut in an extremely hard brown shell so usually sold shelled. Can be used as a snack, in main course and sweet dishes, in confectionery, for nut butter and macadamia nut oil.

Peanuts

Also called groundnuts and monkey nuts. Two oval, creamy nuts in brown skins are encased in a soft, creamy brown, wrinkled shell. The shells are in fact pods of a leguminous plant which grows underground. The shell and skin can be removed with the fingers. Popular as a snack, in main course and sweet dishes. Used to make peanut oil and peanut butter.

Pecans

A long, ridged, oval nut in two segments, similar to a walnut in shape, enclosed in a hard, red flecked, brown shell. Available in halves or chopped. Can be used in meals and sweet dishes.

Pine Nuts

Also known as pignolias. A small, soft, off-white kernel from the core of some species of pine trees. Popular in main course and sweet dishes.

Pistachio Nuts

A small, bright green, soft nut in a pinkish brown, wrinkled skin in a brittle, creamy shell, often split open. A popular snack in the Mediterranean and the Middle East. Used in meals, sweet dishes and in nut butter.

Walnuts

An oval, ridged nut formed in two segments, similar to a pecan, in a hard, creamy brown shell, also formed in two segments. Sold in halves and chopped. Used in sweet and main course dishes, available pickled and used for walnut oil.

What to look for in seeds

Linseeds

Tiny, dark orange seeds of the flax plant, also ground into linseed meal. Used in bread and muesli for their protein and fiber value.

Mustard Seeds

Tiny, dark brown or cream seeds of the mustard plant. Used in curries, sauces and wholegrain mustard.

Pepitas

Also known as pumpkin kernels. A dull green flat oval kernel in a flat oval white shell. Used as a snack, in main course dishes and health bars (slices).

Poppy Seeds

Tiny, round black seed of the poppy plant. Used whole or crushed in curries and in baked products.

Sesame Seeds

Tiny, flat round white seed of the sesame plant. Used raw or toasted in meals and sweet dishes, for tahini paste and sesame oil.

Sunflower Seeds

Small, flat oval, beige seed in a fawn and black striped shell. Used raw or roasted, for snacks, in meals and health bars (slices), and for sunflower oil.

VEGETABLES IN THE VEGETARIAN DIET

Vegetables obviously have a very important place in a vegetarian diet. There is a bountiful variety to choose from, at least a different one for every week of the year. Many people declare that they could quite happily turn to vegetarianism once they realise how many good dishes can be made with them. Vegetables can be classified as green leaf, roots and tubers, pods and seeds or fresh legumes, vegetable fruits, bulbs, stalks, shoots and thistles and fungi. Most vegetables should be stored in the refrigerator, but some bulbs, roots, tubers and hard skinned fruits can be stored in a cool well ventilated dry place.

Nutritional value of vegetables

Vegetables have long been the guardians of good health. Mothers and grandmothers with little formal knowledge of nutrition have always insisted their children eat up their vegetables. And they're right to do so—one of the simplest ways to improve one's diet is to eat more vegetables. Vegetables are a source of plant protein. If you combine a range of vegetables with dairy products in a lacto-vegetarian diet, you are supplying the body with the right balance of essential amino acids or, in simpler terms, a complete protein.

Vegetables also provide a very useful source of vitamins C, B, A and E, potassium, phosphorus, iron, calcium and zinc and dietary fiber. Dark green leaf vegetables, such as spinach and Swiss chard (or silverbeet), are rich in vitamins A and C and in iron. Broccoli and cabbage are rich in calcium and vitamin B. Carrots are a good source of vitamin A, potatoes a good source of vitamin C. Mushrooms are an invaluable source of vitamin B12 in the vegetarian diet which helps prevent anaemia. The pods and seeds, or fresh legumes group, is an important source of plant protein, zinc and vitamin B.

Vegetables have a negligible fat content and a high water content, so they are ideal for a weight-reduction diet.

What to look for in vegetables

Green Leaf

Spinach, cabbage, Brussels sprouts, broccoli and lettuce are all important leaf vegetables. Lettuce, endive and witlof (chicory) are usually used raw in salads but can also be lightly cooked. Spinach and cabbage, often cooked, can also be used raw in salads! Sorrel, Swiss chard, silverbeet, kale and vine leaves are also green leaf vegetables. There is also a big variety of Chinese green vegetables available including bok choy, Chinese broccoli and Chinese cabbage.

Whatever the variety or size of leaf, a glossy green leaf is always a good indication of freshness.

Roots and Tubers

Roots and tubers are grown underground. Roots are the enlarged fleshy end root of a plant, such as a carrot. Tubers are the enlarged part from which the plant stalks and roots develop, such as a potato. Roots and tubers are regarded as staple vegetables because most of them are available all year round and they store well. They include turnips, parsnips, beets (beetroot), rutabaga (swede), kohlrabi, celeriac, sweet potatoes, Jerusalem artichokes, salsify and scarzonera. Choose firm, dry roots and tubers, free of lumps of dirt.

Pods and Seeds/fresh Legumes

The French green bean is the most popular edible pod, the green pea the most popular edible seed. Other pods are wax beans, runner beans, navy (haricot) beans, snow peas (mange-tout) and sugar snap peas. Other seeds are broad beans and sweet corn. Choose young crisp pods and seeds for the best taste.

Vegetable Fruits

Vegetable fruits develop from flowering plants. They include the attractive collection of eggplant (aubergine), red, green, butter yellow and now purple bell peppers (capsicum), cucumber, okra, tomatoes and the big squash family of zucchini (courgette), choko (chayote), squash, marrow and pumpkins. These versatile vegetables are used in many national traditional dishes. Big does not necessarily mean beautiful in this group, but natural ripening on the plant or vine does contribute to a good natural taste. Choose firm, undamaged vegetables.

Bulbs

Bulbs are short underground stems with fleshy overlapping leaves. The most well known are onions and garlic, essential for developing an enticing taste in lovingly prepared food. This group also includes the popular leeks, scallions (spring onions), French shallots and chives. Choose firm, shiny undamaged bulbs.

Stalks, Shoots and Thistles

Stalks and shoots come from plants in which the stalk and stems become thick. They include celery, fennel bulb, cardoon (popular in Italy), seakale and asparagus. They are valued for their crisp, refreshing texture and many may be enjoyed raw. The globe artichoke is a thistle, valued for its tender, delicious heart. A firm texture is a good indication of freshness in this group.

Fungi

Fungi covers edible mushrooms. Once gathered wild, most varieties of mushroom are cultivated now and are available all year round. The varieties include champignons, morels, chanterelles, caps and truffles.

DAIRY PRODUCTS

Dairy products include milk, cheeses, yogurt, cream, sour cream, butter, ghee, buttermilk and ice cream. They play an important role in a healthy lacto-vegetarian diet. All dairy products should be stored in the refrigerator.

Nutritional value of dairy products

Milk is important as a source of animal protein supplying all the amino acids essential for health. Milk protein supplements cereal protein when eaten together. Milk is also an important source of calcium, often low in a vegetarian diet, and a valuable source of phosphorus, potassium and vitamins A, D and B.

Cheese is a concentrated form of milk so is a valuable source of protein and calcium, phosphorus, potassium, vitamins A and D.

Yogurt has the same nutrients as milk but slightly more concentrated.

Cream has a high fat content, contains a little calcium and small quantities of vitamins A, D, E and the B complex vitamins.

Sour cream has a similar nutritive value to cream.

Butter also has a high fat content and is a good source of vitamins A and D and some E.

Ghee is nutritionally similar to butter.

Buttermilk has a similar nutritional value to yogurt.

Ice cream ingredient labels should be studied to assess their nutritive value. They are usually a mixture of frozen milk, cream, sugar, eggs, fruits and nuts, cocoa and coffee.

HORS D'OEUVRES

The expression 'hors d'oeuvre' means 'outside of the course'. It is an additional dish served to stimulate the appetite at the beginning of a meal, and so it is also known as the 'appetizer' or the 'first course'. We often order an hors d'oeuvre when we're enjoying a meal in a restaurant, but there are also occasions when you'll want to serve them at home.

There's a wonderful selection of vegetarian hors d'oeuvre recipes here for you to choose from, and hopefully you will be inspired to serve them when you are entertaining. When planning your menu, remember that the hors d'oeuvres should be light and delicate, especially if you want to enjoy a delicious dessert after the main course, but also give a little extra thought to how they may nutritionally complement a well-balanced meal.

Many of the recipes are complete protein dishes: Three Salads for Fall (Autumn), Smoked Cheese and Berry Salad, Andalusian Asparagus Tapas, Red Curried Couscous in Lettuce Rolls, Stuffed Zucchini Flowers, Stuffed Figs, Mushrooms with Macadamia Sparkling Sauce, Eggplant Puftaloons, Creamy Eggs on Pumpernickel and Creamed Eggs with Spinach Mango Chutney. These contain animal protein in the form of eggs or cheese, often in an exciting variety such as smoked, tangy feta and creamy quark. These are ovo-vegetarian, lacto-vegetarian or lacto-ovo-vegetarian dishes, as indicated by the egg and milk symbols at the top of the recipes.

The vegan recipes contain plant protein only. Vegetables and salads are complemented by nuts in Three Salads for Spring, Tapenade Stuffed Squash and Salade Baumanière and by a legume in Peperonata with Beans. Choose a legume or cereal based main course to follow these hors d'oeuvre for a complete protein meal.

Many of the recipes are vitamin-packed dishes. Mushroom and Pistachio Terrine and Spring Rolls are both rich in vitamins B and C, and Tropical Melon Duet and Grelette Sauce are rich in vitamin C. And Vegetable Pakoras, Samosas and Felafel are all good sources of iron and dietary fiber.

Many of the recipes are cool, light, and refreshing, while some are hot and spicy and more suitable for cooler weather!

Serve the hors d'oeuvres with imagination, so that they please the eye as well as the palate, and you will be thrilled with the compliments!

Three salads for spring, p.24

THREE SALADS FOR SPRING

SERVES 8

The great chefs of France all have their own version of this dish. This one was inspired by the late Alain Chapel and Louis Outhier.

1.

2 bunches asparagus, trimmed

1 cup (1 punnet) strawberries

1/2 teaspoon horseradish cream

finely grated rind of 1 orange

2 teaspoons orange juice

freshly ground black pepper

2.

1/2 lb (250 g) button mushrooms

8 tablespoons French dressing (page 205)

1 tablespoon chopped parsley or snipped chives

3.

14 oz (440 g) canned artichoke hearts, drained, quartered and thinly sliced

1/4 cup pecans, halved and chopped

8 tablespoons French dressing (page 205)

Salad 1: Trim ends off asparagus spears and trim coarse leaves from stalks. Rinse asparagus in cold water, then place in a plastic bag, loosely bunched, and cook in a microwave oven on High setting for 4–5 minutes, or until tender. Alternatively steam asparagus for 5 minutes until tender-crisp. Hull strawberries and mix to a puree in a blender or food processor, then add horseradish, orange rind, orange juice, and pepper and mix well.

Salad 2: Trim mushroom stalks and brush caps clean. Slice mushrooms thinly and place in a bowl, add dressing and herbs and mix until well coated.

Salad 3: Mix artichokes with pecans and dressing. To assemble salad: Put a portion of salads 1, 2 and 3 on each of 8 plates, beginning with a serving of the asparagus coated with the strawberry sauce, and adding the mushroom and then the artichoke salads.

THREE SALADS FOR FALL (AUTUMN) ♟🏠

SERVES 8

The idea for this salad comes from a Pacific Islander friend. Use English spinach or buy prepared baby spinach leaves.

1.

2 avocados
8 tablespoons French dressing
(page 205)

2.

4 tamarillos
4 tablespoons French dressing
(page 205)
1 tablespoon snipped chives

3.

1 small bunch spinach
8 tablespoons crème fraîche
1 hard-boiled egg
2 tablespoons pine nuts, toasted

Salad 1: Cut avocados in half lengthwise and remove stones, then cut each into quarters and remove skin carefully. Cut each quarter into thin segments.

Salad 2: Slice the top and bottom off each tamarillo then peel skin off neatly using a vegetable peeler. Cut tamarillos into thin round slices.

Salad 3: Pick the good quality tender leaves from the bunch of spinach, wash, drain then shake dry in a clean cloth. Tear spinach leaves into a bowl, add crème fraîche and toss until well coated. Separate egg white from egg yolk. Chop egg white finely and sieve egg yolk.

To assemble salad: Arrange 1 sliced quarter of avocado in a fan shape on a third area of each of 8 individual entree plates. Coat each with 1 tablespoon French dressing.

Arrange 1/2 sliced tamarillo, overlapping the slices, on a third area of each entree plate. Sprinkle each with 2 teaspoons French dressing and 1/2 teaspoon snipped chives.

Place dressed spinach on remaining third of the entree plates, sprinkle with chopped egg white, sieved egg yolk and toasted pinenuts.

SMOKED CHEESE AND BERRY SALAD

SERVES 4

This is a light salad which is good to serve before a rich main course. Fish eaters may like to substitute the smoked cheese with smoked salmon and serve it for Thanksgiving or Christmas dinner.

4 cups mixed salad greens

4 tablespoons blueberries

4 tablespoons raspberries

4 oz (125 g) smoked cheese

1 quantity French dressing (page 205) using light olive oil and raspberry white wine vinegar

Buy the pre-prepared salad greens for speed and convenience. Pick them over and place in a bowl with the berries. Cover and chill until ready to serve. Cut cheese into thin shavings or julienne strips.

To serve, sprinkle dressing over salad greens and berries and toss lightly. Divide salad between 4 plates, sprinkle cheese over the top of each one and serve.

SALADE BAUMANIÈRE

SERVES 8

This is my adaptation of the 'house salad recipe' from the famous Oustau de Baumanière restaurant at Les Baux de Provence in France. Non-vegetarians can add 4 slices prosciutto, cut in julienne strips. Either way, it has proved stunningly popular with my friends and students.

Salad:

1 romaine (cos) lettuce

1/2 cup julienne strips of celery, sliced obliquely

8 button mushrooms, trimmed and thinly sliced

14 oz (440 g) canned artichoke hearts, or hearts of palm, drained, quartered and thinly sliced

1 avocado, peeled, quartered and thinly sliced

8 radishes, thinly sliced

6 teaspoons pine nuts

6 teaspoons slivered almonds

6 tablespoons French dressing (page 205)

Sauce:

1 cup (8 fl oz/250 ml) cream

2 tablespoons lemon juice

pinch of salt

freshly ground black pepper

Salad: Wash lettuce, drain, then shake dry in a clean cloth, chill in refrigerator until crisp.

Tear the lettuce into a chilled salad bowl. Sprinkle remaining ingredients on top in given order.

Finally add French dressing, toss gently and serve immediately accompanied by the sauce.

Sauce: Stir cream together with lemon juice and pepper. Pour into a serving bowl, sprinkle generously with ground pepper.

Pear and pecan salad with tarragon cream (top), p.40; Andalusian asparagus tapas (front), p.28

27

ANDALUSIAN ASPARAGUS TAPAS

SERVES 4

This is a Spanish version of asparagus vinaigrette.

20 thick or 32 thin green asparagus spears, approximately 2 bunches

2 slices wholewheat (wholemeal) bread

4 cloves garlic, crushed

4 tablespoons olive oil

1 tablespoon white wine vinegar

1 teaspoon sweet paprika

pinch of salt

2 hard-boiled eggs, shelled and chopped

Wash asparagus stems and snap off woody ends. Poach in a frying pan of gently boiling water for 5–10 minutes, until tender, or place loosely in a clean plastic food storage bag, twist neck and fold under to seal, then cook in a microwave oven on High setting for 3–5 minutes, until tender. Cooking time varies according to thickness of asparagus stems. Remove and plunge immediately into a bowl of iced water to refresh and retain brightness. Drain well. Trim crusts from bread and rub or process into breadcrumbs. Gently fry breadcrumbs and garlic in olive oil until golden. Add vinegar, paprika and salt and leave to cool. Pour dressing over asparagus, sprinkle eggs over top and serve.

MUSHROOMS VINAIGRETTE

SERVES 12

1 lb (500g) button mushrooms

1 cup (8 fl oz/250 ml) olive oil

4 tablespoons tarragon or basil white wine vinegar

2 teaspoons fine white (caster) sugar

1/2 teaspoon mustard powder

12 grinds black pepper

2 tablespoons chopped gherkin

2 tablespoons chopped parsley

2 tablespoons chopped capers

Trim ends of stalks of mushrooms. Brush mushrooms clean or wipe with a clean, damp cloth and place in a large bowl.

Put olive oil, vinegar, sugar, mustard, pepper and chopped gherkin, parsley and capers into a large screw-top jar and shake well until ingredients are mixed together.

Pour dressing over mushrooms, cover and allow to chill in refrigerator for 1 hour.

Mushrooms Vinaigrette are very appetizing served chilled as part of an antipasto.

Red Curried Couscous in Lettuce Rolls

SERVES 8

Couscous, a wheat specialty of North Africa, shows its versatility when enhanced with the red curry paste of Thailand in this delectable entree.

1 cup (6 oz/175 g) couscous

3/4 cup (6 fl oz/185 ml) boiling vegetable stock

1 tablespoon sunflower oil

1 clove garlic, crushed

1 small leek, thinly sliced

1/2 teaspoon red curry paste

1 teaspoon chopped coriander (cilantro) root

1 tablespoon chopped coriander (cilantro) leaves

finely grated rind of 1 lime

2 teaspoons lime juice

2 tablespoons finely chopped sun-dried red pepper (capsicum)

8 large lettuce leaves

1/2 cup (4 oz/125 g) quark or mascarpone

4 tablespoons light sour cream

Place couscous in a bowl, pour boiling stock over and leave to stand for 3 minutes, stirring occasionally with a fork, until stock is absorbed.

Heat oil and gently fry garlic and leek until soft. Stir in curry paste then couscous, cilantro root and leaves, lime rind and juice and sun-dried red pepper. Stir over a medium heat for 2 minutes then cool.

Meanwhile, blanch lettuce leaves by dipping quickly into boiling water, then wash in iced water to retain freshness. Spread lettuce leaves out on work surface and spoon red curried couscous equally onto each one in a 'cigar' shape. Fold stalk of lettuce over couscous, then fold sides over, and roll up tightly to form a neat cylinder. Make 8 lettuce rolls by this method.

Place in a single layer in a large microwave-safe casserole dish, cover and cook in a microwave oven on High setting for 6–8 minutes until hot. Alternatively, steam the lettuce rolls for 5 minutes until hot.

Mix quark with sour cream. Serve lettuce rolls on 8 individual entree plates each accompanied by a tablespoon of quark mixture.

AVOCADO AND CUCUMBER SORBET

SERVES 8

An unusual tasty sorbet which stimulates those gastric juices and aids the digestion of a rich meal, but also doubles as a delicious appetizer.

2 large avocados

2 cucumbers

1/2 cup (4 fl oz/125 ml) cold water

1 tablespoon white wine tarragon or basil vinegar

1/2 teaspoon salt

1/4 teaspoon white pepper

1 egg white

cherry tomato segments, lime wedges and fresh herbs to garnish

Cut avocados in half, remove stone and peel and place flesh in a blender or food processor. Cut cucumber into quarters lengthwise, remove seeds with a metal spoon and remove skin. Cut cucumber flesh into chunky pieces and add to avocado. Mix avocado and cucumber to a puree, then add water gradually and mix until smooth. Add vinegar, salt and pepper and mix again to combine. Whisk egg white until stiff and fold into mixture.

Place mixture into an ice cream churn and mix according to instructions until a smooth crystal texture is formed. If you do not have a churn, place in a shallow refrigerator container and freeze until crystals have formed almost to the middle. Then take out and whip in a mixer and return to the freezer.

Chill the sorbet in the freezer until ready to serve. It looks attractive served in individual flute-shaped stemmed glasses or pottery goblets and garnished with tomato segments, lime wedges and sprigs of herbs.

Avocado and cucumber sorbet

MUSHROOMS WITH MACADAMIA SPARKLING SAUCE

SERVES 8

Serve this elegant dish as a light first course.

24 medium size mushroom cups

macadamia nut oil for brushing

1/2 cup (4 fl oz/125 ml) sparkling grape juice

6 egg yolks

2 tablespoons light sour cream or creme fraîche

1 teaspoon apple cider vinegar

pinch of white pepper and salt

1 cup (4 oz/125 g) ground macadamia nuts

Remove stalks from mushrooms for later use in a soup or casserole. Wipe mushroom cups clean, then brush with oil and cook in a microwave oven on High setting for 1 minute; or place them with tops uppermost under a broiler (grill) until tender.

Place grape juice, egg yolks, sour cream, vinegar, pepper and salt in the top of a double boiler. Whisk over gently bubbling water, using a wire whisk, until mixture thickens to the consistency of a creamy mousse. Remove from heat. Sprinkle 1 teaspoon ground nuts on each mushroom, coat with 1 tablespoon sauce and sprinkle another 1 teaspoon nuts on top. Place under a hot broiler (grill) for 30 seconds or until golden and hot.

Arrange 3 mushrooms on 8 individual entree plates and garnish with salad greens.

MUSHROOM AND PISTACHIO TERRINE ♀

SERVES 6–8

This looks impressive on a buffet table garnished with ribbons of zucchini (courgette), yellow and green, and yellow tear-drop tomatoes. Or serve for an entree on individual plates with Grelette sauce (page 36) and salad greens.

1 small bunch spinach, stalks trimmed off

1 onion, finely chopped

2 cloves garlic, crushed

1 tablespoon polyunsaturated oil

1/2 lb (8 oz/250 g) mushroom cups, finely chopped

2 tablespoons bran, oat, barley or rice

3 tablespoons chopped parsley

1/2 cup (2 oz/60 g) finely chopped pistachio nuts

4 cups broccoli florets

1 egg white

2 eggs, beaten

1/4 teaspoon ground nutmeg

1 cup (8 fl oz/250 ml) cream or soy drink

salt and pepper

Blanch spinach by plunging into a large pan of boiling water until soft. Drain and refresh immediately by placing in a bowl of iced water, to retain its bright green appearance. Drain spinach well on kitchen paper towels. Line a terrine or loaf tin with spinach leaves, reserving some for the middle layer.

Gently fry onion and garlic in oil until soft. Add mushrooms and cook quickly over a higher heat until darkened. Drain off any excess moisture. Stir in bran, parsley and nuts.

Cook broccoli by steaming or in a microwave oven. Mix broccoli to a coarse textured puree in a blender or food processor.

Whisk egg white until stiff and fold into mushroom mixture. Place into the terrine, spread smooth and cover with more spinach. Mix broccoli puree with remaining ingredients and season to taste with salt and pepper. Spread broccoli mixture level in the terrine and cover with any overhanging spinach leaves. Cover with greased foil and a lid.

Stand in a hot-water bath and bake at 400°F (200°C) for 3/4–1 hour or until firm. Cool before turning out.

Serve terrine warm or chilled.

PEPERONATA
BRAISED PEPPERS, TOMATOES AND ONIONS

SERVES 10–12

This Italian dish may be served hot as an accompaniment to a main course or served cold as antipasto.

1 1/2 tablespoons butter or margarine

3 tablespoons olive oil

1 lb (500 g) onions, thinly sliced

2 lb (1 kg) green and red peppers (capsicum) peeled, seeded and cut into strips

2 lb (1 kg) tomatoes, peeled, seeded and coarsely chopped

1 teaspoon wine vinegar

1/2 teaspoon salt

freshly ground black pepper

1/2 cup cooked red kidney beans

Heat butter and oil in a frying pan over medium heat, add onions and fry, stirring frequently for 10 minutes, until soft and golden.

Stir in peppers, cover and cook over a low heat for 10 minutes. Add tomatoes, vinegar, salt and pepper and cook, covered, for 5 minutes. Remove lid and cook over a high heat for a further 5 minutes, or until almost all liquid is reduced, stirring frequently. Stir in beans then chilli and serve hot.

ARTICHOKES WITH MUSTARD MANGO CHUTNEY

SERVES 4

4 globe artichokes

8 tablespoons natural yogurt

Mustard Mango Chutney:

1 small onion, finely chopped

2 teaspoons mustard seeds

1/4 teaspoon sunflower oil

2 tablespoons sparkling apple juice

2 tablespoons rice wine vinegar

1 tablespoon brown sugar

2 teaspoons wholegrain mustard

1 mango, peeled and coarsely chopped

chives for garnish

Wash artichokes, trim stalks level with leaves, discard tough leaves from base and trim tops level with scissors. Cook by boiling in water with lemon juice or by steaming until tender. Alternatively wrap individually in clear plastic wrap and cook on High setting in a microwave oven for approximately 15 minutes. Keep warm.

Mustard Mango Chutney: Gently fry onion and mustard seeds until onion is soft. Add all remaining ingredients, bring to the boil then cover and simmer for 15 minutes until thick and pulpy. Leave to cool to room temperature.

Serve warm artichokes topped with yogurt, spoon chutney over the top and garnish with chives.

Peperonata (top); Red curried couscous in lettuce rolls (front), p.29

GRELETTE SAUCE

SERVES 6–8

This refreshing homemade tomato sauce was first sampled in a chateau in southwest France. A gracious complement to many vegetarian dishes from terrines to tofu balls, it is well worth the trouble to make.

1 lb (500 g) vine-ripened tomatoes

1/2 cup (4 fl oz/125 ml) fromage blanc (page 208)

1 tablespoon crème fraîche or light sour cream

1 tablespoon ketchup (tomato sauce)

juice of 1 lemon

1/2 teaspoon chopped parsley

1/2 teaspoon chopped tarragon

1/2 teaspoon salt

pinch of white pepper

Blanch tomatoes, cut in half through flower (or circumference) and gently press each half in the palm of your hand and squeeze out excess juice and seeds. Add juice and seeds to a soup or casserole. Cut tomato flesh into tiny dice.

Place fromage blanc in a bowl, add crème fraîche and whisk together. Add all remaining ingredients except tomato and whisk well. Stir in tomatoes and adjust seasoning to taste.

TAPENADE STUFFED SQUASH

SERVES 8

A delightful combination of crunchy refreshing squash and robust black olive filling make these very eye-catching as well as delicious.

12 yellow baby squash

12 green baby squash

Tapenade:

2 tablespoons olive oil

2 cloves garlic, crushed

1/2 cup (2 oz/60 g) crushed salted peanuts

1/2 cup stoneless black olives

2 tablespoons capers

1 tablespoon tomato paste

2 tablespoons parsley sprigs

1 teaspoon lemon juice

freshly ground black pepper

Slice stalks level on squash so that they stand upright. Arrange in a steamer spread out like the hands of a clock, 12 at a time, for 5 minutes. Or cook in a micro-wave oven arranged in the same way on a covered plate, on High setting for 2 minutes. Cool then slice off tops and scoop out soft flesh.

Tapenade: Heat oil and gently fry garlic for 1 minute, add peanuts and stir-fry for 2 minutes. Add to all remaining ingredients and mix to a paste in a food processor or blender. Add pepper to taste. Spoon tapenade neatly into squash.

Arrange 3 stuffed squash per portion on individual entree plates and serve accompanied with salad greens.

TROPICAL MELON DUET

SERVES 8

Choose melons that exude a sweet perfumed aroma from the stem end—this indicates a mature, ripened melon.

1 cantaloupe (rockmelon)

1 honeydew or other green-fleshed melon

juice of 4 limes

1 teaspoon finely chopped ginger

4 tablespoons flaked coconut, toasted

julienne strips of lime rind for garnish

Cut cantaloupe and honeydew in half and remove seeds. Scoop out the flesh, using a melon ball scoop, and place in a bowl. Add lime juice and ginger, cover and chill until serving time.

To serve, spoon into individual dessert dishes, sprinkle coconut on top and garnish with julienne of lime.

FRUIT CURRY

SERVES 6–8

This is a good first course to serve on a hot summer's night or as part of an Indian meal.

1 oz (30 g) solidified coconut oil or polyunsaturated margarine

1 small onion, finely chopped

1 teaspoon ginger root, finely chopped

2 teaspoons curry paste, medium strength

1 cup (8 fl oz/250 ml) vegetable stock

1/2 cup (4 fl oz/125 ml) coconut milk

2 bananas, sliced

juice of 1 lemon

1 peach, peeled and sliced in wedges

1 cup stoneless cherries

1 ripe pear, chopped

2 tablespoons natural yogurt

toasted flaked coconut for garnish

Melt solidified coconut oil and gently fry onion and ginger until onion is soft and transparent. Add curry paste and stir over heat for 1 minute. Add stock and coconut milk and bring to the boil stirring.

Sprinkle bananas with lemon juice. Fold all prepared fruit into the curry sauce and heat through gently.

Serve in individual bowls topped with a teaspoon of yogurt and sprinkled with toasted flaked coconut.

Following page: Stuffed figs (front left), p.40; Tropical melon duet (front right); Smoked cheese and berry salad (top right), p.26

STUFFED FIGS

SERVES 8

Feta cheese is the protein food featured in this delicious Greek-inspired entree.

8 ripe figs

6 1/2 oz (200 g) feta cheese, crumbled

4 tablespoons thinly sliced scallions (spring onions)

8 black olives, stoned and sliced

freshly ground black pepper

Wash and dry figs, cut in half from top to bottom. Scoop out fig seeds and pulp into a bowl. Add all remaining ingredients and mix together. Season to taste with pepper. Spoon mixture back into fig shells. Serve slightly chilled garnished with snow pea sprouts or watercress.

PEAR AND PECAN SALAD WITH TARRAGON CREAM

SERVES 8

1 large egg

2 tablespoons fine white (caster) sugar

3 tablespoons tarragon vinegar

3 fl oz (100 ml) thickened cream

4 pears

juice of 1 lemon

1 small lettuce (possibly mignonette)

1 cup (125 g) pecans, coarsely chopped

Beat egg and sugar together until thoroughly mixed, then gradually beat in vinegar. Pour mixture into the top of a double boiler and heat over simmering water, stirring continuously, until mixture thickens. Remove from heat and allow to cool.

Whip cream until it just begins to thicken then fold it into the tarragon mixture.

Peel pears, cut in half lengthwise and remove the core with a melon ball scoop. Place in a microwave dish, brush with lemon juice then cover and cook on Medium setting for approximately 8 minutes or until pears are tender. Alternatively, poach pears in a large frying pan for 10 minutes or until tender. Stand until warm but do not allow to turn brown.

To serve, place half a pear on a crisp lettuce leaf on 8 individual entree plates and spoon tarragon cream over. Sprinkle pecans on top and serve immediately.

VEGETABLE PAKORAS

SERVES 8

This Indian appetizer or snack uses chick pea (garbanzo bean) flour for the batter. It is available at health food stores and Indian general stores where it is also called besan flour.

Batter:

1 1/2 cups (6 oz/185 g) chick pea flour

1 teaspoon salt

1 tablespoon ground cilantro (coriander)

2 teaspoons ground cumin

1 teaspoon ground turmeric

1 teaspoon garam masala

1/2 teaspoon cayenne pepper

1 1/4-1 3/4 cups (10-14 fl oz/ 300-425 ml) water

1 lb (500 g) mixed prepared vegetables, use cauliflower florets, finger-long pieces of carrot and zucchini (courgette), eggplant (aubergine) cut in 3/4 inch (2 cm) cubes

ghee or vegetable oil for deep frying

Batter: Place the chick pea flour, salt and spices in a mixing bowl. Make a well in the middle; add and mix in sufficient water until it forms a coating batter consistency.

To finish pakoras: Dip vegetable pieces into batter. Deep fry at 350°F (180°C) in batches, for 5 minutes or until golden brown and cooked all the way through. Drain well on kitchen paper towels.

Serve hot or warm. Try complementing with chutney and Yogurt with Cucumber with Tomato (page 212)

❖ DID YOU KNOW THAT THE USE OF FLOWERS FOR COOKING DATES BACK TO 3000BC IN CHINESE CUISINE? STUFFED ZUCCHINI FLOWERS ARE NOW ON THE MENU IN MANY FASHIONABLE RESTAURANTS AND THERE IS A DELICIOUS RECIPE FOR THEM ON THE FOLLOWING PAGE.

STUFFED ZUCCHINI FLOWERS

SERVES 8

Zucchini (courgette) flowers are a delightful conversation piece around the dinner party table. You can also use this filling in zucchini if the flowers are not available.

16 zucchini flowers or 8 long slim zucchini

4 zucchini, trimmed

8 oz (250 g) quark

2 teaspoons tomato paste

1 teaspoon minced chili

1 tablespoon snipped chives

2 egg whites

Red Pepper Sauce (page 150) for serving

Wash zucchini flowers carefully and drain on a clean cloth. Steam the 4 zucchini for 5 minutes, or cook in a clean food storage bag in a microwave oven on High setting for 2 minutes. Cut in half lengthwise and scoop out all flesh into the bowl of a food processor. Mix to a puree, add quark, tomato paste, chili and chives and mix for a few seconds to combine. Whisk egg whites until stiff and gently fold into the quark mixture.

Spoon stuffing into the zucchini flowers and steam for 2–3 minutes or until warm. To serve spread some Red Pepper Sauce on 8 individual entree plates and place 2 stuffed zucchini flowers in the middle of each.

VEGETABLES IN THAI COCONUT CREAM

SERVES 4

12 scallions (spring onions)

1 slim young leek

1 long slim carrot

2 cloves garlic, crushed

2 teaspoons finely chopped ginger

1/2 teaspoon minced chili

2 teaspoons finely chopped cilantro (coriander) root

1/4 cup shredded cilantro (coriander) leaves

1 cup (8 fl oz/250 ml) coconut cream

Trim and peel vegetables and cut into 3/4 inch (2 cm) julienne strips. Steam vegetables or cook in a microwave oven until tender-crisp.

Place all remaining ingredients in a saucepan and bring to the boil. Add vegetables and gently reheat.

Serve in four small individual soufflé dishes accompanied by naan or garlic bread for dunking.

Vegetables in Thai coconut cream

SAMOSAS

MAKES 28–30, SERVES 12–15

Serve Samosas as an appetizer for an Indian meal or as a spicy party fingerfood with a refreshing yogurt-based sauce to accompany or dip into.

Filling:

2 potatoes, about 1/2 lb
(8 oz /250 g)

1 tablespoon vegetable oil

1/2 teaspoon mustard seeds

1/2 teaspoon cumin seeds

1 small onion, finely chopped

1/2 teaspoon ground turmeric

1 cup frozen peas, thawed

1/2 teaspoon salt

1 tablespoon water

1 tablespoon chopped cilantro
(coriander) or mint

1 teaspoon garam masala

1 teaspoon minced chili

Pastry:

1 cup (4 oz/125 g) all-purpose
(plain) flour

1 cup (4 oz/125 g) wholewheat
(wholemeal) flour

1/2 teaspoon salt

4 tablespoons ghee

1/2-3/4 cup (4-6 fl oz/125-185 ml)
cold water

ghee or vegetable oil for deep
frying

Filling: Cook potatoes, with skin on, until tender, then peel and cut into 1/2 inch (1 cm) cubes. Heat oil in a frying pan and fry mustard and cumin seeds until mustard crackles and bursts. Add onion and stir-fry for 5 minutes until soft and golden brown. Stir in turmeric, peas, potatoes, salt and water, cover and simmer for 5 minutes. Transfer mixture to a bowl, add remaining ingredients, mash lightly and leave to cool.

Pastry: Sift flours and salt into a mixing bowl. Add ghee and cut in with a round-bladed knife or mix in a food processor. Add sufficient cold water to mix to a stiff dough. Knead for 5–10 minutes on a lightly floured surface until dough is smooth and elastic.

To finish samosas: Divide dough into 14–15 equal pieces. Roll each piece out to a round 5 inches (12 cm) in diameter. Cut the rounds in half. Shape each half round into a cone or triangle (as for a paper icing bag) and seal overcapping edges with cold water.

Put 1 tablespoon filling into each cone, seal open ends together with cold water, then roll edge over to seal and decorate.

Deep fry at 350°F (180°C) a few at a time for 10–15 minutes, turning occasionally, until pastry is cooked. Drain on kitchen paper towels.

Serve hot; may be accompanied by Yogurt with Mint, Onion and Chili (page 210).

SPRING ROLLS

Eggless spring roll pastry sheets or wrappers are available from the freezer department of most leading supermarkets and from Asian general stores.

16 spring roll pastry sheets, about 8 1/2 inches x 8 1/2 inches (215 mm x 215 mm)

Filling:

1 tablespoon peanut or vegetable oil

1 onion, finely chopped

2 cloves garlic, crushed

1 teaspoon finely chopped ginger

1 carrot, grated

2 stalks celery, finely chopped

2 cups thinly shredded Chinese cabbage

1/2 cup thinly shredded bamboo shoots

2 tablespoons soy sauce

2 teaspoons sweet chili sauce

2 teaspoons cornstarch (cornflour)

1 tablespoon water or vegetable stock

1 egg, beaten, for sealing

peanut oil or vegetable oil for deep frying

Filling: Heat oil in a wok or heavy-based frying pan and stir-fry onion for 5 minutes. Add garlic and ginger, stir-fry for 2 minutes. Add carrot, celery, cabbage and bamboo shoots, stir-fry for 5 minutes. Stir in soy and sweet chili sauces. Blend cornstarch with water until smooth, add to wok and stir until mixture has boiled and thickened. Transfer to a bowl and leave to cool.

To finish spring rolls: Place 2 teaspoons filling diagonally across the middle of a spring roll pastry sheet. Lift the lower triangular corner over the filling and tuck the point under the filling. Fold the two corners in from the sides, one at a time, to enclose the filling and press the points down firmly. Brush the top corner and remaining exposed pastry sheet with beaten egg, then roll the spring roll away from you to form a neat cylinder, sealed by the egg.

Deep-fry spring rolls at 375°F (190°C), five at a time, for 3–4 minutes until crisp and golden brown. Drain well on kitchen paper towels.

Serve hot with Sweet and Sour Sauce (on page 48) or sweet chili sauce.

SUSHI

MAKES 42–56 PIECES, SERVES 12–16

Serve these Japanese rice rolls with tamari, wasabi (Japanese horseradish) and chili sauces for dipping into. They can also be served as a fingerfood at parties. As a guide to quantities, one $1/2$ oz (17 g) packet of sushi nori contains 7 sheets nori and the vegetables weigh $1/4$ lb (100–150 g) each.

3 cups (1 $1/2$ lb/750 g) shortgrain brown rice

6 cups (48 fl oz/1.5 L) water

$1/2$ cup (4 fl oz /125 ml) Chinese rice wine vinegar

$1/2$ cup (4 fl oz/125 ml) honey or rice syrup

7 sheets sushi nori

Filling:

1 long young carrot

1 long zucchini (courgette)

1 small cucumber

1 green banana chili pepper

2 oz (60 g) packet pickled sliced ginger

1 $2/3$ oz (50 g) packet pickled sliced cucumber

1 $2/3$ oz (50 g) packet pickled sliced daikon (Japanese radish)

Rinse and drain rice until rinse water is clear. Place in a heavy-based pan with water, soak for 45 minutes, then bring to the boil, cover and simmer for 45 minutes or until rice has absorbed almost all the water. Turn off heat but leave rice to stand covered for 10 minutes.

Mix vinegar with honey and stir into the rice with a fork, mashing it in thoroughly. Leave rice to cool to room temperature.

Place a sheet of nori on a bamboo mat. Wet your hands in a bowl of salted water to prevent rice from sticking and spread one seventh of the rice over the nori, leaving a 2 inch (5 cm) strip uncovered along the top edge furthest from you.

Filling: Cut vegetables into long thin strips.

Place a selection of prepared vegetable strips in a row on the rice along the edge of nori nearest you, then top with a selection of pickles. Holding the mat, roll it away from you, holding the filling in place so that it is enclosed by the rice. Roll the rice and nori almost to the end, using the bamboo mat, but do not enclose the mat in the roll! Brush the uncovered nori with water then roll up tightly to the end to seal. Roll the completed sushi firmly in the bamboo mat again to give the roll a good shape.

Continue in this method until you have 7 filled sushi rolls. Dip a sharp knife in the salted water and cut each roll into 6 or 8 slices. Turn upright to serve with bowls of tamari, wasabi and chili sauce for dipping.

Sushi

SWEET AND SOUR SAUCE

MAKES 2 CUPS (16 FL OZ/500 ML)

Try serving this as a dipping sauce with Pakoras (page 41) or with broiled (grilled), marinated tofu.

1 tablespoon vegetable oil

2 cloves garlic, crushed

1 green pepper (capsicum) cut in ¹/₂ inch (1 cm) squares

1 carrot, thinly sliced diagonally

1 cup (8 fl oz/250 ml) vegetable stock

1 tablespoon brown or palm sugar

2 tablespoons apple cider vinegar

1 tablespoon soy sauce

1 tablespoon cornstarch (cornflour)

2 tablespoons cold water

Heat oil in a frying pan and stir-fry garlic, capsicum and carrot for 2 minutes. Add stock, sugar, vinegar and soy sauce and bring to the boil, stirring to dissolve sugar. Blend cornstarch with cold water, add to sauce and bring to the boil, stirring continuously, and simmer for 2 minutes before serving.

TZATZIKI

SERVES 8

This Greek appetizer sauce may also be served as a delicious dip with vegetable crudités.

1 cup peeled, seeded, thinly sliced cucumber

1 ¹/₂ cups (12 fl oz/375 ml) natural yogurt

2 cloves garlic, crushed

2 tablespoons shredded mint

The cucumber should be peeled, quartered lengthwise, seeds removed, then thinly sliced or coarsely grated and well drained before combining with yogurt.

Place all the prepared ingredients into a bowl and fold together. Place in a serving bowl, cover and chill for at least 1 hour before serving.

FELAFEL
CHICK PEA BALLS

MAKES 30–32, SERVES 6–8

3/4 cup (3 oz/90 g) fine bulgur (cracked wheat)

1/2 cup (2 oz/60 g) coarsely crumbled pita (Lebanese) or white bread

1 3/4 cups (11 oz/340 g) chick peas, soaked, cooked and drained

4 tablespoons lemon juice

1 1/2 teaspoons crushed garlic

1 1/2 teaspoons ground cilantro (coriander)

1 teaspoon ground cumin

1 teaspoon minced chili

1 teaspoon salt

freshly ground black pepper

oil for deep frying

Place bulgur in a small bowl with sufficient cold water to cover and leave to soak for 15 minutes. Drain well.

Place crumbled bread in another small bowl, add cold water to cover and leave to soak for 15 minutes. Drain breadcrumbs and squeeze dry with fingers.

Place a quarter of the chick peas into an electric blender or food processor, add 2 tablespoons lemon juice, garlic, coriander, cumin, chili, salt and pepper and mix at high speed for 1 minute until mixture forms a smooth puree. Gradually add remaining chick peas, a quarter at a time, and remaining lemon juice and mix to a puree.

Add the bulgur and breadcrumbs and mix well. With clean, cold, wet hands, roll mixture into balls 1 1/2 inches (3 cm) in diameter. Place balls on greaseproof paper and leave to dry at room temperature for 1 hour.

Heat oil to 350°F (180°C) and deep-fry the balls, six at a time, for 2–3 minutes, until golden brown. Drain well and keep warm while frying remaining felafel.

Serve warm; and accompany by Tzatziki (page 48) for an interesting Greek combination.

DOLMATHAKIA LATHERES
STUFFED VINE LEAVES

SERVES 6–8

These may be prepared a few days ahead and stored in the refrigerator. The vine leaves may be bought in delicatessen stores, particularly Greek ones.

5 tablespoons olive oil

1 onion, chopped

1/3 cup wild rice

1/2 cup (4 fl oz/125 ml) water

1/2 teaspoon salt

freshly ground black pepper

1 1/2 tablespoons pine nuts

1 1/2 tablespoons currants

40 canned (or packaged) vine leaves

1 1/2 tablespoons cold water

Heat half the olive oil in a large, heavy frying pan, add onion and cook until soft and transparent. Add rice and stir for 2 minutes until grains are coated with oil.

Add water, salt and pepper and bring to the boil. Reduce heat, cover tightly with a lid or foil and simmer for 30 minutes.

Heat 1 tablespoon of remaining oil in a small frying pan and lightly brown the pine nuts. Add to the rice and stir in the currants.

Bring 6 cups (48 fl oz/1 1/2 L) water to the boil in a large pan. Drop vine leaves into boiling water and blanch or leave for 1 minute. Remove and drain in a sieve and plunge them quickly into a bowl of cold water. Gently separate the leaves and spread, dull side up, on kitchen paper towels to drain.

Cover bottom of a heavy, medium-sized pan with 8–10 vine leaves.

To stuff vine leaves: Place vine leaves dull side up and place a tablespoon of filling in the middle of each leaf. Fold stalk end over and then fold each side over to enclose the filling completely. Starting at the stalk end, roll the vine leaf firmly into a compact cylinder.

Stack stuffed vine leaves side by side, seam side down, in layers in the pan and sprinkle with the remaining 1 1/2 tablespoons oil and cold water. Cover and place over a high heat for 3 minutes, reduce heat and simmer for 30 minutes. Uncover and cool.

To serve: Arrange stuffed vine leaves attractively on a serving dish or individual entree plates, garnish with lemon wedges. You may like to complement this dish with Egg and Lemon Sauce (on the following page).

Salade Baumanière, p.26

Saltsa Avgolemono
EGG AND LEMON SAUCE

SERVES 6–8

3 eggs

1 tablespoon cornstarch (cornflour)

1/8 teaspoon salt

1 cup (8 fl oz/250 ml) vegetable stock

3 tablespoons lemon juice

Beat eggs in a mixing bowl with cornstarch and salt until light in texture and appearance. Boil stock, then pour slowly into egg mixture, whisking continuously.

Pour mixture into the top of a double boiler and cook over gently bubbling water, whisking continuously until sauce thickens. Remove from heat and stir in lemon juice.

Eggplant Puftaloons

SERVES 4

8 slices eggplant (aubergine), about 1/2 inch (1.5 cm) thick and 3 inch (7.5 cm) circumference

1 2/3 oz (50 g) soy cheese, black pepper flavoured

1/4 cup (1 oz /30 g) ground peanuts

1/2 teaspoon minced chili

Batter:

1 cup (4 oz/125 g) chick pea (besan) flour

1 teaspoon baking soda (bicarbonate of soda)

3/4 cup (6 fl oz/185 ml) ginger ale or ginger beer

oil for deep frying

Remove peel from eggplant, cut a pocket in each slice with a sharp pointed knife. Sprinkle with salt and leave to stand in a colander to drain for 30 minutes. Drain well.

Slice cheese thinly. Mix nuts with chili. Divide cheese evenly between slices of eggplant and force it into the pockets with the point of a knife. Press 1 rounded teaspoon of peanut mixture into each pocket and seal by pressing opening.

Batter: Mix all ingredients together, leave to stand for 30 minutes to soften if possible.

To finish: Dip eggplant slices into batter and deep-fry a few at a time in hot oil for 4 minutes, turning to cook evenly. Drain well on kitchen paper towels.

Serve hot with a Mint and Coconut Chutney (on the following page) or Yogurt with Mint, Onion and Chili (page 210).

MINT AND COCONUT CHUTNEY

MAKES 1½ CUPS (12 FL OZ/375 ML)

2 cloves garlic, halved

1 inch (2.5 cm) ginger, sliced

2 teaspoons ground turmeric

2 tablespoons mango chutney

½ cup (1½ oz/45 g) unsweetened (desiccated) coconut

1 cup mint leaves

½ cup cilantro (coriander) leaves

1 tablespoon curry paste

1 tablespoon vinegar

3 ⅓ fl oz (100 ml) coconut milk

3 ⅓ fl oz (100 ml) light sour cream

Place garlic, ginger, turmeric, chutney and coconut in a blender or food processor and mix until finely chopped. Add mint and cilantro (coriander), mix until chopped. Add remaining ingredients and mix again until combined. Chill in the refrigerator until ready to serve.

MINI STRUDELS

SERVES 12

Tempeh is a high-protein food made from soy beans. It is also rich in vitamin B12 which is often lacking in a vegetarian diet. White miso is made from rice and soy beans.

6 ½ oz (200 g) tempeh or tofu

2 tablespoons white miso

1 tablespoon tamari

1 teaspoon sesame oil

1 tablespoon toasted sesame seeds

1 tablespoon lemon or lime juice

freshly ground black pepper

1 large carrot, cut in julienne strips

1 zucchini (courgette), cut in julienne strips

6 scallions (spring onions), cut in julienne strips

10 sheets filo pastry

2 oz (60 g) polyunsaturated margarine, melted

Slice tempeh finely or crumble the tofu. Mix with the white miso, tamari, sesame oil and seeds, lemon juice and pepper. Blanch vegetables and drain well. Brush a sheet of filo with melted margarine, place another on top. Continue brushing and layering 5 sheets of filo and then cut the layers into 6 equal pieces. Divide half the tempeh mixture over the filo pieces, top with half the vegetables. Roll up neatly to form 6 mini strudels.

Repeat these steps with the remaining filo and filling to make a further 6 mini strudels. Place on a baking tray, brush with margarine and sprinkle with more sesame seeds. Bake at 375°F (190°C) for 15 minutes or until cooked.

Serve with a vegetable sauce and a salad garnish.

Following page: Stuffed vine leaves (front), p.51; Tzatziki (top right), p.48; Saltsa avgolemono (front left), p.52; Chickpea balls (top left), p.49

CREAMY EGGS ON PUMPERNICKEL

SERVES 4

4 hard-boiled eggs

4 scallions (spring onions),
thinly sliced

3/4 cup (6 fl oz/185 ml)
mayonnaise

1 tablespoon lemon juice

1 tablespoon chopped
black olives

1 tablespoon chopped
green olives

1 tablespoon chopped sun-dried
tomatoes

8 small slices or 20 small rounds
pumpernickel bread

sliced Lebanese cucumber and
pickled lemon for serving

Remove shell from eggs and chop well. Mix with scallions, mayonnaise and lemon juice. Mix olives with sun-dried tomatoes. Spread egg mixture neatly on top of pumpernickel bread and top with olive mixture. Serve on individual plates with sliced Lebanese cucumber and pickled lemon.

CREAMED EGGS WITH SPICED MANGO CHUTNEY

SERVES 8

This dish looks sensational but requires patience to prepare the egg shells; however your patience will be rewarded with the compliments!

8 very fresh large eggs

2 teaspoons butter or margarine

1/2 teaspoon salt

pinch of white pepper

1 tablespoon fromage blanc (page 208)

1 tablespoon finely chopped onion

1 tablespoon finely snipped chives

2 tablespoons mango chutney

1 teaspoon minced chili

16–24 asparagus spears, trimmed, cooked and cooled

Slice the tops off the eggs carefully with a fine serrated knife 1/2 inch (1 cm) above the widest part of the eggs. Empty the egg shells and reserve 6 eggs for the dish and 8 shells. Wash egg shells carefully in cool water and drain on a clean cloth.

Beat the eggs together. Melt butter in a saucepan, then pour eggs in. Place over a low heat and stir with a wooden spoon or a wire whisk until eggs thicken to form a cream. Remove from heat and stir in salt, pepper, fromage blanc, onion and chives, then adjust seasoning to taste. Select fleshy fruit pieces when measuring mango chutney, chop if necessary then mix with chili.

Place egg shells into 8 egg cups, then fill them with the creamed eggs. Top eggs with the spiced mango chutney and place tops of shells on top at an angle.

Place 2–3 asparagus spears on the side of each egg cup and serve cold at room temperature, with an egg spoon or teaspoon.

SOUPS

I cannot imagine a winter season without soup, delicious soup. I prepare a large pan of soup every weekend, so we have a bowl of steaming hot 'comfort food' to come home to on the first night of the week. It also provides a popular and nourishing after-school snack for growing children, and helps keep them away from junk food alternatives.

The soup recipes in this chapter are very practical, as you can prepare most of them in approximately 30 minutes. You can produce impressive hearty soups in a surprisingly short time by using time-saving kitchen helpers—a food processor, a microwave oven, a pressure cooker, as well as canned legumes, canned tomatoes, preserved minced garlic, ginger and chili, stock cubes or powder, and concentrated liquid stock. For the purists, however, I have given a very good recipe for home-made Vegetable Stock, which you can use immediately or freeze for later use.

Hot winter soups are satisfying in the menu, but cold summer soups also have their place. They are light and refreshing and there are many to choose from. A vegetarian soup should have that extra little bit of nourishment and this can be done very easily.

There are many soups in this chapter that qualify as a complete protein dish. Cream of Sorrel Soup and Lettuce and Tarragon Soup both contain eggs. Leek and Potato Soup with Millet and Vegetable Minestrone combine a grain with a legume. Tomato and Chayote (Choko) Soup and Split Pea Soup combine a legume with a dairy product.

Protein rich legume soups such as Green Pea Soup, Pea Soup Dutch Style and Five Bean Soup, and others not quite so rich in protein content, such as Chestnut Soup and Vegetable Corn Chowder, all become complete protein meals when served with a grain. Crunchy wholewheat (wholemeal) bread rolls, wholewheat toast or wholewheat croutons are delicious and nutritious accompaniments. Yogurt also helps increase the protein content of a soup as well as enhancing the taste.

Following the lighter textured soups with a nut, cereal or legume based main course will also give you a complete protein meal. Cold soups such as Avocado and Asparagus, which is a good source of vitamin E, and Gazpacho, which is a good source of vitamin C, can be followed by a nut, cereal or legume based salad for a balanced hot weather meal.

Finally, for low-calorie soups, try the Blushing Broccoli Soup and the Chinese Noodle Soup. Soups are a versatile dish, and the recipes in this chapter range from traditional soups popular with the family, to new and fashionable dishes suitable for entertaining.

Red lentil soup, p.77; Cream of carrot soup with barley, p.70

VEGETABLE STOCK

MAKES 5 CUPS (40 FL OZ/1.25 L)

This is a good basic stock to use in soups and other dishes. Freeze it in 1 cup quantities for convenience. Vegetable stock is also available in handy cubes and powder and a concentrated liquid stock is available in sealed packs.

1 tablespoon olive oil
1 large onion, chopped
2 carrots, sliced
1 stalk celery, sliced
1 cup chopped turnip or pumpkin
6 cups (48 fl oz/1.5 L) water
1 bay leaf
2 cloves
6 peppercorns
4 stems parsley
1 tablespoon miso or yeast extract
salt and pepper

Heat oil in a large pan, add all vegetables, cover and sauté over a low-medium heat for 5 minutes, shaking pan frequently to loosen and move vegetables. Add water, bay leaf, spices and parsley, bring to the boil covered and simmer gently for 1 1/2 hours. Stir in miso and season to taste with salt and pepper. Strain stock and use as required.

❖ SOUP IS A GOOD FOOD TO PREPARE AND FREEZE FOR LATER USE IN A BUSY HOUSEHOLD. ADD ONLY HALF THE STOCK IF YOU ARE PREPARING SOUP SPECIFICALLY FOR FREEZING. IT TAKES UP LESS ROOM IN THE FREEZER AND IT WILL DEFROST MUCH QUICKER. ONCE THAWED, ADD THE OTHER HALF OF THE STOCK, BRING TO THE BOIL, SERVE AND ENJOY.

VEGETARIAN CORN CHOWDER

SERVES 6

1 onion, chopped

2 potatoes (about 1 lb/500 g), diced

2 cups (16 fl oz/500 ml) vegetable stock

1 teaspoon yeast extract

1 teaspoon tabasco sauce

2 teaspoons chopped rosemary

13 oz (400 g) canned corn niblets, drained

1/2 cup (4 fl oz/125 ml) soy drink

white pepper

Place all ingredients except corn, soy drink and pepper into a pan. Bring to the boil covered and simmer for 20 minutes. Stir in corn and soy drink and heat through gently. Add pepper to taste.

Serve hot accompanied by bran crispbread or rye crispbread.

LEEK AND POTATO SOUP WITH MILLET

SERVES 6

This soup is similar to a Vichyssoise and may be served hot or cold. To save time for a family meal, mash the soup with a potato masher.

2 large leeks, thinly sliced

1 large onion, finely chopped

2 tablespoons butter or margarine

1 large potato, peeled and thinly sliced

1/2 cup (3 1/3 oz/100 g) millet

3 cups (24 fl oz/750 ml) vegetable stock, made with stock cubes

1 1/4 cups (10 fl oz/300 ml) light sour cream or soy drink

salt and white pepper

snipped chives for garnish

Gently fry leeks and onion in butter in a large, heavy-based pan until soft, about 5 minutes. Add potato, millet and stock and bring to the boil, covered, then simmer for 15–20 minutes or until potato and millet are tender.

Mash potato and vegetables in pan to form a smooth texture, or cool soup then mix to a puree in a blender or food processor.

Stir sour cream into soup and season to taste with salt and pepper.

Serve hot or chilled garnished with snipped chives.

CREAM OF PUMPKIN SOUP

SERVES 6–8

Cook the pumpkin in a microwave oven to save time and you can produce a steaming pot of this delicious and attractive soup in less than 30 minutes.

3 cups (24 fl oz/750 ml) vegetable stock

1 cup peeled, chopped fresh or canned tomatoes

1 onion, finely chopped

1 bay leaf

2 cups mashed cooked pumpkin

salt

1/4 teaspoon white pepper

pinch of ground cloves or ginger

1 tablespoon lemon juice

1 cup (8 fl oz/250 ml) cream or light soy drink

1 tablespoon pepitas, optional

chopped chives or parsley for garnish

Place stock, tomatoes, onion and bay leaf in a pan, cover and simmer for 10 minutes. Remove bay leaf and allow to cool.

Mix to a puree in an electric blender. Return to pan, add pumpkin, salt to taste, pepper, cloves and lemon juice, and simmer for 1 minute. Stir in cream or soy drink and pepitas if desired and heat through.

Serve soup immediately, garnished with chopped chives or parsley, accompanied by croutons or warm Cornbread (see 166).

❖ ALLOW 1 CUP (8FL OZ, 250ML) SOUP PER PORTION WHEN CALCULATING THE NUMBER OF SERVINGS. CREAMY SOUPS MAY BE ACCOMPANIED BY CROUTONS WHICH ADD TEXTURE AND EXTRA NOURISHMENT, PARTICULARLY IF MADE FROM WHOLEGRAIN BREAD.

Cream of pumpkin soup

GAZPACHO

SERVES 8

This has been one of my family's best-loved summer soups for many years. The original version was served on the Queen Mary as she voyaged between the USA and Britain. You can cut down on the chilling time required before serving by having the juice and vegetables chilled before preparation.

24 fl oz (750 ml) canned tomato juice, chilled

4 mediumsize tomatoes, sliced

1 cucumber, peeled, seeded and chopped

1 small red pepper (capsicum), seeded and chopped

1 small green pepper (capsicum), seeded and chopped

1 onion, chopped

1 tablespoon parsley sprigs, optional

1 tablespoon chives, optional

juice of 1 lemon

3 tablespoons vegetable oil

2 tablespoons white vinegar

salt to taste

Place half juice and half prepared vegetables into an electric blender and mix to a mushy puree, not smooth. Pour into a soup tureen or bowl. Puree remaining juice and vegetables, add herbs if desired and remaining ingredients and mix well. Pour into soup tureen, cover and chill for 1–2 hours before serving.

Serve in chilled soup bowls accompanied by Corn-bread (page 166) if you like.

CHILLED WATERCRESS AND SWEET POTATO SOUP

SERVES 6–8

This recipe works well with any sweet potato. Native spinach or wild greens may be used in place of the watercress.

1 onion, chopped

2 tablespoons butter or margarine

2 cups peeled cubed sweet potato

3 cups (24 fl oz/750 ml) vegetable stock

2 cups tightly packed watercress sprigs, washed

finely grated rind and juice of 1 lemon

1 cup (8 fl oz/250 ml) natural yogurt

extra watercress sprigs or snow pea (mange-tout) sprouts for garnish

Gently fry onion in butter, in a large pan, until soft and golden. Add sweet potato and stock, bring to the boil, then cover and simmer for 15 minutes, or until tender. Add watercress, lemon rind and juice and simmer for 2 minutes.

Cool, then mix soup to a puree in a blender or food processor. Stir in yogurt, cover and chill thoroughly.

Serve soup cold garnished with watercress sprigs.

JERUSALEM ARTICHOKE SOUP

SERVES 6

The Jerusalem artichoke is the tuber of a variety of sunflower, native to Canada, and is no relation to the globe artichoke. Its sweet, nut-like taste combines well with cream and navy (haricot) beans in this soup.

2 lb (1 kg) Jerusalem artichokes

1/4 cup (2 oz/60 g) polyunsaturated margarine

2 onions, chopped

4 cups (32 fl oz/1 L) vegetable stock

1 cup cooked navy (haricot) beans

1/8 teaspoon ground nutmeg

1/8 teaspoon ground cardamon

1 cup (8 fl oz/250 ml) cream or soy drink

pepper

3 tablespoons chopped parsley for sprinkling

Scrub Jerusalem artichokes with a vegetable brush then peel thinly. Don't worry about the skin between the knobs because it is like the skin of a new potato when cooked. Melt margarine in a large pan and gently fry onion until soft. Slice artichokes, add to pan, cover and sauté for 5 minutes, shaking pan frequently. Add stock, bring to the boil and simmer covered for 10 minutes. Mix soup to a puree and return to pan. Add beans, spices and cream, heat through gently and add pepper to taste. Serve hot sprinkled with parsley.

BLUSHING BROCCOLI SOUP

SERVES 8

You can prepare and serve this in less than 30 minutes if you use a microwave.

2 tablespoons butter or
polyunsaturated margarine

1 onion, finely chopped

6 cups (48 fl oz/1.5 L) vegetable
stock

3 medium beets (beetroot)

1lb (500g) broccoli

1 teaspoon apple cider vinegar

salt and pepper

buttermilk for serving, optional

Melt butter in a large pan and gently fry onion until soft. Add stock, bring to the boil covered, then simmer for 10 minutes. Meanwhile, peel and quarter beets, and steam for about 15 minutes until tender, or cook in a clean, plastic food storage bag in a microwave oven, on High setting, for 8 minutes, or until tender. Trim and wash broccoli, microwave as for beets on High setting for 5–8 minutes, until cooked. Mix beets, then broccoli to a puree in a food processor, or blender, add to pan and heat through until boiling. Add vinegar and season to taste with salt and pepper.

Serve soup in individual bowls with two tablespoons of buttermilk stirred into each portion, accompanied by wholewheat bread rolls or toast.

SCOTTISH BARLEY BROTH

SERVES 8

The Scots are renowned for making tasty nutritious meals out of plain basic ingredients. This broth is a good example.

1 onion, diced

1 leek, thinly sliced

2 carrots, diced

2 tablespoons butter or margarine

2 cups diced rutabaga (swede)
or turnip

8 cups (64 fl oz/2 L) vegetable
stock

1 teaspoon yeast extract

1/4 cup quick-cooking barley

1/4 cup barley bran

8 oz (250 g) Brussels sprouts,
thinly shredded

Place onion, leek, carrots and butter in a large, heavy-based pan, cover and sauté for 2–3 minutes, shaking pan over heat, until butter is absorbed. Add all remaining ingredients except sprouts, bring to the boil and simmer covered for 30 minutes, or cook in a pressure cooker for 10 minutes. Add Brussels sprouts and simmer for 2 minutes.

Serve with Scottish baps or oatcakes.

Scottish barley broth

ASPARAGUS AND AVOCADO SOUP

SERVES 6

Asparagus and avocado have become symbols of elegant epicurean eating and the less you add to them the finer they taste. This cold soup combines them and should be served just below room temperature to allow the subtle taste to be enjoyed.

1 lb (500 g) asparagus spears

4 cups (32 fl oz/1 L) cold vegetable stock

1 large ripe avocado

2 tablespoons French dressing (page 205)

6 tablespoons light sour cream

white pepper

3 tablespoons ground almonds, optional

Snap tough stalks off the bottom of each asparagus spear. Cook by steaming, or poaching in water to cover in a frying pan, or in a clean food storage bag in a microwave oven on High setting for 3 minutes. Reserve a few heads and mix remaining asparagus to a puree in a blender or food processor with half the stock. Pour into a bowl. Cut avocado in half, remove stone and peel carefully. Slice avocado and mix to a puree with dressing and remaining stock. Add to asparagus puree. Stir in cream and pepper to taste. Cover and chill for 1 hour only for the best results.

Serve cold, sprinkled with ground almonds if you like, garnished with reserved asparagus heads.

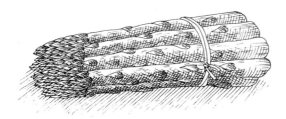

LETTUCE AND TARRAGON SOUP

SERVES 8–10

2 large heads lettuce, washed and crisp

3 tablespoons butter or margarine

2 small white onions, finely chopped

1 tablespoon tarragon leaves

2 tablespoons all-purpose wholewheat (plain wholemeal) flour

8 cups (64 fl oz/2 L) vegetable stock

1 cucumber

4 egg yolks

1 1/4 cups (10 fl oz/300 ml) soy drink

salt, pepper, nutmeg

1 tablespoon wholegrain mustard

Cut lettuce into ribbons. Melt butter and gently fry onion until transparent. Stir in lettuce and tarragon and cook gently for 5 minutes until lettuce is soft. Stir in flour and gradually add half the stock, stirring continuously. Simmer covered for 15 minutes. Peel and deseed cucumber, then cut into fine matchsticks.

Allow soup to cool a little then puree in a blender. Return to pan and add rest of stock. Prepare a liaison by beating together the egg yolks and soy drink, then stir into them some of the warm soup and stir this back into the soup. Season with salt, pepper and nutmeg. Add the cucumber and mustard and reheat without allowing to boil! Serve hot with garlic bread.

TOMATO AND CHAYOTE SOUP

SERVES 6–8

A light refreshing soup, ideal to serve in the summertime.

1 onion, chopped

1 teaspoon minced chili

2 tablespoons butter or polyunsaturated margarine

2 lb (1 kg/about 8) chayotes (chokos), peeled, cored and chopped

6 cups (48 fl oz/1.5 L) vegetable stock

1 lb (500 g) ripe tomatoes or 14 oz (425g) canned tomatoes

2 tablespoons farina (semolina)

14 oz (440 g) canned pinto beans

1 cup (8 fl oz/250 ml) natural yogurt

2 tablespoons shredded basil or mint

Gently fry onion and chili in butter in a large pan until soft and golden. Add chayotes and stock, bring to the boil covered and boil gently until they are tender, about 15 minutes. Cool, then mix to a puree. Core tomatoes and mix to a puree with farina, add with beans to chayote puree. Bring soup to the boil, then reduce heat and stir in yogurt. Season to taste with salt and pepper. Add basil just before serving.

Serve with cornbread or wholewheat rolls, making a complete protein meal.

Note: Zucchini make an acceptable substitute for chayotes.

GREEN PEA SOUP

SERVES 6–8

This soup is a lighter, fresher version of the traditional English 'Mushy Pea Soup'.

1lb (500 g) frozen peas

2 tablespoons butter or margarine

2 white onions, finely chopped

2 tablespoons all-purpose wholewheat (plain wholemeal) flour

5 cups (40 fl oz/1.25 L) vegetable stock, made with stock cubes

1/2 cup (4 fl oz/125 ml) light sour cream or natural yogurt

extra sour cream or yogurt for serving

Thaw peas in a colander under running cold water, drain well.

Heat butter in a large, heavy-based pan, add onions, cover and sauté over a medium heat until soft, shaking pan frequently. Add peas and flour and stir over heat for 1–2 minutes. Add stock and bring to the boil stirring continuously. Cover and simmer for 5 minutes.

Cool soup then mix to a puree in a food processor or blender. Return to pan, stir in light sour cream and reheat gently.

Serve hot with 1 tablespoon sour cream or yogurt , accompanied by wholewheat croutons or toasted wholewheat muffins for a complete protein meal.

CREAM OF CARROT SOUP WITH BARLEY

SERVES 6

1 tablespoon butter or margarine

1 large onion, finely chopped

1 stick celery, thinly sliced

1 lb (500 g) carrots, finely chopped

5 cups (40 fl oz/1.25L) vegetable stock

2 teaspoons tomato paste

1/2 cup (3 oz/100 g) quick-cooking barley

1 tablespoon cornstarch (cornflour)

2 tablespoons cold water

1 teaspoon soy sauce or tamari

pepper

1/2 cup (4 fl oz/125 ml) light sour cream, optional

chopped parsley to garnish

Melt butter in a heavy pan, add onion and celery, cover and sauté over a medium heat, shaking pan frequently until vegetables have absorbed all the butter.

Add carrots, stock and tomato paste, bring to the boil, then simmer covered, for 30 minutes or until carrots are tender. Cook barley in boiling water for 20 minutes, drain well. Cool soup, then mix to a puree in an electric blender or food processor. Return puree to pan. Add barley. Blend cornstarch smoothly with water, add to carrot puree and bring to the boil, stirring continuously. Add soy sauce and season to taste with pepper. Stir in the sour cream, if used, and simmer.

Serve soup hot, sprinkled with chopped parsley.

Green pea soup

CREAM OF SORREL SOUP

SERVES 8

This is a very nourishing soup, being rich in protein, iron, zinc and B vitamins.

8 oz (250 g) fresh sorrel

1 tablespoon olive oil

4 cloves garlic, crushed

1 tablespoon yellow mustard seed

1/2 teaspoon salt

1/8 teaspoon white pepper

8 cups (64 fl oz/2 L) vegetable stock

4 eggs

Wash sorrel, drain well and pat dry. Trim leaves from stalks and shred leaves coarsely.

Heat oil in a heavy-based pan and fry garlic and mustard seed until mustard 'pops'. Stir in sorrel, salt and pepper, then add stock, cover and bring to the boil and simmer for 15 minutes.

Cool soup then mix to a smooth puree in a blender, about 2 minutes. Return puree to pan. Beat eggs together until smooth and frothy.

Just before serving, heat soup through until just coming to boiling point, then quickly remove from heat and pour in the beaten eggs, whisking soup continuously. The egg coagulates on contact with the hot soup, giving a light airy texture.

Serve immediately.

VEGETABLE MINESTRONE

SERVES 8

This can be prepared quickly by using canned navy (haricot) beans in place of the dried beans which are authentic to the Genoese minestrone. Wholewheat (wholemeal) pasta increases the nutritional value of this tasty soup. This is a complete protein dish.

2 tablespoons olive oil

1 onion, chopped

2 cloves garlic, crushed

8 cups (64 fl oz /2 L) vegetable stock, made with stock cubes

2 carrots, thinly sliced

2 stalks celery, chopped

1/4 small cabbage, thinly shredded

2 tomatoes, chopped

1 cup frozen peas

1 cup green beans, cut in 3/4 inch (2 cm) lengths

1/2 cup macaroni or wholewheat (wholemeal) pasta

16 oz (420–500 g) canned navy (haricot) beans

2 tablespoons chopped parsley

salt and pepper

grated parmesan cheese for serving, optional

Heat oil in a large heavy-based pan and gently fry onion and garlic until soft and transparent.

Add stock, carrots, celery, cabbage and tomatoes, cover and bring to the boil then simmer for 20 minutes. Add peas, green beans and macaroni and simmer for 10 minutes or until macaroni is tender.

Stir in navy beans and parsley and season to taste with salt and pepper.

Serve hot sprinkled with parmesan cheese.

Following page: Cream of sorrel soup (top), p.72; Lettuce and tarragon soup (left), p.69; Asparagus and avocado soup (right), p.68

BORSCH

SERVES 10–12

Raw, grated beets (beetroot) makes this Russian soup an attractive pink. Beet juice is also great for brightening up creamy mashed potato!

1/3 cup (3 oz/90 g) polyunsaturated margarine

2 onions, sliced

2 cloves garlic, crushed

8 cups (64 fl oz/2 L) vegetable stock

2 teaspoons vegetable extract

1 bay leaf

sprig of thyme

2 slim carrots, thinly sliced

1 turnip, quartered and thinly sliced

2 stalks celery, thinly sliced

1/2 small cabbage, thinly shredded

3 tomatoes, chopped

1 lb (500 g) beets, peeled and grated

freshly ground black pepper

natural yogurt or buttermilk for serving

Melt 2 tablespoons margarine and gently fry onion and garlic for 5 minutes until soft but not burned. Add half the stock, vegetable extract, bay leaf and thyme and bring to the boil covered and simmer for 30 minutes.

Heat remaining margarine in a large pan and gently fry carrots, turnip, celery and cabbage until soft but not browned, stirring frequently. Strain onion stock and add to pan with remaining stock and simmer covered for 30 minutes. Add tomatoes and beets and simmer for a further 15 minutes or until vegetables are tender. Add pepper to taste.

Serve soup hot with a soup spoon of yogurt or buttermilk added to each portion.

CHESTNUT SOUP

SERVES 6

1 lb (500 g) chestnuts

1 carrot, chopped

1 onion, chopped

1 tablespoon polyunsaturated margarine

2 bay leaves

6 cups (48 fl oz/1.5 L) vegetable stock

1 cup (8 fl oz/250 ml) soy drink

6 Brussels sprouts, thinly shredded

salt and pepper

Make a horizontal slash in the flat side of the chestnuts with a sharp, pointed knife. Place in a pan with water to cover and boil for 3 minutes. Remove pan from heat, take out 3 nuts at a time and using the knife, remove the shell and inner skin.

Sauté carrot and onion in margarine in a large covered pan, shaking occasionally, until onion is soft. Add chestnuts, bay leaves and stock, bring to the boil and simmer covered until chestnuts are tender, about 30 minutes. Remove bay leaves and mix soup to a puree. Add soy drink, Brussels sprouts and salt and pepper to taste and heat through before serving.

FIVE BEAN SOUP

SERVES 8–10

1 onion, diced

1 clove garlic, crushed

1 teaspoon chili powder

1 tablespoon vegetable oil

4 cups (32 fl oz/1 L) vegetable stock

1 carrot, sliced

1 stalk celery, sliced

2 bay leaves

14 oz (425 g) canned tomatoes

1/2 cup (4 fl oz/125 ml) tomato paste

1 cup thinly shredded cabbage

14 oz (440 g) canned 4 bean mix

14 oz (440 g) canned black-eyed beans

1 teaspoon apple cider vinegar

Gently fry onion, garlic and chili powder in oil in a large pan. Add stock, carrot, celery and bay leaves, bring to the boil covered and simmer for 20 minutes. Add tomatoes, tomato paste and cabbage and simmer for 10 minutes. Stir in beans and vinegar and return to the boil.

Serve soup accompanied by warm cornbread or wholewheat bread rolls for a complete protein dish.

RED LENTIL SOUP

SERVES 6

This delicious, traditional Phoenician recipe was given to me by a Lebanese restaurateur. He insisted that the lemon was essential to enhance the dish. Accompany with torn pita (Lebanese) bread for a complete protein dish.

2 cups (12 oz/400 g) red lentils

8 cups (64 fl oz /2 L) vegetable stock

1 onion, quartered

1 tomato, quartered

2 cloves garlic, crushed

1 1/2 teaspoons ground cumin

salt and pepper

1 tablespoon butter or margarine

1 small onion, finely chopped

1-2 lemons, cut in wedges

Wash lentils under cold running water. Bring the stock to a boil in a large, heavy pan and add lentils, onion, tomato and garlic and simmer for 30–40 minutes or until lentils are tender.

Cool soup and mix to a puree in an electric blender.

Return to pan, heat through for 3 minutes and stir in the cumin, salt and pepper to taste.

Melt butter in a frying pan and fry the chopped onion gently for 10 minutes.

Serve soup hot with fried chopped onion sprinkled on top and accompanied by lemon segments for squeezing into the soup.

PEA SOUP DUTCH STYLE

SERVES 10–12

Whole dried green peas are a very good source of vitamin B1 as well as protein and iron and are the main ingredient in this popular Dutch-style soup.

1 cup (6 oz/185 g) dried green peas

4 cups (32 fl oz/1 L) water

2 tablespoons sunflower oil

4 leeks, thinly sliced

2 stalks celery, thinly sliced

1 lb (500 g) potatoes, cubed

3 cups (24 fl oz/750 ml) vegetable stock

1 tablespoon vegetable extract

1/3 cup shredded celery leaves

1 teaspoon mixed herbs

freshly ground black pepper

Place peas in a bowl, cover with boiling water and leave to stand for 1 hour. Drain. Place peas in a pressure cooker with 4 cups water and cook for 30 minutes (or boil in a pan for 1 hour).

Heat oil and gently fry leeks for 3 minutes, add celery and fry for 2 minutes. Add potatoes, cooked peas and their liquor, stock, vegetable extract, celery leaves and herbs. Bring to the boil covered and simmer for 30 minutes. Cool slightly then mix to a puree and add pepper to taste.

Serve soup hot with wholewheat bread rolls.

THAI MUSHROOM AND COCONUT SOUP

SERVES 4

2 cups (16 fl oz/500 ml) coconut milk

6 thin slices peeled galangal or ginger

2 cloves garlic, crushed

2 stalks lemon grass, thinly sliced

4 kaffir lime leaves, optional

salt to taste

1 tablespoon brown sugar

1 teaspoon minced chili

2 teaspoons chopped cilantro (coriander) root

8 oz (250 g) mushroom cups, sliced

1/2 cup (4 fl oz/125 ml) lime juice

1/4 cup cilantro (coriander) leaves, shredded

Place all ingredients except mushrooms, lime juice and cilantro leaves into a pan and bring to the boil. Add the mushrooms to the pan and simmer until tender, about 10 minutes, or cook them in a covered bowl in a microwave oven on High setting for 2 minutes, then add to pan and simmer covered for 5 minutes. Add lime juice and cilantro just before serving.

Serve garnished with extra cilantro leaves.

Thai mushroom and coconut soup

SPLIT PEA SOUP

SERVES 6–8

The humble dried pea is a rich source of plant protein.

1 cup (6 1/2 oz/200 g) green
dried split peas

2 onions, finely chopped

1 clove garlic, crushed

1 tablespoon polyunsaturated
margarine

1 carrot, diced

1 potato, diced

6 cups (48 fl oz/1.5 L) vegetable
stock

1 tomato, diced

1/4 teaspoon caraway seeds

2 tablespoons brewer's yeast

1 cup (8 fl oz/250 ml) natural
yogurt

mint leaves for garnish

Cover the split peas with boiling water and stand until cold. Gently fry onion and garlic in margarine in a large pan, until soft and golden. Add carrot, potato, stock and caraway seeds, cover and bring to the boil then simmer for 1–1½ hours until peas are tender. Remove potato and carrot with a slotted spoon and reserve. Mix soup to a puree in a blender or food processor and return to pan. Return potato and carrot to soup. Add tomato, brewer's yeast and yogurt and heat through gently before serving.

Serve with a mint garnish and damper, a delicious bread originating in Australia (see Wholemeal and Rye Damper, page 278).

CORN AND EGG SOUP

SERVES 4–6

A quick-to-prepare, tasty, light soup which is good for utilizing leftover egg whites. Serve it with a Chinese meal, for balance of taste, texture and nutritive value.

2 large ears of corn on the cob

4 egg whites

1 tablespoon soy drink

4 cups (32 fl oz/1 L) vegetable
stock

1/4 teaspoon white pepper

2 teaspoons cornstarch (cornflour)

1 tablespoon soy sauce

1 tablespoon mirin or rice vinegar

1 tablespoon obliquely sliced
scallions (spring onions)

cilantro (coriander) for garnish

Remove leaves and silky threads from corn cobs. Slice corn kernels off the corn. Whisk egg whites until stiff then whisk in soy drink. Bring stock to boil in a large pan, add corn and pepper and simmer for 10 minutes or until tender. Blend cornstarch smoothly with soy sauce and mirin, add to soup and stir continuously until it clears and thickens. Remove from heat, quickly stir in egg white mixture until it coagulates.

Serve immediately, sprinkled with scallions and sprigs of cilantro.

CHINESE NOODLE SOUP

SERVES 8

This tasty Chinese soup has a perfect balance of crunchy and soft textures. It is satisfying yet suitable for a weight-reducing diet.

8 dried Chinese mushrooms

4 oz (125 g) tofu

2 tablespoons salt-reduced soy sauce

4 oz (125 g) Chinese noodles

6 cups (48 fl oz/1.5 L) vegetable stock

3 teaspoons white vinegar

1 teaspoon sugar

1 teaspoon chopped ginger

extra 3 teaspoons soy sauce

1/4 cup cooked black beans

1/4 cup thinly sliced bamboo shoots

8 tablespoons watercress leaves

Place dried Chinese mushrooms in a small bowl, cover with 1 cup warm water and leave to soften for 30 minutes. Drain off water, remove and discard mushroom stalks and cut caps in half.

Marinate tofu in soy sauce for 30 minutes. Drain off soy sauce and cut tofu into 1/2 inch (1 cm) squares.

Cook noodles in a large pan of boiling salted water, according to directions on the packet, stirring occasionally. Drain noodles, rinse under cold running water immediately, then drain again.

Place the stock, vinegar, sugar, ginger and soy sauce together in a large pan, bring to the boil and simmer for 1 minute.

Add the mushrooms, noodles, black beans, bamboo shoots and watercress and simmer for 2 minutes. Add the tofu and simmer for a further 1–2 minutes.

Serve in Chinese soup bowls.

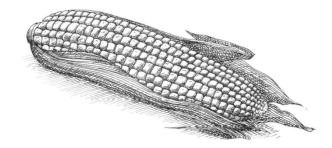

INDIAN SPINACH AND COCONUT SOUP

SERVES 4

1 bunch spinach

2 tablespoons ghee

2 teaspoons mustard seed

1 teaspoon fenugreek

2 teaspoons chopped ginger

4 plump cloves garlic, crushed

2 teaspoons chopped red chili

2 tablespoons wholewheat
(wholemeal) flour

2 cups (16 fl oz/500 ml) water

10 oz (300 ml) can coconut milk

salt

Chop spinach leaves from stalks. Wash well in a sink of cold, salted water, then drain well.

Heat ghee in a heavy-based pan, add mustard seed and fenugreek and fry until mustard crackles or pops. Add ginger, garlic and chili and stir-fry for 1 minute. Add spinach and stir until it softens or wilts. Add flour and stir over a medium heat for 1 minute. Add water and coconut milk and bring to the boil, stirring continuously. Add salt to taste.

Serve hot accompanied by chapatis or naan.

❖ CANNED LEGUMES ARE JUST AS NUTRITIOUS AS HOME-COOKED LEGUMES AND SAVE TIME IN THE PREPARATION OF VEGETARIAN RECIPES. IT IS NOT NECESSARY TO DRAIN THEM WHEN ADDING TO A SOUP OR CASSEROLE, BUT DRAIN AND RINSE THEM IF USING IN A SALAD.

Indian spinach and coconut soup (left); Curried cauliflower and tomato soup (right), p.85

LAKSA

SERVES 12

The popularity of Laksa, a spicy coconut soup with noodles served at restaurants and street stalls in Singapore, is spreading to the Western world. It's a perfect soup to serve in hot or cold weather and if you serve it in Chinese soup/rice bowls with a Chinese porcelain soup spoon, it's really quite easy to handle those noodles. Candlenuts used in this recipe are available at Asian food stores.

2 onions, quartered and thinly sliced

2 cloves garlic, crushed

finely grated rind of 1 lemon

1 tablespoon peanut oil

1 tablespoon chili paste

2 teaspoons ground turmeric

1/2 inch (1 cm) ginger, finely chopped

1/4 cup (1 oz/30 g) candlenuts, finely chopped

4 cups (32 fl oz/1 L) vegetable stock

1 tablespoon sliced lemon grass

1 tablespoon chopped cilantro (coriander) leaves

1 tablespoon tamari

4 cups (32 fl oz/1 L) coconut milk

freshly ground black pepper

For serving:

8 oz (250 g) vermicelli noodles

1 cup bean sprouts

1/3 cup sliced scallions (spring onions)

2 tablespoons lime juice

Gently fry onions, garlic and lemon rind in oil in a large pan. Add chili paste, turmeric and ginger and stir-fry for 1 minute. Add stock, lemon grass, cilantro leaves and tamari and bring to the boil. Add coconut milk and pepper to taste. Simmer gently for 10 minutes.

Boil vermicelli in water to cover for 3 minutes, drain. Assemble bean sprouts, scallions and lime juice.

To serve, divide vermicelli, bean sprouts, scallions and lime juice between 12 soup bowls and ladle hot soup over.

CURRIED CAULIFLOWER AND TOMATO SOUP

SERVES 6

This recipe was inspired by a friend who makes delicious curries, an inheritance from schooldays in India.

1 tablespoon vegetable oil
1 onion, chopped
1 teaspoon cumin seeds
1 teaspoon ground turmeric
1 teaspoon ground coriander
1 teaspoon ground cumin
1/2 teaspoon chili powder
1 lb (500 g) cauliflower
1 medium potato, cubed
14 oz (or 425 g) canned tomatoes
4 cups (32 fl oz/1 L) vegetable stock
2 tablespoons oat bran
salt
natural yogurt for serving, optional

Heat oil in a large pan and gently fry onion with cumin seeds until onion is soft and seeds start to crackle. Add spices and stir-fry for 1 minute. Cut cauliflower into large florets, add to pan with potato, tomatoes and stock. Bring to the boil, cover and simmer for 25 minutes. Add oat bran and simmer for 10 minutes. Cool slightly and mix to a puree. Add salt to taste.

Serve soup hot with a tablespoon of yogurt in each portion.

MAIN COURSES

This chapter is probably the one you will turn to most if you are a vegetarian but I hope semi vegetarians will also find it useful. Whatever your diet, you can find inspiration here for the main meal of the day, which is often the most balanced.

I have attempted to include every variety of vegetable in this book, and in the recipes in this chapter I use fresh leafy greens, roots and tubers, bulbs, stems and stalks, and vegetable fruit. As well, I use fresh pods and seeds, some of which end up in a fascinating range of dried legumes. They are featured in a large repertoire of main course dishes which are attractive and delicious, as well as economical.

The main courses range from Stir-Fried Vegetables, accompanied by a fabulous Macadamia Satay Sauce, and popular international dishes, including Pizza from Italy, Nachos from Mexico, Moussaka from Greece, Kebabs from Korea and Curries from India, all very quick and easy to prepare, to crisp coated patties and fritters, unusually stuffed vegetables, baked vegetable dishes with tasty sauces, international style stuffed pancakes, casseroles, loaves and pies, including a delicious vegetable pie layered with nuts.

All these recipes are based on legumes, nuts, grains, dairy produce and eggs. Served with pasta, rice or another grain (see next chapter), or a simple salad with a sprinkling of nuts, they provide well balanced, complete protein meals.

If you are planning a vegetarian menu for entertaining, I recommend the recipes you can prepare ahead, such as Cabbage and Nut Rolls, Enchiladas with Hot Tomato Salsa, Tamale Pie or Broccoli and Cheese Strudel, so that you can be organised and enjoy your guests' company while they enjoy your food!

All these delicious main course recipes have been methodically tested. They have also been given the seal of approval by my vegetarian family, so I'm sure you will find something here that you, as well as your family and friends, will enjoy.

Macadamia satay sauce (top), p.89; Stir-fried vegetables (front)

STIR-FRIED VEGETABLES

SERVES 4

Stir-fried vegetables is a great dinner standby for busy people. You can use any selection of vegetables, as long as you start off with one of the onion family to develop the initial tastes, and remember to use contrasting shades of vegetables to give eye appeal, because we taste with our eyes first! Add some nuts for protein, whole or ground, or serve with a peanut or Macadamia Satay Sauce (on the following page).

1 tablespoon vegetable oil

2 onions, cut in wedges

1 plump clove garlic, crushed

1 teaspoon finely chopped ginger

2 carrots, thinly sliced diagonally

1 red pepper (capsicum), thinly sliced

1 cup snow peas (mange-tout) or green beans

2 cups shredded Chineses cabbage or Chinese greens

1 tablespoon cornstarch (cornflour)

2 tablespoons salt-reduced soy sauce

2 tablespoons mirin, optional

3/4 cup (6 fl oz/185 ml) vegetable stock or water

Heat oil in a wok or large frying pan. Add onions, garlic and ginger and stir-fry until soft and golden. Add carrots and pepper, stir-fry for 2 minutes. Add snow peas or Chinese greens and stir-fry for a further 2 minutes. Blend cornstarch with soy sauce, add to wok with mirin, if used, and stock and bring to the boil, stirring continuously. Simmer for 1–2 minutes to cook cornstarch.

Serve accompanied by peanut or Macadamia Satay Sauce if desired and brown rice.

❖ ALWAYS DRAIN FRIED FOOD WELL ON KITCHEN PAPER TOWELS BEFORE SERVING. ACCOMPANY FRIED FOOD WITH A LIGHT TEXTURED VEGETABLE OR SHARP FRUIT-BASED SAUCE TO COMPLEMENT THE TASTE AND TEXTURE.

MACADAMIA SATAY SAUCE

SERVES 8

This delicious satay sauce is simple to make and can work out at a third of the price of a processed sauce. It stores well in the refrigerator, for up to 6 weeks, without the coconut milk which can be added later when you use it.

3 cloves garlic, thinly sliced

4 French shallots, thinly sliced

2 red chilies, seeded and finely chopped

5 tablespoons macadamia or peanut oil

1 tablespoon soy sauce

1 tablespoon lemon juice

1 cup (4 oz/125 g) roasted macadamia nuts

1 cup (8 fl oz/250 ml) coconut milk

In a small saucepan, fry garlic, shallots and chilies in 2 tablespoons hot oil until crisp. Drain on kitchen paper towels.

Mix soy sauce and lemon juice, add to pan with another tablespoon of oil and heat gently to blend seasonings.

Mix macadamia nuts in a food processor or blender until coarsely ground. Add remaining oil and mix until finely ground. Stir in crumbled fried garlic, shallots and chilies and soy sauce mixture. May be stored at this stage, otherwise return to saucepan, add coconut milk and stir over a medium heat until hot.

STIR-FRIED LIME TEMPEH

SERVES 4

Tempeh is a protein cultured food made from soy beans. It is also a rich source of vitamin B12, which is often lacking in vegetarian diets. Marinate tempeh for richer taste before cooking.

4 oz (125 g) tempeh, cubed

finely grated rind and juice of 1 lime

2 tablespoons reduced-salt soy sauce

2 teaspoons sesame oil

6 scallions (spring onions), sliced diagonally

1/2 green pepper (capsicum), sliced

1 cup yellow butter beans, sliced diagonally

5 snake beans, sliced diagonally

6 mushroom cups, sliced

1 cup bean sprouts

1 tablespoon chopped cilantro (coriander) leaves

Marinate tempeh in lime juice and rind and soy sauce for at least 30 minutes. Heat oil in a wok or large frying pan and stir-fry scallions and pepper for 1 minute. Add both beans and stir-fry for 2 minutes. Add mushrooms and stir-fry for 1 minute. Finally stir in tempeh with marinade, bean sprouts and cilantro (coriander) and stir-fry until heated through.

Serve with rice.

SPEEDY PIZZA

You can 'throw' this dinner together and serve it within 10 minutes if you use a pre-cooked pizza base or round of foccacia bread and a processed napoletana sauce. Turn the oven on first at 450°F (220°C), put your feet up and watch the TV news for 10 minutes before starting!

1 shrink-wrapped round of foccacia bread or pre-cooked pizza base

1 leek, thinly sliced

1 tablespoon olive oil

1 cup (8 fl oz/250 ml) Napoletana Sauce (page 117)

1/2 cup (2 oz/60 g) grated cheddar cheese

4 tablespoons grated parmesan cheese

olives, capers and/or chopped peppers (capsicum) for topping are optional

Place foccacia bread in oven at 450°F (220°C) for 5 minutes. Gently fry leek in oil until soft, stir in napoletana sauce. Remove foccacia from oven, spread sauce evenly over top almost to edge. (Place foccacia in a flan ring if sauce is too runny). Sprinkle cheddar cheese then parmesan cheese over the top and add optional toppings. Return to oven for 5 minutes.

Serve accompanied by a crisp green salad.

SPEEDY NACHOS

This dish can be 'thrown' together for a quickly prepared dinner. Another bonus is that children, particularly teenagers, love it.

2 large onions, chopped

1/4 cup (2 oz/60 g) butter or margarine

8 oz (250 g) jar taco sauce, medium strength

10 oz (310 g) can red kidney beans, rinsed and drained

2 cups (8 oz/250 g) grated cheddar cheese

6 oz (200 g) pkt corn chips

Gently fry onions in butter until soft and golden. Stir in taco sauce and kidney beans and heat through gently. Pour mixture into a large, shallow microwave-safe dish. Cover with half the grated cheese, then a layer of corn chips and finally sprinkle with remaining cheese. Cook in a microwave oven on Medium setting for 8-10 minutes, until cheese has melted and mixture is hot in the middle. If you don't have a microwave, this is not so speedy, however, cook in an oven at 350°F (180°C) for 20-30 minutes.

Serve topped with a dollop of Guacamole (page 264) and/or sour cream, and a crisp green salad.

Vegetable almond fritters (top), p.100; Stir-fried lime tempeh (front), p.89

CRUNCHY SALSA TACOS

SERVES 4–6

Sunflower kernels provide the crunch in these tacos. Try the sunflower kernels roasted in tamari for something different.

1 onion, chopped

1 tablespoon vegetable oil

12 oz (375 g) jar chunky Mexican salsa

13 oz (425 g) can pinto (borlotti) beans

3 tablespoons tomato paste

3 tablespoons sunflower kernels

12 taco shells

grated cheese, diced tomato, shredded lettuce and bean sprouts for serving

100Gently fry onion in oil until soft. Stir in salsa, beans, tomato paste and sunflower kernels and bring to a gentle boil. Meanwhile, heat the tacos in the oven at 350°F (180°C) for 10–15 minutes.

To serve, spoon hot salsa into taco shells and serve topped with cheese, tomato, lettuce and sprouts.

RATATOUILLE WITH SPINACH

SERVES 4

This versatile Mediterranean vegetable dish may be served hot or cold.

2 tablespoons olive oil

1 clove garlic, crushed

2 onions, chopped

1 green pepper (capsicum), seeded and chopped

1 small eggplant (aubergine) (about 1 lb/500 g), coarsely chopped

4 zucchini (courgette), sliced

3 tomatoes, cut in wedges

2 cups spinach leaves

3 tablespoons ground almonds

salt and pepper

Heat oil in a heavy-based pan and gently fry garlic and onions until soft. Add remaining vegetables, except spinach, cover and simmer for 20–30 minutes. Stir in spinach leaves and heat until wilted. Add almonds and season to taste with salt and pepper.

Serve hot with hot brown rice or cold with a rice salad.

KOREAN TOFU KEBABS

MAKES 12, SERVES 6

This is a delicious barbecue recipe. Try your own mixture of vegetables.

1 lb (500 g) firm tofu

1 eggplant (aubergine), about 1 lb (500 g)

8 oz (250 g) button mushrooms

1/2 bunch plump scallions (spring onions)

1 red pepper (capsicum)

12 bamboo skewers

Marinade:

4 tablespoons sugar

4 tablespoons sesame seeds

2 cloves garlic, crushed

1/2 teaspoon ground chili

1 tablespoon all-purpose (plain) flour

1/2 cup (4 fl oz/125 ml) soy sauce

juice of 2 lemons or 4 limes

2 tablespoons oil

1/2 cup chopped scallions (spring onions)

Cut tofu into 1/2 x 1 inch (1 x 2.5 cm) squares. Cut eggplant into 1 inch (2.5 cm) cubes. Brush mushroom caps with a clean brush and trim stalks. Cut shallots half lengthwise if large. Cut peppers into 3/4 inch (2 cm) squares.

Marinade: Mix all ingredients together. Marinate tofu and vegetables in marinade for 1–2 hours.

Thread tofu and vegetables onto 12 bamboo skewers. Place on an oiled hot plate over a hot charcoal barbecue or under a hot broiler (grill) and cook for 10 minutes, turning frequently and brushing regularly with marinade.

Serve with brown rice and Bean Sprouts and Spinach Salad (see 177) if liked.

Following page: Soy bean casserole (top right), p.126; Napoletana sauce (front left), p.117; Tofu balls (front right), p.113; Cajun casserole, (top left) p.132

Cauliflower and Broccoli au Gratin

SERVES 4

Au gratin vegetables are tasty, satisfying, cold-weather dishes. The combination of white and green, with an onion for texture and a glossy smooth sauce, rich with cheese, makes this particular version very tempting.

8 oz (250 g) trimmed cauliflower

8 oz (250 g) trimmed broccoli

1 large white onion, cut in wedges

1/4 cup (2 oz/60 g) butter or polyunsaturated margarine

4 tablespoons (1 1/3 oz/40 g) wholewheat (wholemeal) flour

2 cups (16 fl oz/500 ml) milk or soy drink

1 cup (4 oz/125 g) grated cheddar or soy cheese

2 teaspoons wholegrain mustard

salt and white pepper

2 tablespoons grated parmesan cheese

1 cup (4 oz/125 g) walnut halves for sprinkling

Wash cauliflower and broccoli in salted water, drain and cut into florets and slice the stalks. Steam all vegetables together or cook in a microwave oven until just tender.

Melt butter in a saucepan, stir in flour and cook over a medium heat for 1–2 minutes, stirring continuously. Add milk and bring to the boil, stirring continuously. Add cheese and mustard and stir until cheese melts. Season to taste with salt and pepper.

Place hot vegetables in an au gratin or heatproof serving dish, cover with hot sauce, sprinkle with parmesan cheese and walnuts. Place under a hot broiler (grill) until golden and bubbling hot.

Serve accompanied by sautéed potatoes and broiled (grilled) tomatoes.

MACADAMIA NUT PATTIES

SERVES 4

Complement these rich nut patties with the sharp taste of Gooseberry Sauce (below).

1 onion, finely chopped

1 clove garlic, crushed

2 teaspoons polyunsaturated margarine

$1/3$ cup (1 $3/4$ oz/50 g) bulgur (cracked wheat), soaked overnight in cold water

1 teaspoon chopped ginger

juice of 1 lemon or 2 limes

2 tablespoons wholewheat (wholemeal) flour or crushed wheat-based breakfast cereal

macadamia nut oil for frying

Gently fry onion and garlic in margarine until soft and golden. Drain bulgur and squeeze dry. Mix all ingredients together and shape into 8 equal-sized, round patties.

Heat oil in a heavy frying pan over a medium heat and fry patties for 2 minutes on both sides, turning carefully. Reduce heat to low and continue frying for 5 minutes on both sides. Drain well on kitchen paper towels.

Top with Gooseberry Sauce if desired, and serve with an interesting salad, such as Bean Sprouts and Spinach Salad (page 177).

GOOSEBERRY SAUCE

SERVES 4

This is an old, unusual English recipe which the British foodies enjoy with their freshly caught broiled (grilled) trout. It's a delicious accompaniment to nut-based fritters and Macadamia Nut Patties (above).

8 oz (250 g) gooseberries, fresh, frozen or canned

$1/2$ cup (4 fl oz/125 ml) water, or juice from canned berries

2 tablespoons sugar, omit if using canned berries

pinch of ground nutmeg

finely grated rind of 1 lemon

Top and tail gooseberries, place in a pan with water, sugar and nutmeg. Cover and stew gently until tender, about 10–15 minutes. Cool then mix to a puree in a blender or food processor. If using canned berries, puree them with $1/2$ cup juice and nutmeg only. Return to pan, add lemon rind and reheat before serving.

MEXICAN LENTIL BURGERS

SERVES 6

For a speedy, nourishing complete protein meal, serve these burgers with lemon brown rice (page 158) and Guacamole (page 264).

1 cup (4 oz/125 g) green lentils

1/4 cup sliced scallions (spring onions)

4 oz (130 g) can corn niblets, drained

1/2 cup diced red pepper (capsicum)

1 teaspoon minced chili

1 egg

1 cup (2 oz/60 g) wholewheat (wholemeal) breadcrumbs

cornmeal for coating

oil for frying

Rinse lentils then cook in boiling salted water until tender, about 15 minutes. Drain well and mash in a bowl. Add all remaining ingredients and mix well. Divide into 12 equal portions and shape into round burger shapes and coat with cornmeal.

Fry burgers for 1–2 minutes on both sides to seal, then reduce heat and gently fry for 5 minutes on both sides or until cooked through. Drain well on kitchen paper towels before serving.

QUICK VEGETARIAN MOUSSAKA

SERVES 4

This recipe uses a processed tomato-based pasta sauce, canned beans and a microwave oven to make it quick and easy to prepare.

1/2 cup (4 fl oz/125 ml) olive oil

8 Japanese eggplant (aubergine), sliced, or 2 cups cubed eggplant

1 onion, chopped

13 oz (425 g) can borlotti beans, rinsed and drained

2 cups (16 fl oz/500 ml) tomato-based pasta sauce, napoletana, cacciatore or similar

2 eggs, beaten

1 cup (8 fl oz/250 ml) natural yogurt

Heat oil and fry eggplant until soft and browned, transfer with a slotted spoon to a shallow microwave-safe dish.

Gently fry onion until soft, add to eggplant. Place beans on top and cover with pasta sauce. Mix eggs with yogurt and spread over the top of the sauce.

Cook in a microwave oven on Medium setting for 10–12 minutes until heated all the way through.

Serve with multi-grain rice.

Quick vegetarian moussaka

THAI POTATO AND TOFU CAKES

SERVES 4

A lovely light texture combined with fragrant Thai seasonings makes these cakes very appetizing, particularly when accompanied by Thai Apricot Salad (page 202).

1 lb (500 g) potatoes, red-skinned, such as Pontiac or Desiree

4 oz (125 g) tofu

juice of 2 limes

2 cloves garlic, crushed

1 teaspoon finely chopped ginger

1 teaspoon finely chopped lemon grass

1 teaspoon finely chopped cilantro (coriander) roots

2 tablespoons chopped cilantro (coriander) leaves

1 tablespoon sweet chili sauce

salt to taste

oil for frying

Cook and mash potatoes. Dice tofu and marinate in lime juice for 30 minutes. Place all ingredients together in a bowl and mix well. Spread level, divide into eight equal portions and shape each into a neat round cake shape.

Heat sufficient oil to coat bottom of frying pan and fry cakes over a medium-high heat for 1 minute on both sides. Reduce to a low heat and gently fry for a further 6–7 minutes on both sides. Drain on kitchen paper towels.

Serve hot.

VEGETABLE ALMOND FRITTERS

SERVES 4

1 large carrot, grated

1 large potato, grated

2 zucchini (courgette), grated

1/2 cup (2 oz/60 g) ground almonds

2 tablespoons chopped parsley

1 tablespoon all-purpose wholewheat (plain wholemeal) flour

1 egg, beaten

equal quantity sesame seeds and wholewheat (wholemeal) flour to coat

oil for frying

Mix all ingredients together in a bowl, except coating. Spread mixture level and divide into eight equal portions. Shape each portion into a neat fritter and roll in sesame seeds and wholewheat flour until evenly coated.

Heat sufficient oil to coat bottom of frying pan and fry fritters for 1 minute over a medium-high heat, turn over carefully and fry for 1 minute on other side, then reduce heat to low and gently fry for 6 minutes on both sides or until cooked all the way through. Drain on kitchen paper towels.

Serve with hot crisp wholewheat bread rolls.

DOMATES DOLMASI
STUFFED TOMATOES
SERVES 6

This is a sophisticated Lebanese recipe. The tomatoes have an unusual filling of brown rice, almonds, currants and herbs.

1 cup (8 oz/250 g) brown rice
3 onions, finely chopped
4 tablespoons olive oil
2 tablespoons slivered almonds
1 tomato, chopped
2 tablespoons currants
1 tablespoon chopped mint
1 tablespoon marjoram
1 tablespoon cider vinegar
1/2 cup (4 fl oz/125 ml) water
1 teaspoon raw sugar
salt and pepper
6 large vine-ripened tomatoes
1 cup (8 fl oz/250 ml) vegetable stock
2 tablespoons butter or margarine
chopped parsley for garnish

Boil rice for 30 minutes, drain well. Fry onions gently in oil in a pan for 10 minutes, but don't brown. Add rice, almonds, chopped tomato, currants, herbs, cider vinegar and water and simmer for 15 minutes or until water is reduced. Add sugar and salt and pepper to taste.

Wash tomatoes and cut a lid from the top of each. Scoop out pulp, being careful not to break the skins. Fill tomatoes with filling and arrange side by side in a large shallow baking dish. Carefully pour in stock and dot tomatoes with butter.

Bake at 350°F (180°C) for 15–20 minutes.

Serve sprinkled with chopped parsley, accompanied by couscous and salad.

SWEET POTATO LATKES WITH CAPER SAUCE

SERVES 6

This traditional Jewish dish becomes more nourishing with the addition of 'besan' or chick pea flour.

1 lb (500 g) sweet red potato (kumara)

1 lb (500 g) potatoes

1 onion, finely chopped

1 cup (4 oz/125 g) chick pea flour

3/4 teaspoon baking powder

2 eggs

salt and pepper

1 tablespoon chopped parsley

1 tablespoon snipped chives

oil for frying

Caper Sauce:

1 tablespoon vegetable oil

1/2 cup thinly sliced scallions (spring onions)

2 tablespoons soy drink

1/2 cup (4 fl oz/125 ml) light sour cream

2 teaspoons lemon juice

1 tablespoon capers

Coarsely grate potatoes and drain well. Place potatoes in a mixing bowl with all remaining ingredients and mix together. Cover and leave to stand for 1 hour. Heat sufficient oil for shallow frying in a frying pan and drop large spoonfuls of mixture from the point of the spoon into the oil, as for small pancakes, and fry until golden brown on both sides and cooked in the middle, about 5 minutes. You should make approximately 12 latkes. Drain well on kitchen paper towels and keep hot until ready to serve.

Caper Sauce: Heat oil and gently fry scallions. Remove from heat and stir in remaining ingredients.

Serve warm or cold with the latkes.

Carrot balls (top), p.116; Sweet potato latkes with caper sauce (front)

CABBAGE AND NUT ROLLS

SERVES 4–8, ACCORDING TO APPETITE

This is a vegetarian version of a traditional Polish recipe. A delicious satisfying dish to serve on a cold winter night.

13 ½ oz (425 g) can sauerkraut

⅓ cup (2 oz/50 g) brown rice

1 large green cabbage

1 tablespoon vegetable oil

2 onions, finely chopped

1 clove garlic, crushed

¾ cup (3 oz/100 g) walnuts, chopped

¾ cup (3 oz/100 g) hazelnuts, chopped

4 oz (125 g) mushrooms, chopped

2 teaspoons paprika

1 tablespoon chopped parsley

1 teaspoon salt

¼ teaspoon freshly ground black pepper

2 eggs, beaten

13 oz (410 g) can tomatoes

1 ½ cups (12 fl oz/375 ml) vegetable stock or water

1 cup (8 fl oz/250 ml) light sour cream

Drain sauerkraut and soak in cold water for 10 minutes. Drain well and squeeze dry.

Cook rice in boiling salted water for 30 minutes. Drain and rinse under cold running water.

Carefully remove 8 large outer leaves from cabbage. Allow cold water to flow between the leaves to loosen them. Place leaves, one by one, in a large pan of boiling water and blanch for 1–2 minutes only, until soft but not too limp. Remove leaves and drain in a colander until just cool enough to touch, then drain well on kitchen paper towels.

Heat oil and gently fry onion and garlic for 5 minutes. Stir in nuts, mushrooms, paprika, parsley, salt and pepper and cook, stirring continuously, for a further minute. Remove from heat, and cool.

Mix rice and eggs into mixture. Spread drained cabbage leaves on a clean working surface and remove any hard core, using kitchen scissors. Place an eighth of filling on the base of each cabbage leaf. With the base end of the cabbage leaf nearest you, fold bottom over filling, fold each side over neatly and roll up firmly in a roll shape. Place sauerkraut in the bottom of a greased flameproof casserole dish and place stuffed cabbage rolls on top. Mix tomatoes and stock together and pour over cabbage rolls. Bring to the boil then cover and simmer gently for 45 minutes or transfer to a moderate oven at 350°F (180°C) for 45 minutes.

Place cabbage rolls on a warm serving plate and keep hot. Stir sour cream into sauce and sauerkraut and heat through. Pour sauce over cabbage rolls and serve.

STUFFED MARROW

SERVES 4

This is a 'cheap and cheerful' dish, particularly if you grow your own vegetables. Serve accompanied by a salad sprinkled with nuts for a complete protein meal.

2 cups (16 fl oz/500 ml) vegetable stock

1/2 cup (3 1/3 oz/100 g) buckwheat groats

1 marrow, approx. 1 lb (500 g)

1 tablespoon olive oil

1 onion, finely chopped

1 small kohlrabi or turnip, grated

2 tablespoons tomato paste

2 tablespoons chopped parsley

1/2 teaspoon paprika

Bring the stock to the boil in a pan, add buckwheat groats and simmer for 15 minutes or until cooked. Drain well.

Cut marrow in half lengthwise, remove and discard seeds and scoop out flesh leaving a 1/2 inch (1.5 cm) 'shell'. Chop the flesh. Heat oil and fry onion until soft. Add marrow flesh and kohlrabi and fry, stirring occasionally, for 3 minutes. Stir in tomato paste, parsley, paprika and buckwheat.

Brush inside of marrow shells with melted margarine and spoon filling into them. Bake at 350°F (180°C) for 25 minutes. Serve with a salad.

STUFFED EGGPLANT ROLLS

SERVES 4

Stuffed long thin slices of eggplant are much easier to serve than stuffed eggplant halves. You can use the remaining eggplant in Caponatina Salad (page 185). This dish can be prepared in advance so it's good to use when entertaining.

2 long, plump eggplant (aubergine)

wholewheat (wholemeal) flour

oil for frying

2 cups cooked brown rice (2/3 cup raw)

1/2 cup cooked peas

1/2 cup diced mushrooms

1/4 cup diced red pepper (capsicum)

2 hard-boiled eggs, chopped

1/2 cup (2 oz/60 g) cheddar cheese, grated

salt and pepper

1 cup (8 fl oz/250 ml) white sauce

1 cup (8 fl oz/250 ml) Napoletana sauce

Cut 4 long, thin slices out of the middle of both eggplant. Dip in flour and fry in hot oil on both sides to soften. Drain well on kitchen paper towels.

Mix together all remaining ingredients, except sauces, and season to taste with salt and pepper. Divide mixture equally between slices of eggplant, placing at one end, then roll eggplant up and secure with a toothpick.

Place stuffed eggplant rolls in a single layer in a shallow baking dish. Coat with white sauce, then with Napoletana Sauce (page 117). Cover with foil and bake at 375°F (190°C) for 30 minutes, removing foil for last 5 minutes.

Serve hot with Feta with Radicchio Salad (page 190) or a crisp green salad.

PEPERONI RIPIENI
STUFFED PEPPERS

SERVES 4

This Italian recipe has a delicious risotto-style filling in the peppers. Use your microwave oven to cut down on the preparation time.

5 sweet red or green peppers (capsicum)

2 tablespoons olive oil

1 cup chopped eggplant (aubergine)

1 onion, chopped

2 cloves garlic, crushed

2/3 cup (6 oz/185 g) brown rice

2 cups (16 fl oz/500 ml) hot vegetable stock

1/4 cup (1 oz/30 g) ground hazelnuts

4 tablespoons grated parmesan cheese

2 tablespoons shredded basil

salt and pepper

Wash and dry peppers. Deseed 1 pepper and chop finely. Trim stalks level with flesh on remaining peppers and slice 1/2 inch (1 cm) from other end and reserve. Remove seeds and cores. Stand peppers stalks down, near the edge of a shallow microwave-safe dish and place in microwave oven on High setting for 5 minutes.

Heat half oil in a frying pan and gently fry chopped pepper and eggplant until soft.

Heat remaining oil in a heavy-based pan and gently fry onion and garlic until soft. Add rice and stir-fry for 2 minutes. Add 1/2 cup hot stock and simmer rice, stirring, until absorbed. Reheat three times, simmering and stirring occasionally. Stir in eggplant mixture, hazelnuts, cheese and basil and season to taste with salt and pepper.

Spoon rice mixture into peppers, top with reserved slices and cook in the microwave on Medium setting for 20 minutes or until rice and peppers are tender.

Serve with a crisp green salad.

Domates dolmasi (front), p.101; Peperoni ripieni (top)

WHOLEWHEAT PÂTE BRISÉE

This pastry has a higher proportion of fat to flour than shortcrust pastry, so it's particularly good for rolling out thinly for quiches and tarts. Add 2 tablespoons bran or wheatgerm to flour for nourishment.

1 1/2 cups (6 oz/185 g) all-purpose wholewheat (plain wholemeal) flour

1/2 cup (4 oz/125 g) salted butter or polyunsaturated margarine

3-5 tablespoons iced water

Sift flour into the bowl of a food processor. Cut butter into small cubes, add to flour and mix for 20 seconds or until mixture resembles breadcrumbs. Add 3 tablespoons water and mix for 20 seconds. If dough has not come together, scrape down, add another tablespoon of water and mix for 20 seconds. Repeat with more water if necessary until dough leaves sides of bowl cleanly, but do not overmix. Turn dough out onto a lightly floured surface, preferably marble in a hot climate, and toss or knead very gently until smooth underneath. Pat into a round cake, wrap in waxed (greaseproof) paper and chill in refrigerator for at least 30 minutes before using. This pastry freezes well.

SWISS CHEESE TART

SERVES 4–6

A delicious tart which the Swiss serve in small portions for an entree or in larger portions as a family dish. Add bran to the pastry and sprinkle the tart with pepitas and sesame seeds to add extra nutrition.

6 oz (185 g) wholewheat pâte brisée (above) with bran

Filling:

1 tablespoon olive oil

1 onion, finely chopped

1/4 teaspoon paprika

1 cup (4 oz/125 g) emmanthal cheese, grated

1 cup (4 oz/125 g) gruyère cheese, grated

2 eggs, beaten

1/2 cup (4 fl oz/125 ml) cream

1/2 cup (4 fl oz/125 ml) milk

1/4 teaspoon ground nutmeg

salt to taste

1 tablespoon pepitas

1 tablespoon sesame seeds

Make pastry and chill for 30 minutes before using.

Filling: Heat oil and gently fry onion and paprika until soft and transparent. Mix with cheese, eggs, cream, milk, nutmeg and salt to taste.

To finish: Roll out pastry on a lightly floured surface to a round and line a 9 inch (23 cm) shallow flan tin. Bake 'blind' in a hot oven at 425°F (220°C) for 10 minutes. Remove 'blind' filling and bake a further 10 minutes. Pour cheese filling carefully into pastry case, sprinkle with pepitas and sesame seeds. Bake at 350°F (180°C) for 10 minutes, then increase to 425°F (220°C) and bake for a further 15 minutes or until firm, puffed and golden brown.

Serve hot accompanied by a rice salad and a crisp green salad.

PUMPKIN, CARROT AND HERB RING

SERVES 8

True vegans may substitute the eggs in this dish with a yolk-free egg mix and the cheese with tofu.

1 lb (500 g) butternut pumpkin, peeled and seeded

1 lb (500 g) carrots

3 tablespoons polyunsaturated margarine

freshly ground black pepper

2 cups (16 fl oz/500 ml) vegetable stock

8 oz (250 g) button mushrooms, diced

2 teaspoons olive oil

2 tablespoons finely chopped scallions (spring onions)

1 tablespoon finely chopped chervil or parsley

1 tablespoon finely chopped dill

1/2 cup rice bran

4 eggs

1/2 cup (2 oz/60 g) grated reduced-fat cheese

Cut pumpkin into small even-sized cubes. Slice carrots.

Heat margarine in a large heavy-based pan, add pumpkin and carrots and cook until lightly browned.

Add pepper and stock and cook over a medium heat for 30 minutes or until liquid has evaporated and vegetables are tender.

Fry mushrooms in a small frying pan in olive oil. Add scallions, chervil and dill, remove from heat.

Beat eggs in a large bowl, add pumpkin, carrot and mushroom mixtures, bran and cheese and mix together lightly. Brush the inside of a ring tin with polyunsaturated oil, line base of ring with waxed (greaseproof) paper and fill with mixture.

Cover ring with foil, stand in a hot-water bath and cook at 375°F (180°C) for 45 minutes or until firm. Turn ring out carefully on to a serving dish and serve hot with Asparagus Sauce (below) and new potatoes.

Note: A carrot and herb ring can be made by using 2 lb (1 kg) carrots instead of the mixture of pumpkin and carrots.

ASPARAGUS SAUCE

SERVES 4

12 oz (375 g) asparagus or 11 oz (340 g) can asparagus

1/2 cup (4 fl oz/125 ml) vegetable stock

pinch of white pepper

salt

2 tablespoons natural yogurt or Fromage Blanc (page 208)

Wash and trim asparagus and poach in a frying pan of boiling salted water until tender, drain well. Alternatively, cook in a microwave oven. Simply drain if using canned asparagus.

Slice asparagus coarsely and mix to a puree, in a blender or food processor with the stock, pepper and salt to taste. Add yogurt and mix for a few seconds.

Heat sauce slowly in a heavy-based, ceramic-lined saucepan or in the top of a double-boiler over gently bubbling water. Serve hot.

GRATIN DAUPHINOIS

SERVES 6-8

Potatoes and cheese are a delicious combination. This was a popular 'dish of the house' during my short career as a restaurateur.

2 cups (16 fl oz/500 ml) soy drink

2 lb (1 kg) medium sized potatoes

2 eggs

1/2 teaspoon salt

12 grinds black pepper

12 grinds nutmeg

1 clove garlic

2 cups (8 oz/250 g) gruyère or cheddar cheese, grated

Bring milk to boiling point then cool. Peel potatoes, dry well then slice thinly using a food processor. Beat eggs with salt, pepper and nutmeg. Peel and cut garlic and rub over a large au gratin dish or shallow ovenproof dish then brush with melted butter.

Layer potatoes and cheese in dish, finishing with a cheese layer. Carefully pour egg mixture over. Bake at 400°F (200°C) for 30 minutes, then at 350°F (180°C) for 30 minutes or until set and golden brown.

Serve hot as a main course, accompanied by a salad and sprinkled with chopped nuts.

ZUCCHINI FRITTATA

SERVES 6

This is an Italian egg pancake, usually cooked in a frying pan then browned under a broiler (grill) when softly set. However if you cook it in the oven, like a crustless quiche, in a ceramic quiche or crème brûlée dish, it looks more stylish for serving.

1 plump clove garlic, crushed

2 tablespoons olive oil

3 zucchini (courgette), thinly sliced

1 tablespoon wholewheat (wholemeal) flour

6 eggs

2 tablespoons chopped parsley

1 teaspoon salt

1/4 teaspoon white pepper

1/2 cup (4 oz/125 g) cottage or ricotta cheese

1/3 cup natural yogurt

1/4 cup grated cheese for sprinkling

1 teaspoon poppy seeds for sprinkling

Gently fry garlic in oil. Mix zucchini with flour, add to pan and stir-fry gently until golden. Beat eggs lightly in a mixing bowl, add zucchini mixture and all remaining ingredients. Pour into an oiled ceramic quiche dish, sprinkle with cheese and poppy seeds and bake at 350°F (180°C) for 25–30 minutes or until firm.

Serve cut into wedges accompanied by a rice salad and a crisp green salad. Alternatively, cool then chill and serve at a picnic.

Zucchini frittata

RUTABAGA BAKE

Born into a Scottish family meant that I ate a lot of rutabaga (swede) as a child. I just love this dish. Serve it with a delicious Sorrel Sauce (below) and accompany with barley or buckwheat for a balanced meal.

2 lb (1 kg) rutabaga (swede)

4 tablespoons rye breadcrumbs

3 tablespoons (2 fl oz/60 ml) soy drink

1/4 teaspoon ground nutmeg

1 teaspoon salt

2 eggs, beaten

2 teaspoons polyunsaturated margarine

2 tablespoons rice bran

Peel rutabaga, cut into chunky pieces and cook in boiling salted water until tender. Drain well then mix to a puree in a food processor or blender.

Soak breadcrumbs in milk, add nutmeg, salt, eggs and rutabaga puree and mix well. Grease a ceramic baking dish with some of the margarine, place rutabaga mixture in it, spread level and dot with remaining margarine. Sprinkle with rice bran.

Bake at 350°F (180°C) for 3/4–1 hour until firm and golden brown.

SORREL SAUCE

Sorrel is a herb with a very distinctive taste. If you cannot buy it, try growing it. Try this sauce with broiled (grilled) mushrooms for a delicious snack or as a tangy accompaniment to Rutabaga Bake (above).

1/4 cup (2 oz/60 g) butter or polyunsaturated margarine

4 plump scallions (spring onions)

2 tablespoons all-purpose (plain) flour

1/2 cup (4 fl oz/125 ml) sparkling grape juice

1/2 cup (4 fl oz/125 ml) vegetable stock

6 green peppercorns

1 cup sorrel leaves, firmly packed

1/4 cup basil or thyme

1/2 cup (4 fl oz/125 ml) light sour cream or soy drink

salt and pepper

1 teaspoon lemon juice

Melt butter in a saucepan and gently fry scallions. Add flour and stir continuously over a medium heat for 1 minute. Add grape juice and stock and bring to the boil, stirring continuously. Stir in peppercorns, sorrel and herbs, simmer for 10 minutes. Mix sauce to a puree, return to saucepan, add sour cream and heat through gently. Season to taste with salt and pepper and stir in lemon juice.

CHEESE AND LEEK CHARLOTTE

SERVES 4

This recipe is a 'cheat soufflé' for those who feel intimidated by the French dish. It has a soufflé-like texture and tastes delicious accompanied by a crisp salad.

2 leeks, very thinly sliced

1 tablespoon butter

3 large eggs, beaten

1 cup (2 oz/60 g) wholewheat (wholemeal) breadcrumbs

1/2 cup (2 oz/60 g) cheddar cheese, grated

2 tablespoons chopped parsley

pepper to taste

1 tablespoon sesame seeds

1 tablespoon wheatgerm

1 tablespoon grated parmesan cheese

2 egg whites, stiffly whisked

Gently fry leeks in butter until soft and moist. Add all remaining ingredients except sesame seeds, wheatgerm parmesan and egg whites and mix together. Gently fold in whisked egg whites.

Pour mixture into a buttered oval pie dish or soufflé dish and sprinkle with sesame seeds, wheatgerm and parmesan. Bake at 350°F (180°C) for 30 minutes or until firm.

Serve hot accompanied by a crisp salad.

TOFU BALLS

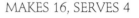

MAKES 16, SERVES 4

These light textured high-protein tofuballs taste delicious.

12 oz (375g) firm tofu, squeezed dry

1/4 cup (1 oz /30 g) chopped walnuts

1 egg, beaten

1 tablespoon miso paste

1 small onion, finely chopped

3 tablespoons chopped parsley

finely grated rind of 1 lemon

1/4 cup (1/2 oz/15 g) wholewheat (wholemeal) breadcrumbs

1/4 teaspoon pepper

2 tablespoons wholewheat (wholemeal) flour, if required

vegetable oil for frying

Mash tofu with a fork or mix in a food processor until well crumbled. Add all remaining ingredients in given order, adding wholewheat flour only if necessary to bind. Roll mixture into 16 even-sized balls in clean, cold hands. Heat oil in a frying pan and shallow fry tofuballs until golden brown, turning frequently. Drain on kitchen paper towels and serve with Napoletana Sauce (page 117) or Sweet and Sour Sauce (page 46) on a bed of rice or pasta.

Following page: Swiss cheese tart (left), p.106; Cheese and leek charlotte (middle), p.113; Curried spinach and lentil tart (right), p.120

CARROT BALLS

SERVES 4

This dish is particularly enticing in cold weather when it is important to include rich sources of vitamin C in the daily menu.

2 lb (1 kg) carrots

2 tablespoons butter or margarine

4 oz (125 g) mushrooms, finely chopped

1/4 cup thinly sliced scallions (spring onions)

1/4 teaspoon ground ginger

salt and pepper

egg and crushed wheat-based breakfast cereal for coating

oil for deep frying

Peel carrots and slice thinly. Cook in boiling salted water for 15 minutes or until tender. Drain, then mix to a puree in a blender or food processor. Squeeze the carrot puree, a quarter at a time, in a clean cloth, then place in a mixing bowl.

Heat butter in a small frying pan and gently fry mushrooms, stirring occasionally.

Add mushrooms, scallions and ginger to the carrot puree and mix well, then season to taste with salt and pepper.

Spread mixture on a plate, cover and chill in refrigerator for 2 hours.

Shape tablespoons of mixture into balls, then coat with beaten egg and crushed cereal.

Deep-fry carrot balls in oil at 375°F (190°C) for 1–2 minutes until crisp and golden brown. Drain well on kitchen paper towels.

Serve carrot balls immediately, accompanied by boiled rice and cheese sauce or Napoletana sauce (page 117).

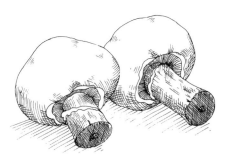

NAPOLETANA SAUCE

MAKES 3 CUPS (24 FL OZ/750 ML)

This is a popular classic sauce from Naples where it is used on pizza, but is equally versatile on top of pasta, or in lasagna. For the best results make it when tomatoes are abundantly in season. Many good processed varieties are also available for a quick alternative standby.

3 tablespoons vegetable or olive oil

2 onions, finely chopped

3 teaspoons crushed garlic

2 lb (1 kg) ripe tomatoes, cored and coarsely chopped or two 14 oz (450 g) cans tomatoes

3/4 cup (6 fl oz/185 ml) tomato paste

1 tablespoon chopped basil

1 tablespoon chopped oregano

1 bay leaf

2 teaspoons sugar

2 teaspoons salt (omit if using canned tomatoes)

freshly ground black pepper

Heat oil in a pan and gently fry onion and garlic for 5 minutes until soft, stirring occasionally. Add all remaining ingredients and bring to the boil stirring. Cover and simmer for 1 hour (30 minutes for canned tomatoes), stirring occasionally. If too thin, simmer uncovered to reduce liquid.

For something different, serve over cooked spaghetti squash/vegetable spaghetti.

CURRIED TEMPEH

SERVES 4

The strong taste of tempeh marries well with curry. Tempeh is made from fermented soy beans and therefore is a good source of protein. It is also a source of vitamin B12.

1 onion, cut in wedges

1 tablespoon vegetable or nut oil

3 teaspoons curry paste, mild strength

2 carrots, sliced

1 stalk celery, sliced

1 cup cauliflower florets

2 medium potatoes, in chunky pieces

2 cups (16 fl oz/500 ml) vegetable stock

4 oz (125 g) tempeh, cubed

1 cup (4 oz/125 g) frozen peas

1 tablespoon lime pickles

Gently fry onion in oil in a pan until soft and transparent. Add curry paste and stir-fry for 1 minute. Add carrots, celery, cauliflower, potatoes and stock, bring to the boil covered, then simmer for 20 minutes. Add tempeh, peas and pickles and simmer for a further 10 minutes.

Serve with brown rice and curry accompaniments.

VEGETABLE AND CASHEW CURRY

SERVES 4–6

This is a popular dish in our house, impressive enough for entertaining, yet easy to prepare, because you use a convenient processed curry paste. The curry matures if you have time to let it stand overnight.

1 large onion, chopped

1 plump clove garlic, crushed

2 tablespoons butter, margarine, or vegetable oil

5 tablespoons good quality korma or medium-strength curry paste

2 carrots, sliced

1 cup coarsely chopped pumpkin

2 potatoes, coarsly chopped

1 3/4 cups (10 fl oz/300 g) can coconut milk

14 oz (450 g) can tomatoes

1 cup green beans or sugar snap peas

10 oz (310 g) can red kidney beans, rinsed and drained

4 tablespoons toasted cashew nuts

Gently fry onion and garlic in butter in a large, heavy-based pan until soft and golden. Add curry paste and stir over heat for 1 minute. Add carrots, pumpkin, potatoes, coconut milk and tomatoes and bring to the boil, stirring occasionally. Cover and boil slowly for 20–30 minutes until vegetables are tender. Wash and trim green beans and steam or microwave until tender-crisp. Stir green beans, kidney beans and nuts into curry and heat through gently.

Serve accompanied by boiled rice, mango chutney, banana and shredded coconut with natural yogurt, tomato and cucumber with safflower dressing and pappadams.

Vegetable and cashew curry (top); Indian egg curry (front), p.121

CURRIED SPINACH AND LENTIL TART

SERVES 6–8

This combination of pulse-legume with cereal, cheese and eggs is very nourishing. You can use commercial sheets of rolled pastry to save time.

8 oz (250 g) wholewheat (wholemeal) pâte brisée with bran (page 108)

Filling:

1/2 cup (3 oz/100 g) red lentils

1 lb (500 g) spinach

1 onion, finely chopped

1 clove garlic, crushed

2 tablespoons butter or margarine

2 eggs

1/2 cup (4 oz/125 g) cottage cheese

2 teaspoons curry paste

1/2 teaspoon salt

3 tablespoons grated parmesan cheese and 1 tablespoon sesame seeds for sprinkling

Make pastry according to recipe and chill.

Filling: Cook lentils in boiling salted water for 15 minutes or until tender, drain well then mash lightly. Trim and wash spinach. Shred spinach leaves and cook in the water clinging to the leaves in covered pan for 5 minutes; drain well. Gently fry onion and garlic in butter until soft and golden. Beat eggs, cottage cheese, curry paste and salt together in a mixing bowl. Add onion mixture, lentils and spinach and mix together.

To finish tart: Roll pastry out to a round and line a deep 20 cm/18 inch flan tin. Line with greaseproof paper and dry beans and bake 'blind' at 425°F (220°C) for 10 minutes. Remove 'blind' filling, spread spinach mixture in pastry case and sprinkle with cheese and sesame seeds. Bake at 400°F (200°C) for 20–30 minutes until filling is set and cheese is golden.

This recipe is also delicious made with Swiss chard (Silverbeet) instead of spinach.

Serve hot or cold; delicious with Curried Rice Salad (page 198) and a crisp green salad. This tart freezes well.

INDIAN EGG CURRY

Often overlooked and underrated, the egg is a rich source of protein and is very versatile. In this Indian curry sauce it becomes a gourmet's delight.

2 cloves garlic, peeled and halved

1 inch (2.5 cm) piece ginger, peeled and sliced

6 tablespoons (unsweetened) desiccated coconut

1 tablespoon poppy seeds

2 oz (60 g) ghee or copha (solidified coconut oil)

2 large onions, thinly sliced

1 cup (8 fl oz/250 ml) natural yogurt

3 teaspoons ground coriander

1 teaspoon chili powder

1/4 teaspoon ground cloves

1/4 teaspoon ground cinnamon

2 green and 2 red chilies, seeded and thinly sliced

1 tablespoon lemon juice

salt

4 hard-boiled eggs

Place garlic, ginger, coconut and poppy seeds in a small blender, processor or coffee mill and mix until ground.

Heat ghee and gently fry onion until soft and golden. Remove with a slotted spoon, pressing well to drain off ghee. Crush onion and mix with yogurt.

Add spices to remaining ghee in pan and fry for 3 minutes, stirring continuously. Add yogurt and onion and bring to a simmer. Cover and simmer for 10 minutes. Add chilies, lemon juice and salt to taste.

Shell eggs and cut in half while still warm. Pour curry sauce over the eggs and serve, accompanied by rice, pappadams or naan, mango chutney or lime pickle and other attractive curry accompaniments.

❖ LENTILS ARE ONE OF THE MOST VERSATILE AND POPULAR LEGUMES IN THE VEGETARIAN DIET BECAUSE THEY ARE THE QUICKEST TO COOK. RED LENTILS COOK IN APPROXIMATELY 15–20 MINUTES, BROWN LENTILS IN ABOUT 25 MINUTES. YOU CAN USE THEM IN SOUPS, PATTIES, PIES, TARTS, LOAVES, CASSEROLES AND CURRIES. THEY ARE VERY POPULAR IN INDIAN CUISINE SERVED AS DHAL, A TASTY CURRY ACCOMPANIMENT.

ENCHILADAS WITH HOT TOMATO SALSA

SERVES 4

This dish is worth all the trouble because it's delicious. Vacuum-packed tortillas are available in leading supermarkets.

Filling:

4 oz (125 g) cream cheese

3 tablespoons light sour cream

1 onion, finely chopped

10 oz (310 g) can red kidney beans, rinsed and drained

Sauce:

6 green banana peppers or 3 yellow peppers (capsicum)

1 lb (500 g) tomatoes, seeded and quartered

2 green chilies, seeded and coarsely chopped

1 tablespoon parsley sprigs

1 egg

3/4 cup (6 fl oz/185 ml) light sour cream

1 cup (8 fl oz/250 ml) cream

salt

8 tortillas

2 tablespoons grated parmesan cheese

Filling: Beat cream cheese with sour cream. Add onion and kidney beans and mix together.

Sauce: Cut peppers in half lengthwise, remove seeds and membrane and place under a red hot broiler (grill) for 5 minutes, moving frequently so that they darken and blister but do not burn. Wrap peppers in a clean, damp cloth, leave a few minutes, then unwrap and rub peppers carefully to remove the skin.

Mix peppers to a puree in a food processor or blender. Add tomatoes, green chilies and parsley and mix together to a puree. Add egg and remaining cream and mix again to a smooth puree. Season to taste with salt if necessary.

To make enchiladas, pour some sauce into a deep round pie plate, dip a tortilla into the sauce, turn over and dip other side. Place on work surface, spoon an eighth of filling along the middle and fold one side over and roll up into a cylinder. Place in a large, shallow baking dish. Continue until all tortillas are filled.

Pour remaining sauce over and sprinkle parmesan cheese on top. Bake at 375°F (180°C) for 15 minutes or until hot and golden.

Serve with a crisp green salad.

TAMALE PIE

SERVES 6–8

This delicious Mexican crustless pie is cooked in a covered casserole dish, but you can serve it in wedges. It's easy to make and economical too.

2 onions, chopped

2 cloves garlic, crushed

2 tablespoons sunflower oil

1 1/2 tablespoons hot chili paste

14 oz (440 g) can corn niblets, drained

13 1/2 oz (425 g) can tomatoes, chopped

1 cup (5 oz/160 g) cornmeal

1/2 cup stuffed olives

1 cup (4 oz/125 g) ground pecans

3 tablespoons grated parmesan cheese

3 eggs, beaten

1 cup (8 fl oz/250 ml) soy drink

3 oz (90 g) polynsaturated margarine

salt and pepper

Gently fry onions and garlic in oil in a heavy-based pan. Add chili paste and stir-fry for 30 seconds. Add corn and tomatoes and cook for 5 minutes, stirring continuously. Stir in all remaining ingredients and season to taste with salt and pepper.

Place mixture in a large greased casserole dish, cover and bake at 350°F (180°C) for 30 minutes.

Serve cut into wedges accompanied by salad.

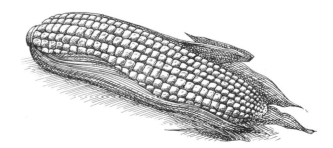

GREEN CURRIED BEAN CRÊPES

SERVES 4

Crêpes made with wholewheat (wholemeal) flour and soy drink will provide some protein and fiber to your diet. Unfilled crêpes, layered with waxed (greaseproof) paper, freeze well. The green curried bean filling may also be served with brown rice.

Crêpes:

1 cup (4 oz/125 g) all-purpose wholewheat (plain wholemeal) flour

1 tablespoon wheatgerm

2 tablespoons bran

2 tablespoons cracked wheat

2 tablespoons melted butter or margarine

3 x 2 oz (60 g) eggs

1 1/4 cups (10 fl oz/300 ml) soy drink

unsalted butter or vegetable oil for cooking

Filling:

1 large onion, chopped

1 clove garlic, crushed

1 teaspoon minced red chili

1 tablespoon vegetable oil

1 teaspoon green curry paste

2 large tomatoes, diced

2 cups green beans

1 cup (8 fl oz/250 ml) natural yogurt

2 tablespoons ground almonds

Crêpes: Place flour, wheatgerm, bran and cracked wheat into a mixing bowl and make a well in the middle. Add remaining ingredients and beat with the back of a wooden spoon to make a smooth batter. Cover and stand for 30 minutes to give a soft textured batter.

Season a 7 inch (18 cm) crêpe pan by melting a little unsalted butter in it, then rub clean with a wad of kitchen paper towels.

To cook the crêpes, melt 1 teaspoon unsalted butter in the seasoned pan over a medium-high heat. Pour in 1/4 cup (2 fl oz/60 ml) batter, tilt pan to swirl batter until the bottom of the pan is covered with a thin layer. Cook until golden underneath, shaking pan occasionally to loosen crêpe, then turn over with a palette knife or toss over and continue cooking until golden brown on other side.

Slide crêpe out onto a heatproof plate; cover with a strip of waxed paper. Continue making and layering crepes in this method. You should make at least 8 crêpes.

Filling: Gently fry onion, garlic and chili in oil in a frying pan until soft. Stir in curry paste, stirring over heat for 1 minute. Add tomatoes and stir-fry for 1 minute. Wash and trim beans, snap into small pieces, add to pan and stir-fry for 2 minutes. Stir in yogurt and almonds and heat through gently without boiling.

To finish: Divide hot bean mixture between 8 hot crêpes, spread evenly to edges. Fold crêpes in half then into quarters and serve. Crêpes can be reheated in a warm oven or microwave oven if they get cold while filling. Nicely complemented by lemon rice.

RUSSIAN BLINI WITH RED CABBAGE ♀

SERVES 6–8

A blini is a Russian yeast pancake made with buckwheat flour. You can speed up the rising process by adding a ground vitamin C tablet (ascorbic acid) to the yeast. This is a delicious dish to serve in cold weather and the blini freeze well.

Blini:

1/4 oz (7 g) packet dry yeast or 1/2 oz (15 g) fresh yeast

1/4 x 50 mg vitamin C tablet

3 tablespoons lukewarm water

1 cup (4 oz/125 g) buckwheat flour

1 cup (4 oz/125 g) all-purpose wholewheat (plain wholemeal) flour

1/2 teaspoon salt

1 1/2 cups (12 fl oz/375 ml) soy drink

1 egg, beaten

2 tablespoons melted polyunsaturated margarine

extra margarine for cooking

Red Cabbage:

2 lb (1 kg) red cabbage

1/2 cup (4 fl oz/125 ml) apple cider vinegar

1 tablespoon raw sugar

1 tablespoon polyunsaturated margarine

1 onion, cooked

1/2 cup canned black beans

2 apples, peeled, cored and sliced

1 onion stuck with cloves

1 bay leaf

1/2 teaspoon caraway seeds

2 tablespoons cranberry or redcurrant sauce

2 tablespoons chopped parsley

salt and pepper

sour cream and sliced scallions (spring onions) for serving

Blini: Dissolve yeast and vitamin C tablet in lukewarm water. Sieve flours into a warm mixing bowl, sprinkle salt around edge and make a well in the middle. Pour yeast mixture into well, add 1/2 cup lukewarm soy drink, egg and margarine. Stir in flour from around edge, then beat to form a smooth batter. Cover with clear plastic wrap, wrap in a towel and stand in a warm place to rise for 30 minutes, then stir in remaining 1 cup boiling soy drink. Cook blini in margarine as for Orange Pancakes (page 294) and keep warm. You should make approximately 18 blini.

Red cabbage: Quarter cabbage, remove core and shred thinly. Mix with vinegar and sugar. Heat margarine in a heavy-based pan and gently fry onion until soft, add beans and apples and cook gently for 5 minutes. Add cabbage mixture, onion with cloves, bay leaf, caraway seeds and 3 cups (24 fl oz/750 ml) boiling water or vegetable stock and bring to the boil, stirring occasionally. Cover and simmer for 3/4–1 hour until cabbage is tender and most of liquid has evaporated. Remove onion with cloves and bay leaf and stir in cranberry sauce and parsley. Add salt and pepper to taste.

Serve hot blini half-covered with the red cabbage and topped with sour cream and scallions.

BROCCOLI AND CHEESE STRUDEL

SERVES 4–6

You can brush the layers of filo pastry with orange juice if on a low-fat diet.

Filling:

1 tablespoon butter

1/2 cup sliced scallions (spring onions)

1 clove garlic, crushed

1 tablespoon brown mustard seed

2 cups broccoli florets

1/2 cup sliced celery

1 cup (8 oz/250 g) cottage or ricotta cheese

1/3 cup (1 2/3 oz/50 g) flaked almonds, toasted

3 tablespoons rolled oats

salt to taste

8 sheets filo pastry

juice of 1 large orange or 1/4 cup (2 oz/60 g) butter, melted

Filling: Heat butter and gently fry scallions, garlic and mustard seeds. Add broccoli and celery and stir-fry for 1–2 minutes until al dente or tender-crisp. Remove from heat, add to cottage cheese, almonds and oats and mix together. Add salt to taste.

To finish: Spread a sheet of filo out and brush with orange juice or melted butter. Put another sheet of filo on top. Continue brushing and layering all the pastry. Place filling along one of the long edges of the pastry and roll up firmly, securing join underneath. Place on a baking tray and brush pastry with melted butter. Bake at 375°F (190°C) for 15 minutes or until crisp and golden.

Serve with Lemon Brown Rice (page 158) and a crisp salad.

SOY BEAN CASSEROLE

SERVES 4

Soy beans are a high protein legume and this is a quick and easy casserole to prepare, so enjoy it often.

1 large onion, chopped

2 cloves garlic, crushed

2 tablespoons olive oil

2 carrots, sliced

1 small green pepper (capsicum), chopped

13 1/2 oz (425 g) can tomatoes

13 1/2 oz (425 g) can soy beans, drained and rinsed

1/2 cup (4 fl oz/125 ml) vegetable stock

1 tablespoon chopped parsley

1 tablespoon chopped thyme

Gently fry onion and garlic in oil in a heavy-based pan for 5 minutes, until soft. Add all remaining ingredients, bring to the boil, stirring, then cover and simmer for 30 minutes or until tender.

Serve with Sheik's Couscous (see 169) or jacket baked potatoes.

Broccoli and cheese strudel

BROAD BEAN AND BARLEY CASSEROLE

SERVES 4

This is a light, low-calorie, complete protein casserole ideal for a weight-reduction diet. The broad bean is high in water content and therefore lower in calories than other beans. Canned lima or butter beans may be used in place of broad beans.

2 cloves garlic, crushed

1 tablespoon sunflower oil

2 leeks, sliced

2 carrots, sliced

1 parsnip, chopped

1 stalk celery, sliced

1 potato, chopped

1 cup Brussels sprouts, halved

2/3 cup (4 oz/125 g) pearl barley or quick-cooking barley

4 cups (32 fl oz/1 L) vegetable stock

8 oz (250 g) mushroom cups, quartered

1 tablespoon chopped thyme

10 oz (310 g) can broad beans

salt and pepper

grated low-fat cheese for sprinkling, optional

Place garlic, oil and all vegetables except mushrooms into a heavy-based pan, cover and saute for 10 minutes, shaking pan frequently. Add barley, stock, mushrooms and thyme, bring to the boil covered and simmer for 30 minutes or until vegetables are tender. Add beans and heat through gently. Season to taste with salt and pepper.

Serve spooned into soup or pasta bowls, and sprinkle with cheese.

TOFU LOAF

SERVES 6–8

This is a high-protein tofu loaf with a moist texture and is simple to prepare. It's delicious hot or cold served with a tomato salad or broiled (grilled) tomatoes.

1 small onion, finely chopped

1 clove garlic, crushed

1 tablespoon polyunsaturated oil

8 oz (250 g) tofu, mashed

8 oz (250 g) cottage cheese

1/2 cup (3 oz/90 g) cashew nuts, chopped

1/2 cup (2 oz/60 g) ground almonds

1/2 cup (1 oz/30 g) wholewheat (wholemeal) breadcrumbs

2 eggs, beaten

1 tablespoon soy sauce

2 tablespoons chopped cilantro (coriander) or parsley

pepper to taste

Gently fry onion and garlic in oil until soft. Add all remaining ingredients and mix together. Place mixture in a greased loaf tin and bake at 350°F (180°C) for 45 minutes or until firm and golden on top.

Serve in slices accompanied by an attractive salad, such as Cherry Tomato and Basil Salad (page 204), and a bowl of brown rice.

HEARTY BEAN LOAF

SERVES 4–6

This loaf combines pulse-legumes with some grains and seeds, as well as eggs, to produce a complete protein dish.

1 onion, chopped

1 leek, sliced

1 tablespoon oil

13 1/2 oz (430 g) can soy beans and one 12 1/2 oz (400 g) can borlotti beans, drained, or total of 3 cups cooked beans

3 tablespoons cracked wheat

1/2 cup sesame seeds, toasted

4 tablespoons peanut butter

3 tablespoons tomato paste

2 eggs, beaten

Gently fry onion and leek in oil. Add to the rest of the ingredients and stir well to combine. Place mixture in a foil-lined loaf tin. Bake at 350°F (180°C) for 3/4-1 hour.

Serve in slices accompanied by Napoletana Sauce (page 117) or Asparagus Sauce (page 109) and freshly cooked vegetables.

LAYERED VEGETABLE AND NUT PIE

SERVES 8

1 tablespoon butter or polyunsaturated margarine

1 onion, chopped

13 1/2 oz (425 g) can tomatoes

1 tablespoon soy sauce

4 cups finely shredded spinach or Swiss chard (silverbeet)

1 cup grated carrot

1 cup grated pumpkin

1 cup grated parsnip

2 tablespoons tahini

2 tablespoons peanut butter

12 oz (375 g) puff pastry or 2 sheets pre-rolled frozen puff pastry, thawed

1/2 cup (2 oz/60 g) almonds, halved

soy drink for glazing

sesame seeds for sprinkling

Heat butter and fry onion until golden brown. Add tomatoes and soy sauce and cook over a high heat for 10 minutes, stirring frequently until tomato liquid has evaporated. Remove from heat and stir in spinach. Mix grated vegetables with tahini and peanut butter.

To finish pie, roll half pastry out to a round and line a 9 inch (23 cm) round pie dish. Place carrot mixture into pastry, pressing down firmly. Cover with a layer of nuts. Spread spinach layer over nuts. Roll out remaining pastry and cover the filling. Trim, seal and decorate edge. Brush top of pie with soy drink and sprinkle with sesame seeds.

Bake at 400°F (200°C) for 15 minutes then at 375°F (190°C) for a further 25–30 minutes until cooked and golden brown.

Layered vegetable and nut pie

CURRIED SPINACH WITH CASHEWS

SERVES 4

This is a light curry and is quick and easy to prepare.

3 tablespoons olive oil

1 leek or onion, finely chopped

1 tablespoon mustard seeds

6 French shallots, finely chopped

1 tablespoon ghee or
polyunsaturated margarine

4 oz (125 g) button mushrooms,
sliced

1 tablespoon curry paste, mild
strength

8 oz (250 g) packet frozen spinach
puree, thawed

4 tablespoons cream

4 tablespoons light sour cream

4 tablespoons cashew nuts

Fry mustard seeds and shallots in ghee until mustard seeds burst and crackle. Add mushrooms and fry for 3 minutes. Stir in curry paste and stir-fry for 1 minute. Add spinach and heat gently, stirring occasionally until heated through. Stir in cream and sour cream and heat through gently.

Serve with cashew nuts sprinkled on top, accompanied by brown rice, pappadams and curry accompaniments.

CAJUN CASSEROLE

SERVES 6

Okra, a rich source of soluble fiber combined with black-eyed beans, a good source of vegetable protein, makes this a nourishing and eye-catching casserole.

1 tablespoon vegetable oil

1 purple (Spanish) onion, chopped

1 cup sliced celery

1 small green pepper (capsicum),
chopped

1 lb (500 g) fresh or 13 1/2 oz
(425 g) can okra, drained

13 1/2 oz (425 g) can black eyed-
beans, drained and rinsed

13 1/2 oz (425 g) can tomatoes

2 tablespoons tomato paste

1 teaspoon chopped red chili

1 cup (8 fl oz/250 ml) vegetable
stock

2 tablespoons chopped parsley
for garnish

Heat oil in a heavy-based pan and gently fry onion, celery and green pepper until soft. Add all remaining ingredients and bring to the boil, stirring. Cover and simmer for 30 minutes if using fresh okra, for 15 minutes if using canned okra.

Serve sprinkled with parsley, accompanied by Quinoa with Greens (see 170) or brown rice.

SPRING GREENS SPANAKOPITA
SPRING GREENS AND SPINACH PIE

SERVES 6–8

Use your imagination and add the spring green vegetables you like best to this delicious Greek spinach pie, based on the following proportions. Serve with a pulse-legume dish for a 'complete protein' meal.

6 scallions (spring onions), thinly sliced

2 zucchini (courgette), finely chopped

2 lb (1 kg) spinach or Swiss chard (silverbeet) or two 16 oz (500 g) packets frozen spinach, thawed and drained

1/4 cup chopped parsley or mint

1 cup shredded lettuce

4 eggs

8 oz (250 g) feta cheese, crumbled

1 teaspoon poppy seeds

1 teaspoon salt

black pepper

3/4 cup (6 oz/185 g) butter

16 sheets filo pastry

2 tablespoons sesame seeds

Heat oil and gently fry leek and scallions until soft, about 5 minutes. Add zucchini and cook for 2 minutes. Wash, drain and shred spinach. Add spinach, herbs and lettuce to pan, cover and simmer for 5 minutes.

Beat eggs, stir in feta, spinach mixture, poppy seeds, salt and pepper to taste.

Brush an 8 x 12 inch (20 x 30 cm) rectangular tin with melted butter. Unwrap filo pastry carefully and unfold 16 sheets. Keep filo pastry covered with waxed (greaseproof) paper and a damp cloth, while not layering it. Place a sheet of filo pastry in the tin and brush with melted butter. Repeat layering and brushing a total of 8 sheets of filo.

Carefully spread spinach mixture into the lined tin. Cover with 8 remaining sheets of filo, brushing each with melted butter, finishing with top sheet. Trim edges of pie neatly with kitchen scissors and fold in neatly. Mark top of pie diagonally into diamonds and sprinkle with sesame seeds.

Bake at 350°F (180°C) for 30–40 minutes, until crisp and golden.

Serve hot, cut into squares or bars, and accompany with Black Bean and Rice Salad (page 200) and broiled (grilled) tomatoes for a delightful nutritious meal.

PASTA, RICE AND GRAINS

Pasta and rice are well known as staple ingredients that are kept in stock in most homes, as you can always produce a good meal from them. Grains, in many unusual varieties, are also a staple ingredient in a vegetarian's kitchen, because these too can provide a delicious, sustaining meal, as well as an accompaniment or side dish. The grain recipes in this chapter will be an enjoyable new food for many of you.

According to recent surveys, many people enjoy pasta at least twice a week. One of the most appealing qualities of pasta is that it is quick to prepare, another is that it is easy to eat, as it slides down topped with a tasty sauce. Pasta is particularly satisfying for vegetarians, because it is a very good source of complex carbohydrate, which is essential for food energy.

I have included my failproof recipe for home-made pasta in this chapter, which is fun to make if you have a pasta machine. But take warning, you will need some helpers in the kitchen to handle it as it grows and grows in length! You can make pasta in many varieties of shapes and thickness, and you can also have fun experimenting, by adding other ingredients such as beets (beetroot) or red peppers (capsicum) to create artistic shades. You will find I use many delicious cheeses in the pasta dishes, because it is hard to break with Italian tradition, but vegans can omit the cheese and still enjoy most of these recipes.

Noodles have also become fashionable because they are as versatile and quick to prepare as pasta. You will discover some delicious, easy-to-prepare Asian-style noodle dishes in this chapter.

Rice is one of the most important grains in the world, and while it is often served as an accompaniment or side dish, main course rice dishes should not be overlooked. I've included recipes for both rice main courses and accompaniments here.

The other grains included are millet, barley, buckwheat, burgul, cornmeal, couscous and quinoa, each featured in at least two recipes, so I hope you will be inspired to try them. Not only do they add interest to a vegetarian menu, but they are also all packed with nourishment.

Finally, the most important meal of the day, the 'break of fast', or breakfast, has not been forgotten. I have included some excellent recipes for your own home-made muesli, which are all perfect partners to fresh fruit and yogurt. You can enjoy pasta, rice and grains throughout the day!

Spinach fettucine al burro, p.140

BASIC FRESH PASTA ♀

SERVES 4 FOR AN ENTREE, 2 FOR A MAIN COURSE

This recipe for home-made pasta always gives successful results and is fun to make. Mechanical pasta machines are usually available from Italian general stores. For fresh wholewheat (wholemeal) pasta, substitute half all-purpose white flour with wholewheat (wholemeal) flour and use large eggs.

1 1/4 cups (5oz/150 g) all-purpose (plain) flour
1 teaspoon olive oil
pinch of salt
2 eggs

Place all ingredients in a food processor, mix for 30 seconds. Turn onto a lightly floured surface and knead gently (as for pastry) until smooth; pasta should look dry, not shiny, when stretched. Cover with clear plastic and allow to stand for 3-5 minutes.

Divide pasta into thirds and knead each until smooth. Work with one third at a time, keeping remainder covered, and roll 7 times, through a pasta machine, set at thickest point, folding into three each time and turning 90 degrees. Roll once on each point (or number), tightening one point at each roll, i.e., from no. 7 to no. 1.

For lasagna, cannelloni, fettucine and spaghetti, stop at no. 3. For angel's hair, ravioli and tortellini, stop at no. 1.

FRESH CHICK PEA PASTA ♀

SERVES 4 FOR AN ENTREE, 2 FOR A MAIN COURSE

Chick Pea fettucine is delicious served with a tomato-based sauce such as Napoletana (page 117) and sprinkled with wheat bran or rice bran for added fiber.

3/4 cup (3oz/90 g) chick pea flour
1/2 cup (2oz/60 g) all-purpose (plain) flour
1 teaspoon olive oil
pinch of salt
2 eggs

Follow Basic Fresh Pasta method.

PASTA VARIETIES

SERVES 4 FOR AN ENTREE, 2 FOR A MAIN COURSE

To 1 quantity Basic Fresh Pasta ingredients, add 1/4 cup all-purpose (plain) flour and the following ingredients before mixing:

Beets (beetroot): 1/4 cup pureed cooked beets.

Herbs: 1/2 cup finely chopped fresh herbs, but omit extra 1/4 cup flour.

Leek and Pepper: 1 large leek, cooked, drained and pureed (to give approx. 1/4 cup), and 1 teaspoon freshly cracked peppercorns.

Hazelnut: 1 3/4 oz (50 g) crushed hazelnuts, but omit extra 1/4 cup flour.

Red Pepper (Capsicum): 1/4 cup pureed, broiled (grilled) and skinned red pepper.

Spinach: 6oz (185 g) fresh spinach, cooked, drained and pureed, or 1/3 cup well drained frozen spinach.

Tomato and Basil: 2 tablespoons tomato paste and 2 tablespoons shredded basil leaves.

PASTA WITH RED PESTO

SERVES 4

This delicious sauce uses red peppers (capsicum) in place of basil in the classic pesto sauce. It looks sensational with a bright pasta variation. Try it with corn pasta as a conversation piece at your next dinner party!

2 cups seeded, skinned red peppers (capsicum), approx. 3 large peppers

2 cloves garlic, crushed

1 tablespoon sun-dried tomatoes

3 tablespoons pine nuts

1/2 cup (4 fl oz/125 ml) olive oil

1/2 cup (2 oz/60 g) grated parmesan cheese

14 oz (or 400 g) corn pasta

fresh herbs for garnish

The peppers can be skinned by placing, halved and seeded, under a red-hot broiler (grill) until blistered, then wrapping in a damp cloth for 5 minutes to create steam. This process makes it easy to remove the skin.

Slice peppers coarsely and place in a food processor or blender. Add garlic, tomatoes and nuts and mix to a puree. Add oil and mix until combined. Add cheese last and mix for a few seconds.

Serve red pesto sauce warm or cold over freshly cooked pasta and garnish with fresh herbs.

Following page: Vegetable pasta with asparagus Brazilia (left), p.141; Buckwheat/Quinoa noodles with pesto (back), p.152; Pasta with red pesto (right), p.137

FARFALLE WITH CREAMY MUSHROOM SAUCE

SERVES 4

Farfalle are 'butterfly' or 'bow tie' shaped pasta. Choose small ones because they expand a lot during cooking.

13 oz (400 g) farfalle

1/4 cup (2 oz/60 g) butter

1 bunch shallots, sliced

2 cloves garlic, crushed

8 oz (250 g) mushroom cups, chopped

3/4 cup (6 fl oz/185 ml) cream

2 tablespoons shredded mint

salt and pepper

grated parmesan cheese for serving

mint sprigs for garnish

Cook pasta according to pack directions. Heat butter and gently fry shallots and garlic until soft. Add mushrooms and cook briskly until they darken. Add cream and mint and salt and pepper to taste and heat through gently.

Serve over freshly cooked pasta, sprinkle with parmesan cheese and garnish with mint. Serve accompanied by a salad.

SPINACH FETTUCINE AL BURRO

SPINACH EGG NOODLES WITH BUTTER AND CHEESE

SERVES 8 FOR AN ENTREE,
4 FOR A MAIN COURSE

This easy-to-prepare, delicious, rich-sauced pasta dish is nicely complemented by a green salad.

1/2 cup (4 oz/125 g) butter or polyunsaturated margarine, softened

1/4 cup (3 fl oz/60 ml) cream or soy milk

1 cup (4 oz/125 g) grated parmesan cheese or reduced-fat cheddar cheese

1 lb (500 g) spinach fettucine

freshly ground black pepper

extra 1 cup (4 oz/125 g) grated parmesan cheese for serving.

Beat butter, cream and parmesan cheese together until light and fluffy. Use an electric hand-beater to save time. Cook fettucine in a large pan of boiling salted water, stirring immediately with a pasta fork or wooden spoon to prevent sticking, until al dente or just tender to the bite.

Fresh pasta will require 3–5 minutes, dry pasta 8-10 minutes. Drain pasta as soon as it is tender, place in a warm bowl, add sauce and toss gently until every strand of pasta is coated.

Serve sprinkled with black pepper accompanied by a bowl of extra grated parmesan cheese to sprinkle on top and a baby spinach leaf side salad.

VEGETABLE PASTA WITH ASPARAGUS BRAZILIA

SERVES 2

You could rename this dish 'Cupboard Love Pasta' because all the ingredients can usually be found stored in your cupboards. It's a perfect dish to make when you don't know what to have for dinner. Try replacing the vegetable pasta with rye, soy or legume pasta for extra nourishment.

2 tablespoons butter or margarine	Melt butter in a saucepan and gently fry onion and garlic for 5 minutes, until golden. Cut asparagus into 1 inch (2.5 cm) lengths. Add asparagus, nuts, cream and cheese and parsley to pan and heat through, stirring frequently.
1 small onion, finely chopped	
1 clove garlic, crushed	
11 oz (340 g) can asparagus, drained	
1/2 cup (2 1/2 oz /75 g) finely chopped Brazil nuts	Serve sauce over freshly cooked pasta, garnished with parsley sprigs, accompanied by extra grated parmesan cheese for sprinkling and a crisp green salad.
1/2 cup (4 fl oz/125 ml) cream or soy milk	
1/4 cup (1 oz/30 g) grated parmesan cheese	
1 tablespoon chopped parsley	
6 oz (200 g) approx. vegetable pasta, cooked	
sprigs of continental parsley	

PASTA SHELLS WITH THREE CHEESES

SERVES 4

This is a delicious rich pasta dish to serve in cold weather. You can use any variety of cheeses you have in the refrigerator, but try to have a blue variety, a good melting cheese like Swiss, Gouda or Edam and a mature cheese for grating.

13 oz (400 g) vegetable pasta shells	Cook pasta in boiling, salted water until al dente, according to pack directions. Drain well, return to pan. Mix pasta with the butter and cheeses over a low heat. Add pepper to taste then add cream and toss carefully until all pasta is cooked and sauce is hot.
2 tablespoons butter or polyunsaturated margarine	
3 1/3 oz (100 g) gorgonzola cheese, crumbled	
3 1/3 oz (100 g) mozzarella cheese, grated	Serve garnished with herbs and accompany with a crisp green salad.
4 oz (125 g) grated parmesan cheese	
freshly ground black pepper	
10 fl oz (300 ml) cream or soy drink	
chopped herbs for garnish	

GOAT'S CHEESE AND SPINACH RAVIOLI

SERVES 8 AS AN ENTREE, 4 AS A MAIN MEAL

1 ¹/2 lb (750 g) sheets of fresh pasta

Filling:

2 teaspoons butter or polyunsaturated margarine

¹/4 cup sliced shallots

2 cups shredded spinach

6 ¹/2 oz (200 g) goat's milk feta cheese

freshly ground black pepper

soy milk for sealing

Filling: Melt butter and gently fry shallots until soft. Cover spinach and cook in a microwave oven on High setting for 1 minute, or blanch in boiling water for 1 minute; refresh in cold water. Drain cooked spinach well, squeezing out any excess moisture. Mix shallots with spinach and crumbled feta cheese, season to taste with pepper.

To make ravioli, place in sheet of pasta flat on a work surface. Place teaspoon of mixture on the pasta, 4 across by 5 down, leaving plenty of space around each spoonful. You should use half the mixture. Brush pasta with soy milk and cover with a second sheet of pasta. Press down firmly between filling to seal well, then cut into squares using a pasta wheel cutter or a sharp knife. Press edges of each ravioli square to seal well. Repeat this process with remaining pasta and filling.

Cook ravioli in a large pan of boiling salted water for 5 minutes or until pasta is cooked. Drain well.

Serve with Red Pepper Sauce (page 150) or other tomato pasta sauce.

Goat's cheese and spinach ravioli, with Red pepper sauce, p.15

Sicilian Macaroni

SERVES 4

Add a cup of cooked pulse-legumes to fennel sauce for a complete protein meal.

12 oz (375 g) fennel bulb or celery

3 tablespoons olive oil

2 onions, sliced

freshly ground black pepper

1/2 cup (2 oz/60 g) pine nuts

1/2 cup(3 oz/90 g) raisins (or sultanas)

8 oz (250 g) short thick macaroni

1/2 cup (2 oz/60 g) grated parmesan cheese

Wash and trim fennel. Cook in 8 cups (64 fl oz/2 l) boiling salted water for 10–15 minutes, until tender. Drain well, reserve cooking liquor, then gently squeeze fennel dry and chop coarsely.

Heat half oil and gently fry onions until golden. Sprinkle with pepper to taste. Stir in fennel, pine nuts and raisins, then cover and cook for a few minutes. If too thick, add some fennel cooking liquor.

Bring fennel cooking liquor to the boil, add macaroni and boil according to instructions until al dente; drain well. Mix macaroni with half the fennel sauce.

Place half the macaroni and sauce in the bottom of an oven-proof dish. Sprinkle half the cheese over. Cover with remaining macaroni mixture, spread remaining sauce over, and sprinkle with remaining cheese. Cover and bake at 375°F (190°C) for 20 minutes.

Mushroom and Pecan Ravioli

SERVES 6–8

You can use won ton wrappers for this ravioli. It is easier to handle than fresh pasta and is already pre-cut to a convenient size.

1 tablespoon olive oil

2 scallions (spring onions), thinly sliced

4 oz (125 g) mushrooms, finely chopped

1/3 cup (1 1/2 oz/45 g) pecans, finely chopped

1/2 cup (4 oz/125 g) cottage cheese

freshly ground black pepper

60 small square won ton sheets, approx. 8 oz (250 g)

soy milk or water for sealing

Heat oil and gently fry scallions and mushrooms for 5 minutes. Remove from heat, stir in pecans and cottage cheese and season to taste with pepper.

Spread won ton sheets on work surface and place 2 teaspoons mixture in the top quarters of the sheet. Brush edges with milk, fold bottom of sheet over to top and press to seal around edge and in between 2 fillings. Cut in half to form 2 squares of ravioli. Continue in this method until all are filled. You will have 120 small pieces of ravioli.

Cook in boiling salted water for 2 minutes or until the ravioli floats.

PASTA AND EGGPLANT TIMBALE

SERVES 6–8

Timbales are usually baked in a soufflé dish. This one also looks elegant baked in a 8 1/2 inch (21 cm) ring tin. You will have some filling left over if you use a ring tin, so this can be heated and served in the middle of the ring.

8 oz (250 g) penne pasta

2 eggplant, approx. 12 oz (375 g) each

olive oil for frying

all-purpose wholewheat (plain wholemeal) flour for coating

2 eggs, beaten

6 tablespoons grated parmesan cheese

3 cups (24 fl oz/750 ml) tomato-based pasta sauce

10 oz (310 g) can butter beans, drained

1/3 cup (1 1/3 oz/40 g) pine nuts

1/4 cup soy grits

1/2 cup cooked peas

1 hard-boiled egg, chopped

1 oz (30 g) mozzarella cheese, diced

Cook pasta in boiling salted water according to directions until al dente. Drain well.

Cut eggplant lengthwise 1/4 inch (5 mm) thick. Fry eggplant in hot oil on both sides until lightly golden. Drain on kitchen paper towels. Dip eggplant in flour then coat with egg mixed with half the parmesan cheese. Fry the coated eggplant again until golden brown, drain well. Cut a large round out of one slice of eggplant and place on the middle of the bottom of a greased 6 1/2 inch (16 cm) soufflé dish. Line the dish with overlapping slices of eggplant and reserve a third for the top.

Mix penne with half the tomato sauce, beans, pine nuts, soy grits, peas, egg, mozzarella and remaining parmesan. Spoon mixture into the lined dish or tin, cover with reserved eggplant. Spread a little tomato sauce over the top then cover with foil.

Bake at 375°F (190°C) for 25 minutes. Turn out onto a serving plate and serve with remaining hot tomato pasta sauce.

CANNELLONI WITH SPINACH AND PINE NUTS

SERVES 4

Use a can or jar of processed tomato-based pasta sauce in this recipe to save time.

8 cannelloni shells

1 onion, finely chopped

1 tablespoon olive oil

8 oz (250 g) packet frozen spinach, thawed and drained

12 oz (375 g) ricotta or cottage cheese

3 tablespoons pine nuts

1/2 cup (4 fl oz/125 ml) natural yogurt

salt and pepper

2 cups (16 fl oz/500 ml) tomato-based pasta sauce, napoletana or cacciatore

extra pine nuts for sprinkling

low fat mozzarella, thinly sliced, for topping

Cook cannelloni in boiling salted water until al dente, drain carefully.

Gently fry onion in oil until soft, add spinach, remove from heat and stir in well drained ricotta, pine nuts and yogurt and salt and pepper to taste.

Spoon half tomato pasta sauce over the base of an oiled lasagna dish or shallow baking dish. Spoon spinach mixture carefully into the cannelloni shells and place in a single layer on top of the sauce. Cover with remaining sauce and sprinkle with pine nuts. Bake at 350°F (180°C) for 30 minutes or until bubbling hot.

Serve with garlic or pesto bread and a crisp green salad.

❖ USE 3–4 OZ (100–125 G) RAW PASTA PER PORTION FOR A MAIN COURSE; USE 2 OZ (60 G) RAW PASTA PER PORTION FOR AN ENTRÉE. IF RAVENOUSLY HUNGRY OR TRAINING FOR A MARATHON RUN, YOU CAN OF COURSE SERVE MORE!

Cappelletti con la zucca, p.148

Cappelletti con la Zucca
LITTLE PUMPKIN HATS

SERVES 6

This is a very popular pasta dish served in the country trattorias surrounding the Parmesan cheese factory of Parma in Italy.

Stuffing:

3 lb (1.5 kg) pumpkin

8 oz (250 g) freshly grated parmesan cheese

2 tablespoons chopped herbs, parsley, mint, chives, tarragon

1/2 teaspoon freshly grated nutmeg

freshly ground pepper

1 1/2 cups (6 oz/185 g) all-purpose (plain) flour

3/4 cup (3 oz/90 g) all-purpose wholewheat (plain wholemeal) flour

1 teaspoon salt

Three 2 oz (60 g) eggs

1 egg yolk

3/4 cup (6 fl oz/185 ml) water

Peel pumpkin, cut into chunky pieces 1 inch (2.5 cm) thick, place in a clean plastic food storage bag and cook in microwave oven on High setting for 15 minutes or until tender. Boil pumpkin if you do not have a microwave oven, and drain well. Mash pumpkin, mix with parmesan, herbs, nutmeg and pepper to taste.

Prepare pasta as directed. Roll out one band at a time, i.e., one-sixth of dough. Cut into circles 3 inches (8 cm) in diameter.

Place a little pumpkin mixture (approx. 1/2 teaspoon) on each circle, and shape into little hats as for tortellini. Spread on a floured cloth.

Boil for 5 minutes. Serve immediately with melted butter and parmesan cheese.

Millet Balls

SERVES 4

These tasty deep fried balls may accompany dishes such as Caponatina Salad (page 185), Ratatouille with Spinach (page 92), or Crunchy Nut and Orange Salad (page 192) with Tofu Mayonnaise (page 209).

3/4 cup (5 oz/150 g) millet

1 1/2 cups (12 fl oz/375 ml) water

1/2 cup snipped chives or sliced scallions (spring onions)

2 cloves garlic, crushed

4 tablespoons hijiki, in 1/2 inch (1 cm) lengths

2 tablespoons tahina

1 1/2 tablespoons tamari or soy sauce

sesame seeds for coating

oil for deep frying

Place millet and water in a heavy-based pan, bring to the boil, then cover and simmer slowly for 25 minutes or until millet has absorbed most of the liquid. Drain off any liquid and leave to cool.

Mix millet with all remaining ingredients. Divide into equal quarters and roll each quarter into a large ball. Roll balls in sesame seeds until well coated. Deep fry balls in hot oil on a medium heat for 5 minutes until golden brown and cooked through. If in doubt cook a further 2 minutes in a microwave oven on High setting or in an oven at 350°F (180°C). Drain well on kitchen paper towels. Serve hot.

SPATZLE

SERVES 8

Spatzle is a Swiss noodle, usually served with Swiss veal, but I serve it with pasta sauces as it is similar to gnocchi but much simpler to make.

Pasta:

2 quantities Basic Fresh Pasta (page 136)

Sauce:

2/3 cup (5 oz/155 g) butter, melted

1 cup (4 oz/125 g) freshly grated parmesan cheese

Bring a large pan of salted water to the boil.

Meanwhile, place flour, salt, eggs, egg yolk and water into a food processor or electric mixer and mix until smooth.

Hold a colander over the pan of boiling water, add spatzle mixture a quarter at a time, and press into water. When spatzle rise to surface remove with a slotted spoon and drain on kitchen paper towels.

Keep warm until all mixture is cooked. Serve hot with a pasta sauce.

SPATZLE WITH SPINACH AND GORGONZOLA

SERVES 4

1 quantity spatzle (above)

Sauce:

1lb (500 g) spinach, cooked

1 cup (8 fl oz/250 ml) cream

4 oz (125 g) gorgonzola, crumbled

1 clove garlic, crushed

1/4 cup (2 fl oz/60 ml) vegetable stock

1 vine ripened tomato, diced

freshly ground black pepper

Cook spatzle according to directions and keep hot.

Sauce: Drain spinach well and mix to a puree in a food processor or blender. Heat cream and gorgonzola in a saucepan over a low heat, stirring until cheese has melted. Add spinach, garlic and stock and simmer for 5 minutes. Add tomato and heat through gently, then season to taste with black pepper.

Serve sauce over hot spatzle, accompanied by a crisp salad.

Tofu Sesame Triangles with Green Noodles

SERVES 4–5

These 'yummy' marinated triangles are delicious to nibble on with drinks, and they make an elegant complete protein meal when served on top of green spinach noodles. You have two marinades to choose from!

11 oz (350 g) firm tofu

3 tablespoons chick pea flour

1/2 cup sesame seeds

oil for frying

8 oz (250 g) spinach noodles

Marinade 1:

1/2 cup (4 fl oz/125 ml) light soy sauce

2 tablespoons sweet chili sauce

Marinade 2:

1/2 cup (4 fl oz/125 ml) teriyaki glaze

4 tablespoons lemon juice

Red Pepper Sauce (below) for serving, optional

coriander sprigs for garnish

Cut tofu into 10 thin square slices and cut each across into triangles. Place triangles in the marinade of your choice and leave for at least 30 minutes. Mix flour with sesame seeds and coat tofu triangles.

Heat oil and fry coated tofu until golden brown on both sides. Drain well. Cook noodles according to directions, drain well.

To serve, divide spinach noodles between serving bowls and spoon remaining marinade over. Pour a little Red Pepper Sauce, if liked, over noodles and top with tofu sesame triangles. Serve garnished with coriander.

Red Pepper Sauce

MAKES 2 CUPS 8 FL OZ (500 ML)

8 oz (250 g) red peppers (capsicum)

1/2 cup sliced French shallots

1 cup (8 fl oz/250 ml) vegetable stock

salt and pepper

1 tablespoon millet or soy grits, optional

Seed and slice red peppers. Place in a pan with all remaining ingredients, cover and bring to the boil. Simmer for 15–20 minutes until vegetables are soft. Puree mixture and adjust to taste with salt and pepper. Serve hot or cold.

Tofu sesame triangles with green noodles

BUCKWHEAT/QUINOA NOODLES WITH PESTO

SERVES 4

Buckwheat or quinoa noodles, both available from health food stores, add some protein and fiber to this delicious, traditional basil sauce. Buckwheat noodles are also known as soba.

8 oz (250 g) buckwheat, or quinoa, noodles

Pesto Sauce:

2 cups fresh basil leaves, tightly packed

1/2 cup (4 fl oz/125 ml) olive oil, chilled

3 tablespoons pine nuts, toasted

2 cloves garlic, crushed

1/2 teaspoon rock salt

3/4 cup (3 oz/90 g) grated parmesan cheese

Cook noodles in a large pan of boiling salted water until al dente. Buckwheat noodles are tender after approx. 8–10 minutes, quinoa noodles take approx. 10–15 minutes, but follow pack directions.

Pesto Sauce: Place all ingredients except parmesan cheese in a food processor and mix well, stopping and scraping down as necessary. Stir parmesan cheese into sauce and mix well.

Serve pesto sauce at room temperature over freshly cooked pasta, accompanied by a crisp green salad.

Pesto sauce can also be added to minestrone just before serving.

SPICY NOODLES

SERVES 4–6

If you enjoy spicy food try these Sichuan inspired noodles topped with irresistable cashews. You can make it in a few minutes.

2 tablespoons peanut oil

1 teaspoon minced red chili

2 tablespoons crushed garlic

2 tablespoons finely chopped ginger

1/2 cup thinly sliced scallions (spring onions)

2 tablespoons sweet chili sauce

2 tablespoons tahina

2 tablespoons soy sauce

1 cup (8 fl oz/250 ml) vegetable stock

8 oz (250 g) Chinese noodles

1/2 cup (2 oz/60 g) roasted cashews

coriander sprigs for garnish

Heat oil in a wok or heavy-based frying pan and stir-fry chili, garlic, ginger and scallions for 1 minute. Add chili sauce, tahina, soy sauce and stock and simmer for 3 minutes.

Cook the noodles in boiling water according to directions, usually 2 minutes. Halve the cashew nuts lengthwise. Drain noodles well and divide between serving bowls. Spoon spicy sauce over, sprinkle cashew nuts on top and garnish with coriander sprigs if you like.

THAI STYLE NOODLES

SERVES 4–6

Serve as a light meal or an accompaniment to a Thai style meal.

1 tablespoon vegetable oil

1 onion, finely chopped

2 cloves garlic, crushed

1 inch (2.5 cm) ginger, thinly sliced

1 inch (2.5 cm) lemon grass, thinly sliced

1 teaspoon minced chili

3 coriander roots, thinly sliced

1/2 cup(4 fl oz/125 ml) vegetable stock

1 tablespoon soy sauce

salt to taste

8 oz (250 g) Chinese noodles, cooked

2 tablespoons chopped coriander leaves

2 tablespoons chopped pistachio nuts

1 carrot, cut in julienne strips

Heat oil and stir-fry onion, garlic, ginger, lemon grass, chili and coriander roots until onion is soft and transparent. Add all remaining ingredients in given order and stir gently until heated through.

Serve in individual bowls.

Following page: Rice balls (top), p.161; Moroccan couscous (right), p.169; Thai style noodles (left), p.153

SOFT FRIED CHOW MEIN

SERVES 4

Any of the fascinating variety of Chinese green vegetables can substitute the Chinese cabbage in this dish. Mushrooms, dried and fresh, provide a good source of B vitamins, iron, zinc and protein.

8 oz (250 g) Chinese noodles

2–3 tablespoons vegetable oil

1 clove garlic, crushed

1 teaspoon finely chopped ginger

1/4 cup diagonally sliced scallions (spring onions)

1 stalk celery, thinly sliced diagonally

4 water chestnuts, thinly sliced

1/2 cup thinly sliced bamboo shoots

8 Chinese dried mushrooms, soaked 30 minutes, drained and thinly sliced

1 cup shredded Chinese cabbage

1 cup (8 fl oz/250 ml) vegetable stock

1 tablespoon cornstarch (cornflour)

1 tablespoon apple juice

2 tablespoons salt-reduced soy sauce

1/2 cup bean shoots

pepper

Cook noodles according to pack directions, drain well.

Heat 2 tablespoons oil in a wok or large frying pan and fry noodles until golden, stirring frequently. Drain and keep warm. Add another tablespoon oil to wok if necessary and stir-fry garlic, ginger and scallions for 2 minutes. Add celery, water chestnuts, bamboo shoots, mushrooms, cabbage and stock, bring to the boil stirring, then simmer for 3 minutes.

Blend cornstarch smoothly with apple juice and soy sauce. Stir into vegetables and bring to the boil stirring continuously, then simmer for 2 minutes. Add bean shoots and season to taste with pepper.

Serve over soft fried hot noodles.

CHOW MEIN WITH CRISP NOODLES

SERVES 4–6

Deep fried Chinese noodles add a crisp texture to this tasty dish. Serve in Chinese bowls and eat with chopsticks.

8 oz (250 g) Chinese noodles

2 tablespoons vegetable oil

1 onion, cut in thin wedges

4 stalks celery, sliced diagonally

8 oz (250 g) mushrooms, sliced

1 1/2 cups (12 fl oz/375 ml) vegetable stock

1 cup water chestnuts, sliced

3/4 cup bamboo shoots, thinly sliced

1 tablespoon cornstarch (cornflour)

3 tablespoons salt-reduced soy sauce

pepper

1 cup bean shoots

extra oil for deep frying

Boil noodles until tender, stirring to separate, then drain and leave to cool.

Heat oil in a wok or large frying pan and stir-fry onion for 2 minutes until transparent; add celery and mushrooms and stir-fry for 2 minutes, then add 1 cup (8 fl oz/250 ml) stock and simmer for 5 minutes. Add water chestnuts and bamboo shoots. Add to vegetables with soy sauce and bring to the boil stirring continuously. Add pepper to taste.

Deep fry cold noodles until golden, drain well on kitchen paper towels. Stir bean shoots into hot vegetables just before serving over deep fried noodles.

FRIED RICE

SERVES 8

4 tablespoons polyunsaturated oil

2 cloves garlic, squashed

2 oz (60 g) slivered almonds

2 eggs, beaten

4 cups cold boiled short grain rice (1 1/3 cups raw rice)

8 scallions (spring onions), thinly sliced

2 tablespoons cooked black beans, optional

2 tablespoons soy sauce

Heat 2 tablespoons oil in a wok or frying pan and gently fry garlic 2–3 minutes; remove when browned and discard. Add almonds and gently fry until golden brown, remove with a slotted spoon and drain.

Add 1 tablespoon oil to pan, heat through then pour in beaten egg and cook as a flat omelette without stirring. Turn when half set, then transfer to a plate. When firm, roll up and cut in strips.

Add remaining tablespoon oil to pan, then stir-fry rice and scallions until hot, add almonds and egg and black beans if used, sprinkle with soy sauce to taste and stir-fry 1-2 minutes or until heated through.

Serve with Asian style food.

Risotto Milanese
MILAN RICE

SERVES 8

This traditional recipe requires a lot of patience during preparation, but the resulting taste and texture is worth every minute of your time. A 'quick cooking' brown rice may be used in place of the white rice.

8 cups (64 fl oz/2 l) vegetable stock; use stock cubes

1/2 cup (4 oz/125 g) butter

1 onion, thinly sliced

2 cups (1 lb/ 500 g) long-grain rice, preferably arborio rice

1/2 cup (4 fl oz/125 ml) dry white wine or grape juice

1 sachet or 1 pinch saffron threads or 1 teaspoon ground turmeric

1/2 cup (2 oz/60 g) freshly grated parmesan cheese

Bring stock to the boil and keep it simmering hot over a low heat.

Melt half butter in a large, heavy pan and gently fry onion until soft but not brown. Add rice and stir-fry until every rice grain is coated with butter. Add wine and boil until almost absorbed, then add 1 cup hot stock and simmer, stirring frequently, until rice absorbs stock and begins to dry out, then add another cup of hot stock.

Continue cooking in this manner, stirring occasionally, until 1 cup of stock remains. Dissolve saffron in remaining stock, add to rice and cook until absorbed. Rice should be tender now.

Finally stir in remaining butter and parmesan cheese off the heat. An Italian risotto is moist and creamy (somewhat like rice pudding!).

Serve immediately.

Brown Rice with Lemon Garlic

SERVES 4

The butter may be omitted for those on a fat-reduced diet.

1 1/4 cups (10 oz/300 g) brown rice

2 tablespoons butter or polyunsaturated margarine

1 clove garlic, crushed

juice of 1 large lemon

2 tablespoons wheatgerm

Cook rice in a pan of rapidly boiling salted water or vegetable stock uncovered, for 30–40 minutes, until tender. Drain, rinse under boiling hot water, drain again. Rinse pan. Melt butter in rinsed pan, add garlic and lemon juice and bring to the boil. Add rice to pan and stir well while heating through.

Serve hot sprinkled with wheatgerm as an accompaniment to a main course.

Risotto Milanese

BROWN RICE WITH SPINACH

SERVES 4–6

Serve with nut, legume or tofu patties for a complete protein meal.

1 bunch spinach or Swiss chard (silverbeet)

2 onions, chopped

1 clove garlic, crushed

2 tablespoons vegetable oil

1 1/2 cups cooked brown rice (1/2 cup raw)

freshly ground black pepper

1 cup (4 oz/125 g) cheddar cheese, grated

Wash and drain spinach. Cut leaves from stems, reserve top half of stems and slice thinly. Shred the leaves.

Stir-fry onions, garlic and sliced stems in oil until onions are soft. Stir in cooked rice and spinach leaves, cover and simmer until leaves wilt. Season to taste with pepper. Stir cheese into hot mixture just before serving.

Serve as an accompaniment to a main meal.

BROWN RICE AND ZUCCHINI BAKE

SERVES 6–8

This is an economical, tasty dish that is easy to prepare. It is also a complete protein meal.

2 onions, chopped

1 tablespoon olive oil

1 tablespoon polyunsaturated margarine

1 red pepper (capsicum), sliced

2 zucchini (courgette), grated

1 cup cooked brown rice (1/3 cup raw)

8 oz (250 g) tofu, diced

1 tablespoon soy sauce

1 cup (8 fl oz/250 ml) soy milk

2 tablespoons wheatgerm

2 tablespoons brewer's yeast

2 tablespoons wholewheat (wholemeal) breadcrumbs

1/2 cup (2 oz/60 g) grated cheese

Fry onions in oil and margarine until soft, add red pepper and fry for 2 minutes. Place fried vegetables in a bowl, add zucchini, rice, tofu and soy sauce and mix together. Place mixture in a greased baking dish and pour soy milk over. Mix all remaining ingredients together and sprinkle over the top. Bake at 350°F (180°C) for 15–20 minutes, or until browned.

Serve with a green salad.

RICE BALLS

SERVES 4

Serve these satisfying rice balls with a vegetable dish and a crisp salad for a well balanced meal.

1 cup brown rice

1 onion, finely chopped

1 clove garlic, crushed

1 tablespoon olive oil

1 carrot, coarsely grated

1/4 cup (2 fl oz/60 ml) thinly sliced celery

1/2 cup (4 fl oz/125 ml) broccoli florets, cooked

1 tablespoon chopped sun-dried tomato

2 teaspoons miso

2 teaspoons sweet chili sauce

2 tablespoons toasted sesame seeds

1 tablespoon sunflower kernels

2 tablespoons bran or crushed breakfast wheat cereal

extra sesame seeds for coating

oil for deep frying

Cook rice, drain well and leave to cool. Gently fry onion and garlic in oil until soft, drain off oil. Mix rice, onion and garlic with all remaining ingredients and shape into 4 equal-size large balls. Toss in sesame seeds. Deep fry rice balls for 4-5 minutes until crisp and golden brown.

Serve with a sweet chili sauce or Sweet and Sour Sauce (page 48) and a crisp salad.

MUSABI TRIANGLES

SERVES 10

A musabi is made by wrapping nori seaweed around a seasoned brown rice mixture stuffed with an umeboshi plum in the middle. An umeboshi is a Japanese salted and pickled plum which aids digestion and helps cleanse the system. They are available from health food stores.

2 cups (1 lb/500 g) short-grain brown rice

4 cups (32 fl oz/1 l) boiling water

1 tablespoon horseradish cream

1 tablespoon rice wine vinegar

2 teaspoons yeast extract

4 tablespoons sunflower kernels

3 tablespoons sesame seeds

10 umeboshi plums, drained

10 sheets nori

Place rice into a pan with boiling water, return to the boil, then cover and cook over a low heat for 45 minutes, or until nearly all the water has been absorbed. Remove from heat and stir in horseradish cream, vinegar, yeast extract, kernels and seeds. Cover and leave to cool in pan for 10-15 minutes.

Take one tenth of the rice mixture and press around an umeboshi plum, shaping into a triangle 1 inch (2.5 cm) thick. Dip fingers in salt water if sticky. Wrap the triangle neatly in a sheet of nori, pressing aroung to seal it. Continue until you have 10 musabi.

RICE AND MILLET PILAF PUMPKINS

SERVES 6–8

This grain pilaf is nice served on its own as an accompaniment to a main course, or it can be used to stuff vegetables like these pumpkins.

1 onion, finely chopped

2 cloves garlic, crushed

1/4 cup (2 oz/60 g) butter or olive oil

1 cup (8 oz/250 g) brown rice

1 cup (6 oz/200 g) millet

5 cups (40 fl oz/1.25 l) boiling vegetable stock

2 tomatoes, diced

1/2 cup chopped parsley

salt and pepper

6-8 medium size golden nugget pumpkins

olive oil with crushed garlic

salt and pepper

Gently fry onion and garlic in butter or oil in a heavy-based pan until soft. Add rice and millet and fry, stirring until all grains are coated. Add boiling stock, simmer covered for 45 minutes, then without lid for a further 10 minutes, stirring frequently. Stir in tomatoes and parsley and add salt and pepper to taste. Serve hot or use to stuff pumpkin.

Cut a slice from tops of pumpkins and scoop out seeds with a metal teaspoon. Brush cavities with olive oil and crushed garlic, sprinkle with salt and pepper. Steam or cook in a microwave oven on High setting until tender and cooked.

Spoon hot pilaf into hot pumpkin shells and serve.

WILD RICE PILAF WITH CHEESE

SERVES 4

Serve this wild rice dish without the cheese as a delicious accompaniment to a main course. It serves 8 as an accompaniment.

1 cup (6 oz/175 g) wild rice

4 cups (32 fl oz/1 l) vegetable stock

1/2 cup (4 oz/125 g) butter

2 onions, finely chopped

2 tomatoes, peeled, seeded and chopped

1 cup (4 oz/125 g) reduced-fat cheese, grated

Rinse rice in cold water and drain. Bring stock to the boil in a large heavy pan, add rice, stir well, cover and cook according to directions on packet, approx. 45–50 minutes on a low heat until rice splits open. Drain rice and keep warm.

Melt butter in large pan, add finely chopped onions and gently fry until transparent. Add rice and finely chopped tomatoes and stir until rice is evenly coated with butter and heated through.

Stir cheese into rice and serve with a salad.

Rice and millet pilaf pumpkins

WILD RICE ASIAN STYLE

SERVES 4–6

Serve as a main course with a crisp salad or as an attractive accompaniment to Korean Kebabs (page 93).

3/4 cup (4 oz/125 g) wild rice, rinsed

2 cups (16 fl oz/500 ml) vegetable stock

2 cloves garlic, crushed

1/8 teaspoon Chinese 5 spices

1 tablespoon peanut oil

1 cup scallions (spring onions), cut 1 1/2 inch (4 cm) long

2 blood oranges (oranges with dark red flesh)

1/2 cup thinly sliced water chestnuts

1 cup (4 oz/125 g) roasted cashew nuts

salt and pepper

Place rinsed rice in a heavy-based pan, add stock, bring to the boil, cover, and simmer for 40 minutes or until tender. Drain if necessary.

Gently fry garlic and Chinese 5 spices in oil for 2 minutes. Add scallions, stir-fry for 1 minute. Peel oranges with a sharp serrated knife, cut segments out and squeeze juice out of remaining membranes.

Add rice, orange segments and juice, water chestnuts and nuts to pan and heat through, stirring occasionally. Season to taste with salt and pepper. Serve hot.

ITALIAN WILD RICE

SERVES 4–6

Serve as an accompaniment for Tofu Balls (page 113), Zucchini Frittata (page 110), and other meals.

1 cup cooked wild rice (1/3 cup raw)

1 cup long-grain rice (1/3 cup raw)

1 onion, finely chopped

1 clove garlic, crushed

1 tablespoon olive oil

1 green pepper (capsicum), sliced

1/2 cup chopped sun-dried tomatoes

1 tablespoon oil from sun-dried tomatoes

1 tablespoon chopped oregano

1 tablespoon shredded basil

salt and pepper

Cook rices according to directions on the pack. Gently fry onion and garlic in oil in a heavy-based pan until soft and golden. Add pepper and fry gently for 2–3 minutes. Add rices, tomatoes, oil from tomatoes and herbs and stir over heat until heated through. Season to taste with salt and pepper.

STIR-FRIED BARLEY

SERVES 4

Barley is a good source of B vitamins and complex carbohydrate. Serve with Tofu Loaf (page 129) for a complete protein meal.

3 tablespoons polyunsaturated oil

1 onion, chopped

1 clove garlic, crushed

1 teaspoon chopped ginger

1/8 teaspoon five star anise

2 slim carrots, sliced diagonally

2 stalks celery, sliced diagonally

1/2 green pepper (capsicum), cut into squares

1 cup shredded Chinese cabbage

juice of 1 lemon

1 cup quick-cooking barley, cooked

1 tablespoon canned black beans, rinsed and drained

Heat oil in a wok or large frying pan and stir-fry onion, garlic, ginger and five star anise for 2 minutes. Add carrots and stir-fry for 2 minutes. Add celery and peppers, stir-fry for a further 2 minutes, then add cabbage and stir-fry for 1 minute. Stir in remaining ingredients, heat through and serve.

BUCKWHEAT PILAF

SERVES 4

Buckwheat is rich in protein. It belongs to the rhubarb family, not the wheat family, and is used to make a porridge in eastern Europe. Serve with a legume dish for a complete protein meal.

1 cup (6 oz/175 g) buckwheat kernels, rinsed

4 cups (32 fl oz/1 l) vegetable stock for cooking

1/4 cup (2 oz/60 g) butter

1 onion, finely chopped

8 oz (250 g) mushrooms, finely chopped

1 small pickled red pepper (capsicum) or 1 small fresh red pepper, chopped

1 cup (8 fl oz/250 ml) natural yogurt

2 tablespoons chopped parsley or dill

Cook buckwheat in boiling stock for 15 minutes. Drain well. Heat butter and gently fry onion for 5 minutes, add mushrooms and cook for 2 minutes, stirring frequently. Add chopped red pepper and simmer for 2 minutes. Add buckwheat, yogurt and herb and stir until heated through.

Serve with a pulse-legume based main course.

BULGUR PILAF

SERVES 4–6

The popular use for bulgur is in the Middle Eastern salad Tabbouleh, but it also gives a very appealing light texture to a pilaf.

1 tablespoon polyunsaturated margarine

2 cloves garlic, crushed

1 cup (5 oz/150 g) bulgur

2 cups (16 fl oz/500 ml) vegetable stock

1 carrot, in julienne strips

5 scallions (spring onions), in julienne strips

1 tablespoon chopped parsley

1 tablespoon poppy seeds

1/4 cup (1 oz/30 g) slivered almonds

grated rind of 1 lemon

1 tablespoon lemon juice

Heat margarine in a heavy-based pan and fry garlic and bulghur for 5 minutes, stirring continuously. Add stock, bring to the boil, cover and simmer for 30–35 minutes until all stock is absorbed and grain is tender. Remove lid and allow to dry out, off the heat, for 5 minutes. Fluff bulgur with a fork, add all the remaining ingredients, mixing together with the fork.

Serve hot as an accompaniment to a main course.

CORNBREAD

Cornmeal is made from maize, a grain which is a native of the Americas. The cornmeal gives cornbread its bright yellow hue and interesting texture. It's delicious served with soup and casseroles.

1 3/4 cup (9 oz/275 g) yellow cornmeal

1 cup(4 oz/125 g) all-purpose (plain) flour

1 tablespoon baking powder

1/4 cup(2 oz/60 g) sugar

2 eggs, beaten

3/4 cup (6 oz/185 g) butter or margarine, melted and cooled

1 1/4 cups (10 fl oz/300 ml) milk or soy milk

Sift cornmeal, flour and baking powder into a mixing bowl. Stir in sugar. Mix eggs with melted butter and milk, pour into middle of dry ingredients and beat until smooth. Pour into a lined and greased loaf tin and bake at 400°F (200°C) for 45 minutes or until cooked. Test with a fine, warm skewer. Turn out carefully and serve warm in thick slices.

Wild rice Asian style, p.164

POLENTA VEGETABLE CUBES
CORNMEAL PORRIDGE

SERVES 12–16

This yellow porridge, made from ground, rolled corn, is a staple grain dish enjoyed in northern Italy. Plain polenta, cut into shapes, then coated with Napoletana sauce, sprinkled with grated parmesan cheese and baked, is delicious. Polenta seasoned with vegetables, cut into cubes and fried, and accompanied by poached egg, is also delicious.

80 fl oz (2.5 L) water

2 teaspoons salt

1 lb (500 g) yellow cornmeal

1 small curly-leaved cabbage, shredded

2 cups grated zucchini (courgette)

1/2 cup (4 fl oz/125 ml) olive oil

1 1/2 cup (6 oz/185 g) grated parmesan cheese

4 tablespoons brewer's yeast or cereal bran

wholewheat (wholemeal) flour

extra olive oil for frying

Bring 8 cups (64 fl oz/2 l) water and salt to the boil in a large heavy-based pan. Blend cornmeal with remaining 2 cups of water, then slowly add to the boiling water, stirring continuously to prevent lumping. Bring back to the boil, then lower heat and cook for 30 minutes, stirring almost continuously. The mixture should be smooth and soft but stiff enough to support a wooden spoon. If too thick stir in more boiling water. This is plain polenta.

Cook cabbage in boiling salted water for 5 minutes, drain well. Gently fry cabbage and zucchini in oil for 5 minutes, until soft. Stir into polenta mixture with cheese and brewers yeast or bran. Spread mixture in a genoese (lamington) tin or shallow rectangular dish and leave to cool. When firm and cold, cut into cubes, coat with flour and fry in hot olive oil, turning until crisp and brown on all sides, about 10–15 minutes. Drain on kitchen paper towels and serve hot with poached eggs to dip into. Alternatively serve with eggs florentine, poached eggs on a bed of spinach puree.

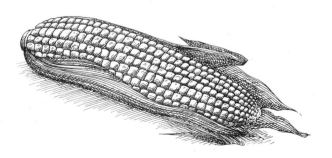

MOROCCAN COUSCOUS

In the countries of north Africa this wheat product is served under juicy casseroles, but you can also use it as a tasty and light accompaniment like rice.

1 cup (6 oz/175 g) couscous

3/4 cup (6 fl oz/185 ml) boiling vegetable stock

2 tablespoons olive oil or polyunsaturated margarine

1/3 cup (1 2/3 oz/50 g) dates, finely chopped

1/4 cup (1 oz/30 g) pistachio nuts, chopped

1 tablespoon chopped marjoram or oregano

1 tablespoon grated orange rind

4 tablespoons orange juice

Place couscous in a bowl, add boiling vegetable stock and leave to stand until all stock is absorbed, about 2–3 minutes. Heat oil in a large frying pan, add couscous and stir continuously over a medium heat for 4 minutes. Remove from heat, add all remaining ingredients and stir through before serving.

SHEIKH'S COUSCOUS

Not as bizarre as its name, this Moroccan-style dish is a lovely accompaniment to bean and vegetable casseroles or stuffed vegetables. Couscous is available in health food stores.

1 lb (500 g) couscous

3 cups (24 fl oz/750 ml) vegetable stock

3 1/4 oz (100 g) butter or margarine

1/2 cup (3 1/4 oz/100 g) cooked chick peas

1 cup (6 oz/185 g) seedless raisins

fresh herbs for garnish

Place couscous in a shallow dish and add an equal volume of boiling salted water (i.e. 1 cup for 1 cup). Leave to stand for 5 minutes, stirring with a fork to separate the grains as the couscous swells.

Place stock in a pan and bring to the boil. Add the butter, chick peas, raisins and couscous and stir with a fork over a low heat for 5 minutes.

Stir well before serving, garnished with sprigs of fresh herbs as an accompaniment to Soya Bean Casserole (page 126) for a complete protein meal.

QUINOA WITH GREENS

SERVES 4

You can serve quinoa like rice. Its light texture combined with some lightly cooked greens make it an attractive accompaniment to a casserole or stuffed vegetables.

1 tablespoon oil

6 scallions (spring onions), thinly sliced

2 cloves garlic, crushed

8 oz (250 g) asparagus spears, sliced

1 cup thinly shredded Chinese cabbage

1 cup thinly shredded choy sum

1 tablespoon shredded basil

2 teaspoons tahina

1 teaspoon lemon juice

1/2 cup (4 fl oz/125 ml) natural yogurt

4 oz (125 g) quinoa

Heat oil and gently fry onions and garlic until soft. Add asparagus and stir-fry for 3 minutes. Add Chinese greens and basil, cover and cook until the greens wilt. Stir in remaining ingredients and heat through gently.

Cook quinoa according to directions; drain well. Add green vegetable mixture and toss gently before serving.

QUINOA PRIMAVERA

SERVES 4

6 1/2 oz (200 g) packet quinoa

Sauce:

2 cloves garlic

1 red skinned onion, cut in wedges

2 tablespoons olive oil

1 choko (chayote), peeled, cored and coarsely chopped

1 zucchini (courgette), thinly sliced

1 cup cherry tomatoes, quartered

1/2 cup (4 fl oz/125 ml) tomato paste

1/2 cup (4 fl oz/125 ml) water

1 red chili, seeded and sliced

salt

1 cup shredded basil

grated parmesan cheese for sprinkling, optional

Cook quinoa according to directions on the pack.

Sauce: Gently fry garlic and onion in oil until soft and golden. Steam or microwave choko until almost cooked. Add choko, zucchini, tomatoes, tomato paste, water and chili to onion and simmer, covered, until juicy and tender. Add salt to taste then stir in half the basil.

Serve sauce over hot quinoa in pasta bowls, sprinkled with remaining basil and parmesan cheese if desired.

Quinoa with greens

HIGH PROTEIN MUESLI

MAKES 14 CUPS

A breakfast of unadulterated cereal grains is a satisfying and healthy way to start your day. There are lots of interesting mueslis to choose from today but many people still prefer to make their own, so this recipe is for you!

2 cups rolled oats
1 cup rolled barley
1 cup rolled triticale
2 cups rolled wheat
1 cup rolled rye
1 cup rolled millet
1 cup (8 fl oz/250 ml) honey
1 cup wheatgerm
1 cup bran
1/2 cup sunflower kernels
1/2 cup pepitas
1/2 cup sesame seeds
1/4 cup roasted buckwheat
1/4 cup alfalfa seeds
1/4 cup linseed seeds
1/4 cup poppy seeds
1 cup chopped dried apricots or
apples
1 cup raisins (or sultanas)

Combine the rolled cereals in a large mixing bowl. Heat honey until thin, pour over rolled cereals and mix well. Transfer to a greased baking tin and bake at 350°F (180°C) for 15 minutes, stir well and roast for a further 15 minutes, stirring every 5 minutes. Remove from oven and leave to cool. Add all remaining ingredients and mix well. Store in clean glass storage jars. Serve with milk, yogurt, buttermilk or fresh or stewed fruit for a healthy high fiber breakfast.

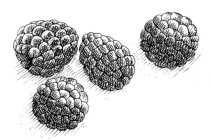

LIGHT MUESLI

MAKES 14 CUPS

This muesli feels light to eat and is lower in calories than most mueslis. Serve it with milk, yogurt or buttermilk for a complete protein breakfast and add some fresh fruit which is a good source of vitamin C.

2 cups rice flakes

2 cups oat bran flakes

2 cups puffed corn

2 cups puffed rice

2 cups puffed millet

2 cups puffed wheat

1 cup raisins (or sultanas)

1 cup dried papaya (pawpaw), chopped

Mix all ingredients together. Store in air-tight glass storage jars. Serve with milk, yogurt or buttermilk and fresh fruit.

CRUNCHY GRANOLA

MAKES 10 CUPS

Here is a way to make your own granola. It is similar to toasted muesli and often forms crunchy pieces during the roasting process. This recipe is a high protein breakfast cereal because of the inclusion of soy grits, and is delicious accompanied with milk, yogurt or buttermilk.

5 cups rolled oats

1 cup rolled rye

1 cup rolled barley

1 cup soy grits

1 cup wheatgerm

1 cup (8 fl oz/250 ml) honey

1/2 cup (4 fl oz/125 ml) safflower oil

1 tablespoon vanilla essence

1/2 cup sunflower kernals

1/4 cup sesame seeds

1/4 cup flaked almonds

Place all cereals in a baking tin. Heat honey and oil until thin, add vanilla and pour over cereals and mix well. Bake at 350°F (180°C) for 15 minutes. Stir well then roast for a further 15 minutes, stirring every 5 minutes, or until mixture forms into crunchy lumps. Remove from oven and cool before storing in glass storage jars. Eat dry as a snack or with milk, yogurt or buttermilk as a breakfast cereal.

SALADS AND ACCOMPANIMENTS

We are blessed with a wonderful variety of salad greens, vegetables and fruits, thanks to the enthusiasm and communication between good cooks and chefs and growers, and to the wonders of modern transportation. When I was a child, most fruits and vegetables were only available during their growing seasons, but now we can enjoy a surprisingly extensive range of them all year round.

It's important to shop carefully for salad greens, vegetables and fruit. Choose crisp, clean, bright leafy salad greens, firm, crisp, unblemished vegetables and firm undamaged fruit. The hydroponic lettuces are particularly good quality and can taste good too, as long as the grower has fed them sufficient nutrients. Prepared salad mixes or 'value-added' salads save time and are very attractive. Look out for arugula, maché or lamb's lettuce, mesculum miniature salad greens, cress salad with flowers, spinach leaf salad and snow pea sprouts. Vine-ripened tomatoes are also a good buy because they usually have a memorable tomato taste and add an eye-dazzling brightness to salad greens.

There are many interesting and unusual salads to choose from in this chapter. Some such as Caesar's Salad, Cheese Fruit and Nut Salad and Feta with Radicchio Salad are hearty and rustic, and may be served as a well balanced meal with some crunchy wholegrain bread rolls, or hot garlic or pesto bread. Others, such as Citrus Green Salad or Tofu and Daikon Salad, are perfect to accompany with a platter of cheeses for a weekend lunch. Some are ideal for entertaining. Potato salads and rice salads are good for buffet parties, while the exotic Oyster Mushroom and Mango Salad is more appropriate for an elegant dinner party. Thai Apricot Salad, Gado Gado Salad and Tropical Papaya Salad complement Asian meals; Beet Salad and Carrot and Peanut Salad are popular with children; and Tabbouleh, Italian Pasta Salad and Tomato and Basil Salad are great for picnics and barbecues.

When I was a student years ago, I was taught that a salad should look as if 'it has floated down from heaven' and I have always remembered this excellent tip. To ensure this light look it is most important that salad greens are well-drained and dried after washing, because limp lettuce looks dreadful and dilutes the delicious taste of the dressing.

I have included recipes for some wonderful dressings, but I encourage you to experiment and be creatively adventurous.

In this chapter you will also find delicious accompaniments or sambals that are excellent served with curry, plus tasty sauces to accompany other vegetarian dishes.

Italian pasta salad, p.194

AVOCADO AND TAMARILLO WINDMILL SALAD

SERVES 4

Tamarillo can be peeled easily with a vegetable peeler.

1 mignonette lettuce or other curly-leaved lettuce

1 large ripe avocado

8 slices bocconcini cheese

2 tamarillo, peeled and sliced

2 tablespoons small basil leaves

1 quantity French dressing (page 205)

Arrange lettuce leaves around the perimeter of a round serving plate. Cut avocado in half, remove stone then cut into quarters and remove skin. Cut avocado quarters into neat wedges and place on top of lettuce like the spokes of a windmill. Place a circle of overlapping bocconcini on top of avocado, working towards the middle of the plate. Place a circle of overlapping tamarillo in the middle of plate. Sprinkle basil leaves and dressing over salad and serve fresh.

❖ YOU CAN SAVE TIME BY USING PRE-PREPARED SALAD MIXES. LOOK OUT FOR UNUSUAL MINIATURE MESCULUM SALAD GREENS, CRESS SALAD, LAMB'S LETTUCE OR MACHÉ, ARUGULA, WITLOF AND SNOW PEA SPROUTS. TRY GROWING LAND CRESS IN A POT IN YOUR GARDEN. THESE SALAD GREENS CAN ADD AN ELEGANT AND ORIGINAL TOUCH TO HORS D'OEUVRES AND MAIN COURSES AND ARE PARTICULARLY IMPRESSIVE WHEN ENTERTAINING.

BEAN SPROUTS AND SPINACH SALAD

SERVES 6–8

This is an unusual salad which is served warm. An ideal accompaniment to nut or pulse-legume dishes.

8 oz (250 g) fresh bean sprouts

1 lb (500 g) spinach, washed and trimmed

3 tablespoons vegetable oil

1 1/2 teaspoons finely chopped garlic

1 1/2 tablespoons finely chopped scallions (spring onions)

1 1/2 tablespoons soy sauce

1 1/2 tablespoons sesame seeds

1/2 teaspoon finely chopped chili pepper

Wash bean sprouts and drain well. Blanch spinach and drain well. Heat oil in a large, heavy-based frying pan and lightly fry the bean sprouts and spinach. Add garlic, scallions and soy sauce and stir well. Add sesame seeds and chili pepper, stirring constantly.

Place on a serving platter and serve warm.

BEET SALAD

SERVES 4

This is a good high-protein salad to take on a picnic. Canned or preserved beets (beetroot) may be used for convenience.

8 oz (250 g) cooked beets (beetroot), diced

1/2 cup (4 fl oz/125 ml) mayonnaise (page 206)

1 tablespoon lemon juice

2 tablespoons chopped dill

1 tablespoon French mustard

4 eggs, hard-boiled

Fold beets into mayonnaise with lemon juice, dill and mustard. Shell eggs and cut into quarters lengthwise. Fold eggs into salad.

Serve chilled accompanied by a crisp green salad and rye or pumpernickel bread.

Following page: Cheese, fruit and nut salad (right), p.184; Cherry tomato and basil salad (top), p. 204; Feta with radicchio salad (front), p. 190

CAESAR'S SALAD

SERVES 4

Serve this salad in pasta bowls or deep soup bowls accompanied by wholewheat (wholemeal) bread rolls for a light meal.

2 thick slices wholewheat (wholemeal) bread

2 teaspoons crushed garlic

peanut oil for frying

2 hard-boiled eggs

1 romaine (cos) lettuce, washed

2 tablespoons julienne strips of sun-dried tomatoes

2 tablespoons salted cashew nuts

2 oz (60 g) parmesan cheese, thinly sliced

Dressing:

2 egg yolks

2 cloves garlic, crushed

1 teaspoon dijon mustard

4 tablespoons olive oil

2 tablespoons oil from sun-dried tomatoes

2 tablespoons white wine vinegar

freshly ground black pepper

Cut crusts from bread, spread garlic over one side and cut bread into small cubes. Fry bread cubes in hot oil until crisp, to make croutons, drain well on kitchen paper towels.

Shell eggs then chop quickly by slicing twice on an egg slicer.

Tear lettuce into 4 individual or 1 large salad bowl, leaving small inner leaves whole. Sprinkle half the croûtons, eggs, tomatoes and nuts over the lettuce. Add the dressing and toss until well coated. Sprinkle remaining croutons, eggs, tomatoes and nuts over the dressed salad and top with thin slices of parmesan cheese (use a cheese slicer).

Dressing: Place all ingredients in a food processor or blender and mix until well combined, adding pepper to taste.

❖ ALWAYS BE FUSSY ABOUT DRYING LETTUCE LEAVES WELL BEFORE USE IN A TOSSED GREEN SALAD. WET LETTUCE DILUTES THE DRESSING, RESULTING IN A DREARY LIMP SALAD AND A THIN DRESSING.

RED CABBAGE COLESLAW

SERVES 8–12

This is an eye-catching, high-fiber salad with a crisp crunchy texture. Serve at a barbecue or with Rice Balls (page 161). Hijiki is a type of seaweed in attractive threads or strings.

4 cups finely shredded red cabbage

1 green apple

2 tablespoons hijiki, soaked in cold water

3 tablespoons thinly sliced scallions (spring onions)

1 cup sliced celery or 1 cup grated celeriac

Dressing:

3/4 cup (6 fl oz/185 ml) orange juice

3 tablespoons apple cider vinegar

1 teaspoon cumin seeds

1 tablespoon ground mustard

Prepare cabbage, 1/8–1/4 cabbage yields approximately 4 cups. Cut apple into quarters, remove core and cut fruit into neat cubes, leaving skin on. Drain hijiki and cut into 3/4 inch (2 cm) lengths. Combine all ingredients in a salad bowl.

Dressing: Mix all ingredients together in a screw-top jar and shake well. Pour dressing over salad, toss well and serve chilled.

181

CHINESE CABBAGE SLAW

SERVES 6–8

1 onion, cut in wedges

1 teaspoon sesame oil

2 tablespoons hot chili paste

2 teaspoons tamarind sauce

12 snake beans, cut in 2 inch (5 cm) lengths

1/2 cup snow peas (mange-tout)

1/2 cup (4 fl oz/125 ml) coconut milk

4 cups shredded Chinese cabbage (celery cabbage)

1/2 cup bean sprouts

1 tablespoon pepitas

2 tablespoons shredded coconut

Gently fry onion in oil until soft, add chili paste, tamarind sauce and snake beans and stir-fry for 2 minutes. Add snow peas and coconut milk and stir-fry for 1 minute. Pour into a bowl and leave to cool. When lukewarm, stir in cabbage, cover and chill. Before serving, stir in the sprouts, pepitas and coconut.

Serve with a barbecue or with Tofu Balls (page 113).

CARROT AND PEANUT SALAD

SERVES 4–6

This is a popular salad to serve to young children with barbecued vegetarian sausages. Carrots are rich in fiber and are a source of vitamins A and C. Omit peanuts and raisins if serving to toddlers.

1 cup (2 oz/60 g) rye or wholewheat (wholemeal) breadcrumbs

1 tablespoon butter or polyunsaturated margarine

2 cups coarsely grated carrot

1/2 cup (2 oz/60 g) salted peanuts

1/2 cup (3 oz/90 g) raisins (or sultanas)

1/4 cup chopped parsley

4 tablespoons French dressing (page 205)

bean sprouts for sprinkling

Fry breadcrumbs in butter until crisp and golden. Adult palates may like to try pumpernickel breadcrumbs. Mix breadcrumbs with all remaining ingredients. Cover and chill before serving, sprinkled with bean sprouts.

Carrot and peanut salad

CELERIAC SALAD

SERVES 4

Celeriac or celery root can be cooked in casseroles or enjoyed raw in a salad. It is difficult to grate as it has a soft spongy texture, so chop it finely in a food processor for this salad.

2 medium celeriac, grated or finely chopped

juice of 1 lemon or 2 limes

1 carrot, grated

3/4 cup (6 fl oz/185 ml) mayonnaise (page 206)

2 tablespoons dijon mustard

1/4 cup (1 oz/30 g) chopped walnuts or pecans

Mix the prepared celeriac with the lemon juice. Add all remaining ingredients and fold together. Chill salad for at least 1 hour before serving.

CHEESE, FRUIT AND NUT SALAD

SERVES 4

Serve this salad for a main meal accompanied by pesto bread or garlic bread. White miso is a paste made from soy beans and rice and is used as a seasoning condiment. It is available at health food stores.

1 small ripe pineapple

1 red apple

1/2 cup seedless green grapes

4 dessert dates

6 oz (185 g) Swiss or Dutch cheese, cubed

1/2 cup (2 oz/60 g) walnuts or pecans

1 rocket lettuce or similar

1 small radicchio lettuce or similar

2 tablespoons shredded coconut, toasted

Dressing:

2 tablespoons sunflower oil

3 tablespoons apple juice

1 teaspoon white wine vinegar

1 teaspoon white miso

1 clove garlic, crushed

1 tablespoon shredded mint

Peel, core and slice pineapple and cut into cubes. Cut apple into quarters, remove core and cut apple into wedges. Cut grapes in half lengthwise. Remove stones from dates, cut into slices. Combine prepared fruits in a bowl. Add cheese and nuts and dressing and toss together. Cover and chill until ready to serve.

Tear lettuces into a salad bowl, add fruits, nuts and dressing and toss together. Sprinkle with coconut and serve.

Dressing: Mix all ingredients together in a screw-top jar and store in refrigerator until required.

CUCUMBER AND RADISH SALAD

SERVES 6-8

2 cucumbers

1 tablespoon red wine vinegar

1/2 teaspoon salt

1 bunch radishes, thinly sliced

3 tablespoons shredded dill

1 small red onion, thinly sliced, optional

1/2 cup (4 fl oz/125 ml) natural yogurt

1/2 cup (4 fl oz/125 ml) light sour cream

freshly ground black pepper

Cut cucumbers into quarters, lengthwise, remove peel and scoop out seeds. Slice cucumbers thinly, place in a bowl and sprinkle with vinegar and salt. Allow to stand for 30 minutes.

Drain cucumber and gently press out excess juices. Place cucumber in a bowl, add all remaining ingredients and fold together. Add pepper to taste.

Serve chilled.

CAPONATINA SALAD

SERVES 8

An Italian recipe, with the character of Sicily, which stores well in the refrigerator for a few days.

1 onion, chopped

1 tablespoon olive oil

1 carrot, sliced

1 stalk celery, sliced

1 small green pepper (capsicum), skinned

1 small red pepper (capsicum), skinned

2 zucchini (courgette), sliced

1 lb (500 g) eggplant (aubergine)

4 tomatoes, chopped

1/2 cup (4 fl oz/125 ml) tomato paste

3 tablespoons water

1 tablespoon raisins (or sultanas)

1 tablespoon apple cider vinegar

8 olives

Gently fry onion in oil in a heavy-based pan until soft. Add carrot and celery, cover and sauté for 5 minutes. Chop peppers and add with zucchini and sauté for another 5 minutes.

Peel eggplant, cut into cubes and steam until cooked or cook in a microwave oven on High setting for 7 minutes. Add to sautéed vegetables with tomatoes, tomato paste, water and raisins. Cover and simmer for 25–30 minutes, stirring occasionally. Allow to cool. Stir in vinegar, place in a serving bowl and sprinkle with olives.

Serve chilled; complements Millet Balls (page 148) or Rice Balls (page 161).

GADO GADO SALAD

SERVES 4–6

This delicious Indonesian salad may be served as a first course or as part of a Southeast Asian meal. You can prepare the spicy peanut sauce quickly if you use processed curry paste and peanut butter.

Sauce:

1 bulb French shallot, finely chopped

1 plump clove garlic, crushed

1 teaspoon minced chili

1 tablespoon peanut oil

2 teaspoons curry paste, medium strength

3 tablespoons crunchy peanut butter

1 cup (8 fl oz/250 ml) water

1 tablespoon soy sauce

2 teaspoons lemon or lime juice

Salad Vegetables:

1 cup green or snake beans, blanched

1 cup diced cooked new potatoes

2 cups shredded Chinese cabbage (celery cabbage)

1 red pepper (capsicum), sliced

1 cup bean shoots

4 hard-boiled eggs, quartered in wedges

Sauce: Gently fry shallot, garlic and chili in oil until shallot is soft. Add curry paste and stir continuously for 1 minute. Add peanut butter, water, sauce and lemon juice and bring to the boil stirring, then simmer for 2 minutes.

Serve sauce in a bowl or a serving platter surrounded by piles of vegetables and eggs.

Gado gado salad (top); Black bean and rice salad (front), p.200

OYSTER MUSHROOM AND MANGO SALAD

SERVES 4

Make this special salad for a special occasion. Cantaloupe (rockmelon) balls may be used when mangoes are not in season. It is ideal if you are on a weight-reduction diet as it is high in fiber and contains no fat.

4 oz (125 g) small oyster mushrooms

1 cup snow peas (mange-tout), blanched and refreshed

1 large or 2 small mangoes, cubed

1 cup snow pea (mange-tout) sprouts

Dressing:

1 clove garlic, crushed

1 teaspoon minced red chili

1 teaspoon minced ginger

1 teaspoon brown sugar

1 teaspoon finely chopped cilantro (coriander) root

2 tablespoons chopped cilantro (coriander) leaves

3 tablespoons lime juice

Brush mushrooms clean, trim stalks if necessary. Slice mushrooms if large. Combine with snow peas, well dried, and mangoes in a salad bowl and top with snow pea spouts.

Dressing: Mix all ingredients together, refrigerate until required. Pour over salad just before serving.

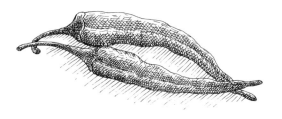

FESTIVE GREEN SALAD

SERVES 12–16

This is a lovely salad bowl to serve at a party buffet or smorgasbord. Add cherry tomatoes, sliced radishes and orange segments for some contrast and texture if desired.

3 different varieties of lettuce

1 cup watercress or snow pea (mange-tout) sprouts

1 bunch asparagus

1 knob fennel or 2 stalks celery, thinly sliced

14 oz (440 g) can artichoke hearts, drained, quartered and thinly sliced

1 tablespoon pitted, sliced green olives

1 avocado pear

1 cup toasted macadamia nuts

2 quantities French dressing (page 205)

Wash lettuces, dry well in a clean cloth, refrigerate in an air-tight container to crisp. Wash watercress sprigs and dry in a clean cloth. Crisp in refrigerator.

Cook asparagus until just tender, refresh in iced water. Prepare fennel, artichoke hearts and olives.

Tear lettuce in bite-sized pieces into a chilled salad bowl, add watercress, asparagus, fennel, artichokes and sliced olives, cover and chill until ready to serve. Just before serving peel avocado pear, remove stone and cut into slices.

Add French dressing to salad and toss gently until salad greens are evenly coated. Arrange avocado slices and macadamia nuts attractively on top and serve fresh.

TOFU AND DAIKON GREEN SALAD

SERVES 6–8

A daikon is a long white radish popular in Japanese cuisine. It turns a beautiful bright pink when marinated in beet (beetroot) juice. Use the juice from canned or boiled beets.

3 1/3 oz (100 g) tofu, diced

2 teaspoons tamari

2 teaspoons lime juice

1/2 cup thinly sliced daikon

4 tablespoons beet (beetroot) juice

1 lettuce, oak leaf, romaine (cos) or mignonette

1/4 cucumber, thinly sliced

1 small green pepper (capsicum), thinly sliced

3 tablespoons French or sunflower dressing (pages 205)

Marinate the tofu in the tamari and lime juice for 1/2–1 hour. Marinate the daikon in the beet juice for 1/2–1 hour, until it turns bright pink.

Tear the washed lettuce leaves into a salad bowl. Add the tofu and marinade, the drained daikon, cucumber and peppers. Chill until ready to serve. Just before serving add dressing and toss gently until all ingredients are lightly coated.

CITRUS GREEN SALAD

SERVES 4

This pretty, refreshing salad is ideal for a low-calorie diet. You can turn it into a main course for 2 people by adding some cottage or ricotta or soy cheese.

1 grapefruit

1 orange

1 small red onion

3 ⅓ oz (100 g) salad greens with edible flowers or cress salad with nasturtium petals

2 teaspoons sesame seeds

Dressing:

4 tablespoons citrus juice from grapefruit and orange

4 tablespoons natural yogurt

Remove skin from citrus fruit, using a sharp serrated knife, taking care to remove all white pith. Cut grapefruit and orange segments out of membrane, working on a plate in order to reserve the juices. Cut onion into very thin segments so that it falls apart like petals.

Place salad greens in a shallow serving bowl, add grapefruit, orange and onion and sprinkle with sesame seeds. Just before serving, 'drizzle' dressing over the salad.

Dressing: Mix together in a screw-top jar until well combined. Store in refrigerator until required.

FETA WITH RADICCHIO SALAD

SERVES 4

Serve this robust salad accompanied by Tabbouleh or wholegrain bread rolls for a well-balanced meal. Daikon is Japanese radish.

8 oz (250 g) feta cheese

1 radicchio or other red lettuce, washed and crisp

1 small red pepper (capsicum), thinly sliced

8 radishes, thinly sliced or ½ cup pickled daikon

1 Lebanese cucumber, thinly sliced

2 heads endive (witlof), thinly shredded

2 tablespoons walnut halves

6 tablespoons French dressing made with hazelnut or walnut oil (page 205)

Drain feta cheese and cut into ½ inch (1.25 cm) cubes. Place all salad ingredients into a salad bowl. Add dressing and toss well just before serving.

Citrus green salad

MUSHROOM AND MINT SALAD

SERVES 6–8

If you happen to be in France or Italy, or you're just feeling extravagant, add a thinly sliced truffle to this salad for a touch of luxury. Mushroom cups have a stronger taste than the younger buttons.

1 lb (500 g) mushroom cups, medium size, thinly sliced

4 oz (125 g) parmesan cheese, shaved or coarsely grated

1 tablespoon poppy seeds

3 tablespoons olive oil

3 tablespoons lemon juice

1 clove garlic, crushed

1 teaspoon wholegrain mustard

8 grinds black pepper

1 tablespoon snipped chives

3 tablespoons shredded mint

butterleaf lettuce for serving

Gently combine mushrooms with cheese and poppy seeds. Place all remaining ingredients, except herbs, in a screw-top jar, cover and shake well, then pour dressing over mushrooms. Cover and marinate at room temperature for 1 hour. Fold herbs in just before serving. Place on top of lettuce leaves for good contrast if desired.

CRUNCHY NUT AND ORANGE SALAD

SERVES 4

Some of the crunch in this salad comes from Belgian endive, also called witlof or chicory, a refreshing vegetable which can be served raw in salads or cooked and served gratinéed.

4 oz (125 g) endive, sliced

2 oz (60 g) roasted cashew nuts

1 yellow pepper (capsicum), sliced

4 yellow squash, cut in wedges

2 oranges, peeled and cut in segments

1/4 cup sliced scallions (spring onions)

1 cup green grapes

1 cup alfalfa sprouts

1 quantity sunflower dressing (page 205)

Combine all ingredients except sprouts with dressing, place in a salad bowl and chill lightly. Serve salad topped with alfalfa sprouts.

Serve accompanied by a rice or grain dish for a balanced protein meal.

ONION SALAD

SERVES 8

This is a French salad which is good to serve al fresco or as antipasto.

4 tablespoons olive oil

2 carrots, chopped

1 1/2 lb (750 g) small pickling onions

1 cup (8 fl oz/250 ml) water

3/4 cup (6 fl oz/185 ml) dry cider

4 tablespoons lemon juice

2 tablespoons tomato paste

1/3 cup (2 oz/60 g) raisins (or sultanas)

2 bay leaves

1/4 teaspoon salt

freshly ground black pepper

pinch of cayenne

1 tablespoon chopped parsley

Heat oil in a large, heavy pan, add carrots, cover and sauté until soft, approximately 5–10 minutes, shaking pan frequently.

Peel onions, add to pan with water, cider, lemon juice, tomato paste, raisins, bay leaves, salt, pepper and cayenne. Bring slowly to the boil, then simmer, partly covered, for 1 hour or until onions are tender and sauce has reduced and thickened.

Cool onion mixture, place in a serving bowl, then cover and chill well.

Before serving, adjust seasoning to taste and sprinkle with chopped parsley.

❖ WHEN ENTERTAINING, IT IS A GOOD IDEA TO PREPARE AS MUCH OF THE FOOD IN ADVANCE AS YOU POSSIBLY CAN. I ALWAYS MAKE SALAD DRESSINGS ON THE DAY OR NIGHT BEFORE A PARTY SO THAT I'M NOT IN A LAST MINUTE PANIC WHEN TOSSING THE SALAD.

PASTA AND BROCCOLI SALAD

SERVES 4

Try serving this quick-to-prepare salad as a main course on a hot night, accompanied by a green salad tossed with 1-2 cups borlotti beans for a complete protein meal.

2 cups small pasta shells

4 cups broccoli florets

4 tablespoons French dressing (page 205)

4 tablespoons thinly sliced scallions (spring onions)

8 tablespoons grated parmesan cheese

2 tablespoons toasted pine nuts

Boil pasta until al dente, drain and cool. Cook broccoli in a clean food storage bag in a microwave oven on High setting for 5 minutes, or steam until just cooked. Add dressing to warm broccoli and leave to cool so that it absorbs the seasoning. When pasta and broccoli are lukewarm, fold together with all remaining ingredients and serve.

ITALIAN PASTA SALAD

SERVES 8

This is a handy salad to prepare ahead of time for a buffet party.

2 cups (5 oz/150 g) rigati pasta

1 cup canned artichoke hearts, quartered

1 cup (1 punnet) cherry tomatoes

1/2 cup sliced sun-dried tomatoes

24 black olives

Dressing:

1/4 cup (2 fl oz/60 ml) olive oil

1 cup (8 fl oz/250 ml) sparkling grape juice

1 tablespoon white wine vinegar

2 tablespoons shredded basil

Cook pasta in boiling water according to pack directions, until al dente. Drain then rinse in cold water. Mix pasta with half the dressing and leave until cold. Add remaining ingredients and dressing and toss well before serving.

Dressing: Mix all ingredients together in a screw-top jar and store in refrigerator until required.

Pasta and broccoli salad

TROPICAL PAPAYA SALAD

SERVES 6–8

This salad is popular in the tropical islands where green papaya (pawpaw) are readily available, often in your own garden! Choose unripe papaya, and grate by hand, as a food processor will make it mushy.

1 green papaya (pawpaw), approx. 2 lb (1 kg)

1 clove garlic, crushed

1 teaspoon minced chili

1 cup snake beans

1 vine-ripened tomato, chopped

1/2 cup (2 1/2 oz/75 g) Brazil nuts, chopped

Dressing:

1 tablespoon macadamia nut oil

3 tablespoons lime juice

salt to taste

1/2 teaspoon palm or brown sugar

1 tablespoon pickled pink ginger, optional

Peel, deseed and grate papaya. Mix with garlic and chili. Cut beans into 1 inch (2.5 cm) lengths and blanch and refresh. Fold beans, tomato and nuts into papaya.

Dressing: Mix all ingredients together. Pour dressing over salad and chill before serving.

PEAR AND BUTTER BEAN SALSA

1 cup yellow butter beans

1/2 cup diced sun-dried red pepper (capsicum) in oil

1 teaspoon minced red chili

juice of 1 lemon

1 quantity sunflower dressing (page 205)

2 large ripe pears, peeled, cored and diced

1 tablespoon chopped cilantro (coriander) leaves

Cook beans only until tender crisp, in a microwave oven or a steamer, refresh in iced water to preserve their natural appearance. Mix with red pepper. Mix chili and lemon with dressing. Pour over beans. Gently mix pears into salad and sprinkle with cilantro (coriander).

Serve chilled.

POTATO AND MUSTARD SEED SALAD

SERVES 4–6

Choose yellow-fleshed potatoes for this salad and leave the skins on for additional dietary fiber.

1 tablespoon macadamia nut oil

1 leek, thinly sliced

2 cloves garlic, crushed

1/2 teaspoon yellow mustard seeds

1/2 teaspoon brown mustard seeds

1/4 teaspoon paprika

1 lb (500 g) yellow-fleshed potatoes

1 cup sliced snake beans

1 stalk celery, sliced

2 tablespoons ground, roasted macadamia nuts

Dressing:

3 tablespoons mayonnaise

3 tablespoons soy drink

1 tablespoon macadamia oil

Heat oil and gently fry leek with garlic, mustard seeds and paprika until leek is soft and seeds crackle. Scrub potatoes, leave skin on and boil or cook in a microwave oven until tender. Cut potatoes into 3/4 inch (2 cm) cubes. Blanch snake beans in boiling water or in a microwave oven, place in cold water to retain a fresh appearance, then drain well. Mix potatoes with snake beans, celery, mustard seed mixture and dressing. Place in a serving bowl and sprinkle with nuts. Tastes best when served at room temperature.

Dressing: Mix all ingredients together, store in refrigerator until required.

POTATO AND SPROUT SALAD

SERVES 6–8

Use waxy new potatoes for the best salads, always mix them with dressing while warm and stand a chilled salad at room temperature for 30 minutes before serving for the best results.

1 lb (500 g) tiny new potatoes

8 scallions (spring onions), thinly sliced

1 cup (8 fl oz/250 ml) light sour cream or tofu mayonnaise (page 209)

juice of 1/2 lemon

1 dill pickled cucumber, chopped

1 green apple, quartered, cored and chopped

freshly ground black pepper

fruit of 1 pomegranate

1 cup snow pea (mange-tout) sprouts or watercress sprigs

1/2 cup mustard and cress or bean sprouts

3 tablespoons grated parmesan cheese, optional

Wash potatoes and cook, with skin on, in boiling salted water until tender. Drain and mix with scallions, sour cream and lemon juice while still warm, to develop a good taste. Leave to cool and fold in dill pickled cucumber and apple and season to taste with pepper. Cover and chill lightly until serving time.

Serve potato salad topped with pomegranate fruit, sprinkled with sprouts and cheese.

CURRIED RICE SALAD

SERVES 6–8

This can be made a day before serving so it's handy to prepare for entertaining. Try serving it with Spinach and Lentil Tart (page 120) for a complete protein meal.

1 cup (8 oz/250 g) long grain rice

1/2 cup (4 fl oz/125 ml) mayonnaise (page 206)

3 tablespoons natural yogurt

2 tablespoons chunky mango chutney

1/2 teaspoon ground turmeric

1/2 teaspoon ground cumin

1/2 cup cooked green peas

1 red pepper (capsicum), seeded and chopped

4 tablespoons pine nuts

salt and pepper

Cook rice in rapidly boiling salted water for 10–12 minutes, until tender. Drain immediately and rinse in cold water to avoid stickiness. Leave in a colander to drain well. Mix mayonnaise with yogurt, chutney and spices. Fold rice, vegetables and nuts into dressing and season to taste with salt and pepper.

Curried rice salad

BLACK BEAN AND RICE SALAD

SERVES 6

Cook the beans and rice a day before use and cool well to avoid a sticky salad. Try accompanying with Gado Gado Salad (page 186).

3/4 cup (5 oz/150 g) black Mexican turtle beans

3 cloves

1 cinnamon stick

1/2 teaspoon salt

2 cups (16 fl oz/500 ml) water

1 cup (8 oz/250 g) multi-grain rice

3 teaspoons cumin seeds

3 tablespoons olive oil

1/2 cup thinly sliced scallions (spring onions)

1/2 cup chopped cilantro (coriander)

1 green chili or jalapeno pepper, finely chopped

2 oranges

1/4 cup toasted pecans

2 tablespoons concentrated orange juice

1 tablespoon rice or cider vinegar

Place black beans, spices, salt and water in a pan, bring to the boil covered, then boil gently for 1 1/2 hours until tender, or cook for 30 minutes in a pressure cooker. Drain, discard spices and cool.

Cook rice in boiling salted water for 30 minutes, drain, rinse and cool.

Fry cumin seeds in 1 tablespoon olive oil in a small frying pan, stirring for 2 minutes. Crush with a mortar and pestle or in a small processor or coffee grinder. Mix beans and rice with cumin, scallions, cilantro and chili.

Grate orange rind finely, remove peel with a serrated knife and cut orange fruit into neat segments. Add orange rind and fruit and pecans to salad.

Mix remaining oil with orange juice and vinegar, pour over salad and toss gently to combine. Season to taste before serving.

TABBOULEH
CRACKED WHEAT SALAD

SERVES 8

Although this salad is readily available from delicatessens and take-away food stores, it is much cheaper to make your own tabbouleh. It keeps well in the refrigerator, so you can make it in advance. You may find it more convenient to substitute your ready-made French dressing for the oil and lemon juice.

2/3 cup (4 oz/125 g) bulgur (cracked wheat)

2 cups chopped continental parsley

1/4 cup shredded mint

3 tablespoons thinly sliced scallions (spring onions)

4 tablespoons olive oil

4 tablespoons lemon juice

1 vine-ripened tomato or 1/2 cup cherry tomatoes, diced

salt and pepper

Soak the bulgur in enough water to cover for at least 30 minutes. Drain very well then wrap in muslin or a clean fine cloth and squeeze well. Place bulgur in a bowl, add all the remaining ingredients and toss together using a fork. Add salt and pepper to taste.

Serve as a salad or use as a sandwich filling.

SAUERKRAUT SALAD

SERVES 4

Sauerkraut is a good source of Vitamin B12 for vegetarians.

13 1/2 oz (425 g) can sauerkraut, rinsed and drained

1 quantity sunflower dressing (page 205)

1 tablespoon ground mustard

1 teaspoon cumin seeds

2 tomatoes, diced

1 green apple, cored and diced

lamb's lettuce (salade de maché) or other small-leaved lettuce for serving

Fold all prepared ingredients together and serve chilled with the lamb's lettuce leaves on the side.

Thai Apricot Salad

SERVES 6

This stylish salad adds a delightful touch of freshness to Thai main course dishes.

1lb (500 g) apricots

1 cup alfalfa bean sprouts

Dressing:

1/4 cup (2 fl oz/60 ml) lime juice

1/4 cup (2 fl oz/60 ml) peanut oil

1 clove garlic, crushed

1 teaspoon chopped ginger

1 teaspoon chopped red chili

2 tablespoons chopped cilantro (coriander)

salt to taste

2 tablespoons roasted peanuts, chopped for sprinkling

Wash and dry apricots, cut in half, remove stones and cut fruit into wedges. Place in salad bowl and sprinkle alfalfa bean sprouts on top.

Dressing: Place all ingredients in a screw-top jar, cover and shake well. Chill until required.

Just before serving, pour dressing over apricots and sprinkle peanuts over the top.

Thai apricot salad

CHERRY TOMATO AND BASIL SALAD

SERVES 6–8

This Italian salad is an ideal attractive and delicious accompaniment to many vegetarian main courses, nut-based dishes in particular, such as Tofu Loaf (page 129), Macadamia Nut Patties (page 97) and Vegetable Almond Fritters (page 100).

1 lb (500 g) cherry tomatoes

2 tablespoons finely chopped basil

finely grated rind and juice of 1 lemon

4 tablespoons French dressing (page 205)

Wash tomatoes in cold water, dry with a clean cloth. Cut tomatoes in half across the flower and arrange in a shallow serving dish. Sprinkle basil, lemon rind and juice over tomatoes, cover and chill until ready to serve. Pour dressing over just before serving.

WINTER TROPICAL SALAD

SERVES 8

This is a delicious mixture to serve when lettuce and salad greens are expensive or unavailable. Serve with a legume-based main course for a satisfying, nutritious meal.

1 avocado pear

1 head of fennel

14 oz (440 g) can hearts of palm

Dressing:

2 tablespoons toasted sesame seeds

3 tablespoons olive oil

1 tablespoon tarragon or basil vinegar, or lemon juice

1/2 teaspoon sugar

1/2 teaspoon wholegrain mustard

1/2 teaspoon salt

6 grinds black pepper

Peel avocado, cut into quarter segments, remove stone and slice flesh approximately 1/4 inch (5 mm) thick. Wash and slice fennel thinly. Drain hearts of palm well, slice thinly. Place all salad ingredients in a salad bowl, cover and chill.

Dressing: Place all ingredients in a screw-top jar and shake until well mixed. Chill dressing.

To serve salad, pour chilled dressing over and serve immediately.

FRENCH DRESSING

MAKES ⅓ CUP

This classic recipe makes 4 tablespoons dressing, sometimes referred to as '1 quantity French dressing' in other recipes throughout this book. You can make up larger quantities and store in a glass jar, with a plastic screw-top lid, in the refrigerator for a few weeks.

3 tablespoons (2 fl oz/60 ml) olive oil

1 tablespoon (⅔ fl oz/20 ml) tarragon white wine vinegar

½ teaspoon fine white (caster) sugar

½ teaspoon mustard powder or wholegrain mustard

¼ teaspoon salt

6 grinds black pepper

1 plump clove garlic, crushed

1 tablespoon chopped herbs, optional

Place all ingredients in a screw-top jar, cover tightly and shake well until evenly mixed.

You may like to experiment with light and virgin olive oils, nut oil, cold-pressed oils, balsamic and herb and fruit vinegars, but this classic recipe remains the one I like best.

SUNFLOWER DRESSING

MAKES ½ CUP (4 FL OZ/125 ML)

Use this dressing for green salads to accompany and complement nut and pulse-legume based main course dishes.

4 tablespoons sunflower oil

1 clove garlic, crushed

1 teaspoon chopped basil

½ teaspoon chopped mint or tarragon

½ teaspoon chopped parsley or chervil

1 tablespoon apple cider vinegar

1 tablespoon lemon or lime juice

¼ teaspoon salt

6 grinds black pepper

Place all ingredients in a screw-top jar, cover with a plastic lid and shake well. Stand for 1–2 hours before use to allow seasoning to develop.

MAYONNAISE

MAKES 1 ½ CUPS (12 FL OZ/375 ML)

Home-made mayonnaise tastes far better than the commercial variety; however, you can get good results by adding lemon juice to taste to bought mayonnaise.

2 egg yolks

½ teaspoon salt

½ teaspoon sugar

½ teaspoon mustard powder

pinch of white pepper

1 teaspoon lemon juice

1 ¼ cups (10 fl oz/300 ml) olive oil, chilled if using a blender or processor

2–3 teaspoons white wine or apple cider vinegar

Place egg yolks in a mixing bowl, add seasoning and lemon juice and mix until smooth, using a wooden spoon or a sauce whisk. Stand the bowl on a damp cloth to prevent slipping.

Add 2 tablespoons oil, 2–3 drops at a time, stirring continuously. Add 1 teaspoon vinegar and mix to the consistency of cream. Continue adding oil slowly, a drop at a time, whisking continuously. As the mixture thickens, add the oil more quickly in a steady stream, whisking to prevent it from becoming too thick.

Alternatively, mix all ingredients, except oil, in a blender or food processor. Add chilled oil gradually, mixing continuously. When complete, the mayonnaise should be stiff enough to hold its shape.

Note: If mayonnaise separates, beat another egg yolk and stir in the curdled mayonnaise, a little at a time. If the mayonnaise is too stiff, add a little cold water.

Bean sprouts and spinach salad (top), p.177; Oyster mushroom and mango salad (front), p.188

CUISINE MINCEUR MAYONNAISE

SLIMMERS' MAYONNAISE

MAKES APPROXIMATELY 1 CUP (8 FL OZ/250 ML)

This recipe is an attempt to reduce the high oil content of the classic mayonnaise, but please note that it still contains a considerable amount of oil, which is fat in nutrition terminology!

1 egg, separated

1 teaspoon wholegrain or dijon mustard

1 teaspoon lemon juice

1 tablespoon light olive oil

4 tablespoons sunflower/polyunsaturated oil

2 tablespoons fromage blanc (below)

salt and pepper

Place egg yolk into a small mixing bowl, add mustard and beat well with a wooden spoon or whisk. Gradually beat in the lemon juice and oils, then the fromage blanc. Add salt and pepper to taste. Whisk egg white to a soft smooth aerated texture and gently stir into the mayonnaise.

Serve or use in place of mayonnaise.

FROMAGE BLANC

MAKES APPROXIMATELY 1 CUP (8 FL OZ/250 ML)

This can be used in place of mayonnaise, and/or egg yolks, in certain recipes, if on a low-cholesterol or reduced-fat diet. It's simple to make!

2/5 cup (3 1/4 oz/100 g) low-fat cottage cheese

1/2 cup (4 fl oz/125 ml) reduced-fat natural yogurt

3 teaspoons lemon or lime juice

Mix all ingredients together in an electric blender or small food processor until smooth and shiny and as thick as lightly whipped cream. Store in the refrigerator until required.

Serve as an accompaniment to vegetable curries and use in Cuisine Minceur Mayonnaise (above).

TOFU MAYONNAISE

MAKES ¾ CUP (6 FL OZ/185 ML)

This recipe contains considerably less oil than classic mayonnaise and consequently has a quarter of the calories.

1 clove garlic, halved

1 teaspoon sliced ginger

1 teaspoon miso

1 tablespoon parsley sprigs

⅔ cup (6 oz/185 g) silken tofu, well drained

2 tablespoons olive oil

6 teaspoons lemon juice

Place garlic, ginger, miso and parsley in a food processor or blender and mix until finely chopped. Add remaining ingredients and mix for 30 seconds or until well blended. Store in the refrigerator. The tofu mayonnaise will keep for 2–3 days only.

CURRIED CHICK PEAS

SERVES 4

Serve this as an accompaniment to a curry main course, such as Indian Curried Eggs (page 121), with a cucumber and yogurt sambal. Use 1 tablespoon curry paste in place of dry spices for convenience.

1 tablespoon vegetable oil

2 onions, chopped

2 cloves garlic, crushed

1 teaspoon mustard seeds

2 teaspoons ground coriander

2 teaspoons ground cumin

1 teaspoon ground turmeric

1 cup (4 oz/125 g) chick peas, cooked

1 cup (8 fl oz/250 ml) liquid from cooking chick peas or 1 cup vegetable stock

2 tablespoons shredded mint

Heat oil and gently fry onion, garlic and mustard until onion is soft. Add spices and stir-fry for 1 minute. Add chick peas and liquid and simmer covered for 30 minutes to develop seasoning. Stir in mint before serving.

To cook chick peas, cover with boiling water and leave to stand and swell for 1 hour until cold, then boil chick peas in fresh boiling water for 1 hour. Drain and reserve 1 cup liquid for this recipe.

INDIAN DHAL

SERVES 6–8

Curried lentils are a nutritious accompaniment to a curry meal.

1 cup (6 1/2 oz/200 g) red lentils

2 cups (16 fl oz/500 ml) vegetable stock

2 oz (60 g) ghee or polyunsaturated margarine

3 onions, sliced

1 tablespoon curry paste, medium strength

Rinse lentils, place in a large pan with stock and bring to the boil, then simmer, without a lid, for 15-20 minutes, until tender and nearly all the liquid has evaporated. Heat ghee in a frying pan and fry onions until golden brown, stirring frequently. Add curry paste to onions and stir-fry for 1–2 minutes. Add the lentils and stir well until heated through.

Serve hot with a curry meal.

YOGURT WITH MINT, ONION AND CHILI

SERVES 4

Try this with Tofu Loaf (page 129) or serve with a curry.

3 tablespoons shredded mint

3 tablespoons finely chopped red or white onion

1/2 teaspoon minced red or green chili

pinch of cayenne

pinch of salt

3/4 cup (6 fl oz/185 ml) natural yogurt

mint leaves for garnish

Mix all ingredients together, cover and chill before serving.

Serve garnished with mint leaves as an accompaniment to a curry.

Potato and sprout salad (top), p.198; Potato and mustard seed salad (front), p. 197

211

YOGURT WITH CUCUMBER AND TOMATO

SERVES 4–8

Lovely with a curry and goes well with Eggplant Puftaloons (page 52).

1 cucumber

1 tablespoon finely chopped red or white onion

salt

1 vine-ripened tomato, diced

1 teaspoon ground coriander

1 teaspoon ground cumin

1/2 cup (4 fl oz/125 ml) natural yogurt

Peel cucumber, cut in half lengthwise and scrape out all seeds, using a small sharp teaspoon. Slice cucumber thinly, then cut across into 1/4 inch (5 mm) slices. Place cucumber in a bowl, add onion and sprinkle with salt. Leave to stand for 5 minutes then drain well, squeezing with clean fingers.

Mix with the remaining ingredients, cover and chill for at least 1 hour for spice seasoning to develop.

Serve as an accompaniment to curry.

YOGURT WITH SPICED POTATO

SERVES 6–8

3 potatoes, cooked with skin on

2 tablespoons peanut oil

1 teaspoon mustard seeds

1 teaspoon cumin seeds

1 small onion, finely chopped

1 teaspoon minced red or green chili

1 cup (8 fl oz/250 ml) natural yogurt

salt

Peel potatoes and cut into 1/2 inch (1 cm) cubes. Heat oil in a frying pan and fry mustard and cumin seeds and onion until mustard seeds 'pop', stirring frequently. Add potatoes and chili and stir-fry until potatoes are coated with the spices. Allow to cool slightly then mix with yogurt and add salt to taste. Cover and chill before serving.

MUSHROOM SAUCE

SERVES 4

Mushrooms are one of the few natural sources of vitamin B12 which is often lacking in a vegetarian diet, so include them in your weekly menu.

8 oz (250 g) mushroom cups

8 French shallots or 1 onion, finely chopped

1 oz (30 g) polyunsaturated margarine

1/2 cup (4 fl oz/125 ml) sparkling grape juice

2 tablespoons chopped parsley

1 teaspoon chopped capers

1 tablespoon bulgur (cracked wheat), soaked in milk or soy drink

Brush mushrooms clean and trim stalks. Chop finely in a food processor or blender. Place mushrooms, French shallots, margarine and grape juice in a saucepan and simmer covered until tender. Add parsley, capers and drained bulgur and heat through.

Serve sauce hot as an accompaniment to a main course.

LEEK AND PEAR PUREE

SERVES 4

This sauce has a delicate appearance, and is a delicious combination of tastes. It complements nut and legume loaves and fritters.

8 oz (250 g) leeks

8 oz (250 g) firm ripe pears

2 tablespoons polyunsaturated margarine

freshly ground nutmeg

salt and pepper

Trim and wash leeks, cut into 2 inch (5 cm) lengths and steam or cook in a clean plastic food storage bag in a microwave oven on High setting for 5 minutes. Alternatively, boil until tender.

Halve pears, remove core and peel. Stew gently in 3 tablespoons water until tender or cook in a covered microwave-safe dish in a microwave oven on High setting for 5 minutes.

Mix leeks and pears to a smooth puree in a blender or food processor. Add nutmeg, salt and pepper to taste.

Serve hot; complements Hearty Bean Loaf (page 129).

DESSERTS AND CAKES

This chapter wasn't big enough for me! I could have included innumerable recipes for delectable desserts and luscious cakes. However, a collection of desserts and cakes appropriate for a vegetarian diet requires a certain discipline in selection.

Many of the desserts in this chapter, such as Caramel Coconut Custard, Almond Junket, Mandarin Muesli Cheesecake and Chocolate Walnut Tart, are rich in eggs, milk, cottage cheese and nuts, and they are nourishing supplements to the main course. Other desserts abound in fresh and dried fruits, as they are rich in vitamins C and B, dietary fiber, and iron. Wholegrain cereals are used in some of the recipes, particularly in the sweet, hot puddings. There is also an unusual variety of home-made ice cream recipes, some classic, others made with silken tofu and soy drink. With the delicious addition of fruit, nuts and chocolate, they are all a perfect joy in any kind of diet!

Fresh fruit is very important in the vegetarian diet and there is an enormous variety to choose from. Fruits tend to be more seasonal than vegetables. There are the delectable berries and juicy stone fruits of summer, the crisp apples, pears and nashi fruit of fall (autumn), the winter and summer citrus and pineapple, the winter exotic fruit, the summer tropical fruit and the luxury of fresh dates and figs. With controlled temperature storage and the wonders of refrigerated transport, some of these fruits are available to enjoy all year round. However, when possible, buy the fruit that is in season, as they are at the peak of their quality. Serve them simply and fresh whenever possible, or puree them and serve as a fruit coulis. Poach them gently or use them in tarts, pies and crumbles, or puree them to use in ice cream or sorbet, served with some delicious petit four.

The selection of cakes and petit four recipes found in this chapter also highlight the use of nuts and seeds, fresh fruit, dried fruit, and even vegetables (carrots and zucchini), and I use wholewheat (wholemeal) flour. There are a few true eggless vegan cakes such as Baklava, Vegan Chocolate Cake and Apple Puree Fruit Cake.

Many of these cakes are so good they can double up as a dessert if served in elegant portions sifted with confectioner's (icing) sugar, with some fresh fruit on the side and a dollop of thick, clotted or whipped cream.

Among this selection of desserts and cakes are some of my best-loved recipes, and many I've adapted for a vegetarian diet. I hope they will delight you, your family and your guests.

Spiced red fruit salad (top), p.216; Strawberry sorbet (front), p.242

SPICED RED FRUIT SALAD

SERVES 8

Fresh fruit salad is refreshing served with junket, egg custard or ice cream, or simply by itself.

2 cups watermelon balls

4 nectarines, sliced in wedges

1 cup (1 punnet) small strawberries

1 cup (1 punnet) redcurrants, optional

1 cup (8 fl oz/250 ml) sparkling grape juice

3 tablespoons raw sugar

1/2 teaspoon mixed spice

1 cup (1 punnet) or 1 can raspberries, pureed

2 tablespoons blanched almonds

Place prepared fruit in a serving bowl. Heat grape juice with sugar and spice until sugar has dissolved, leave to cool. When cold, mix with raspberry puree and pour over fruit. Chill for at least 1 hour before serving. Split almonds in half and sprinkle over fruit salad before serving.

POACHED PEACHES

SERVES 8

A microwave oven cooks these perfectly and keeps the heat down in your kitchen as an added bonus in the hot peach season!

4 large or 8 small, ripe peaches

2 cups (16 fl oz/500 ml) grape juice

1 cup (8 fl oz/250 ml) pear or apple juice

1/2 cup (4 fl oz/125 ml) honey or corn syrup

1 orange, thinly sliced

4 cloves

1 stick cinnamon

Wash peaches in cold water and pat dry. Cut large peaches in half. Place all remaining ingredients in a stainless steel or enamel-lined pan, cover and bring to the boil. Add peaches and poach or stew gently in barely simmering liquid for 10–15 minutes or until peaches are tender. Test with a fine skewer.

Alternatively, place all ingredients together in a microwave-safe mixing bowl, cover with clear plastic and cook in a microwave oven on Medium setting for 8 minutes or until tender, stirring after 4 minutes.

When cool enough to handle, remove peach skins and transfer peaches to a polished glass serving bowl, discard orange, cloves and cinnamon and pour liquid over the peaches. Cover and chill well.

Serve with a fruit sorbet or fruit ice cream.

DRIED FRUIT COMPOTE

SERVES 4–6

Dried fruits are very rich in iron and vitamin B. Use them for snacks, in a packed lunch or for a dessert accompanied by a low-fat yogurt.

1 lb (500 g) dried fruit salad, made up from prunes, apricots, apples, peaches, pears, nectarines and figs

1 tablespoon raw sugar

1 1/2 cups (12 fl oz/375 ml) water

1 cinnamon stick

2 cloves

1/4 teaspoon grated nutmeg

2 tablespoons pine nuts

2 teaspoons sunflower kernels

juice of 1 large orange

Place fruit salad, sugar, water and spices in a saucepan, cover and stew gently for 15 minutes or until tender. Add pine nuts and sunflower kernels, cool then chill in refrigerator. Remove cinnamon stick and cloves, stir in orange juice and serve with natural yogurt.

PRUNE FOOL

SERVES 6

Serve this in small quantities accompanied by crisp petit fours or ice cream. Prunes are a good source of iron and fiber.

8 oz (250 g) dessert prunes

1 cup (8 fl oz/250 ml) water

grated rind of 1 lemon

1/2 cup (4 fl oz/125 ml) sparkling grape juice

3/4 cup (6 fl oz/185 ml) apricot yogurt

Place prunes in a saucepan with water and lemon rind. Bring to a gentle boil covered and stew gently until tender and plump and water has been absorbed, about 30 minutes. Cool prunes and remove stones. Mix prunes to a puree in a food processor, add grape juice and mix until smooth. Fold yogurt in. Serve in individual dessert dishes or a dessert bowl.

Chill before serving.

Following page: Cream of marscarpone with berries (front), p.229; Scottish gingerbread (top), p.256; Poached peaches (right), p.216

Hazelnut Apricot Praline Crêpes ♀

SERVES 8

This is a delicious dessert for a winter dinner party. The crêpes may be made in advance, also the apricot puree and the praline, making it easier to assemble before serving.

16 French Wholewheat Crêpes
(page 221)

Apricot puree:

8 oz (250 g) dried apricots

2 cups (16 fl oz/500 ml) boiling water

juice of 1 large orange

4 tablespoons concentrated orange juice

4 tablespoons raw sugar

Filling:

1 ⅓ cups crushed praline (below

¾ cup (3 oz/90 g) toasted ground hazelnuts

1 ⅓ cups (11 fl oz/330 ml) apricot puree

orange segments and confectioner's (icing) sugar for decoration

Make crêpes and have them warm, ready for filling.

Apricot puree: Cover apricots with boiling water, stand for 20 minutes then stew in a covered pan for 20 minutes or until tender. Cool and mix to a puree in a blender or food processor. Stir in orange juices and sugar.

To finish: Place crêpes flat on a work surface and sprinkle 1 tablespoon crushed praline and ½ tablespoon toasted ground hazelnuts over the middle of each. Spread 1 tablespoon apricot puree over each crêpe then fold crêpes in half. Place on a serving plate or individual dessert plates. Add sufficient water or extra orange juice to remaining puree to make up to 1 cup (8 fl oz/250 ml). Spoon puree over the crêpes and place some orange segments on top. Heat through in a microwave oven or cover with foil and heat in the oven at 400°F (200°C) for 10–15 minutes, until hot.

Serve decorated with sifted confectioner's sugar.

Praline

MAKES 1 ⅓ CUPS

¾ cup (6 oz/175 g) fine white (caster) sugar

¾ cup (3 oz/90 g) chopped almonds

Place sugar in a caramel pan, or a heavy-based saucepan or frying pan, over a very low heat until sugar dissolves and turns light golden, as for caramel.

Add nuts and stir quickly with a metal spoon and, still working quickly, turn out onto an oiled baking tray. Leave to cool and set. When firm, loosen and place in a thick plastic bag and beat with a rolling pin or cleaver until crushed to desired size.

Try using hazelnuts or macadamia nuts in place of almonds.

FRENCH WHOLEWHEAT CRÊPES ♟

MAKES 16

3/4 cup (3 oz/90 g) all-purpose wholewheat (plain wholemeal) flour

1/2 cup (2 oz/60 g) all-purpose (plain) flour

3 x 2 oz (60 g) eggs

1 cup (8 fl oz/250 ml) milk or soy drink

4 tablespoons water

2 tablespoons (1 1/3 oz/40 g) unsalted butter or polyunsaturated margarine, melted

Sieve flours into a mixing bowl, make a well in the middle. Drop eggs into middle of flour and gradually stir in surrounding flour using a wooden spoon. When mixture starts to thicken, gradually add half the milk and beat well with the back of the spoon until batter is smooth. Stir in remaining milk, water and melted butter. Cover and leave to stand at room temperature for 30 minutes before cooking crêpes.

This crêpe batter may also be made by mixing all ingredients together in a blender or food processor.

Make crêpes according to method given in Green Curried Bean Crêpes (page 124) but use a 6 inch (15 cm) crêpe pan.

ALMOND JUNKET ◈

SERVES 6-8

This has a very refreshing, cleansing texture and is good to serve after spicy hot curries or Mexican chili-hot food.

3 tablespoons raw sugar

1/2 teaspoon ground cinnamon

1/2 teaspoon freshly grated nutmeg

2 teaspoons almond extract (essence)

5 cups (40 fl oz/1.25 L) milk

2 junket tablets

2 tablespoons coffee crystal sugar

Mix sugar with spices and almond extract in a mixing bowl. Heat milk to blood heat (lukewarm). Dissolve junket tablets according to instruction in another mixing bowl and pour warm milk onto rennet mixture. Add milk mixture to almond mixture and stir well. Pour into a serving bowl or individual serving bowls and stand in a warm place until almond junket is firm and set like a soft blancmange.

Sprinkle sugar neatly over the top and serve with fresh seasonal fruit or fruit compote.

RASPBERRY ALMOND TRIFLE

SERVES 8

A classic trifle is one of the best desserts to have come out of England. The egg custard sauce adds easily digested protein to its total nourishment. Omit the cream if on a low-fat diet.

3 1/2 oz (100 g) packet sponge fingers, approximately 16

3 tablespoons raspberry jam

1/2 cup (2 oz/60 g) flaked almonds

2/3 cup (5 fl oz/150 ml) orange juice

3 tablespoons sparkling grape juice

1 quantity Egg Custard Sauce (below)

1 1/4 cups (10 fl oz/300 ml) cream

8 oz (250 g) fresh, frozen or canned raspberries

Spread 8 sponge fingers with the jam and use them to line the bottom of a glass serving bowl. Cut remaining sponge fingers into 1 inch (2.5 cm) pieces and scatter over the 'lining'. Sprinkle half the almonds on top. Lightly toast remaining half. Pour orange and sparkling grape juice over and leave to stand at room temperature for 30 minutes.

Make custard and cool. Whip cream until thick. Reserve some of the best berries to decorate the trifle, sprinkle the remainder over the sponge fingers. Pour custard over. Cover gently with whipped cream, swirling to resemble a snow drift. Decorate with reserved raspberries and almonds.

Serve at room temperature for best results.

EGG CUSTARD SAUCE

MAKES APPROXIMATELY 2 1/2 CUPS (20 FL OZ/600 ML)

This is also known as Crème Anglaise. A delicious, much-loved sauce by dessert-aholics as it is used in fruit fools, mousses, ice cream and trifle, as well as an accompaniment to poached fruit, dried fruit compote, hot fruit crumbles, baked and steamed puddings. You can make up half the quantity if desired.

2 1/2 cups (20 fl oz/600 ml) milk or soy drink

1 vanilla pod or 1 teaspoon vanilla extract (essence)

4 eggs

2 tablespoons fine white (caster) sugar

Heat milk or soy drink with vanilla pod in the top of a double-boiler over gently simmering water until lukewarm., leave to infuse for 30 minutes to develop vanilla taste. Beat eggs lightly, add to warm milk and stir continuously over simmering water, using a wooden sauce spoon, until mixture is thick enough to coat the back of a metal spoon. Stir in sugar and vanilla extract, if used, and leave to cool. Custard thickens a little on cooling.

Raspberry almond trifle

CARAMEL COCONUT CUSTARD

SERVES 8

A dessert suitable for ovo-vegetarians as the coconut milk is made with soy drink.

Caramel:

7/8 cup (7 oz/220 g) fine white (caster) sugar

5 tablespoons water

Coconut custard:

4 cups (11 oz/350 g) unsweetened (desiccated) coconut

4 cups (32 fl oz/1 L) soy drink

1/2 cup (4 oz/125 g) fine white (caster) sugar

6 eggs

extra 1/4 cup unsweetened (desiccated) coconut, optional

Caramel: Place sugar and water into a caramel pan or small heavy pan and dissolve over a high heat, stirring frequently with care. Boil syrup over a medium heat until it turns golden. This can take 10-15 minutes. As soon as syrup reaches caramel stage, pour into a soufflé dish and, holding with oven gloves, quickly rotate dish so that caramel coats sides as well as bottom of dish before it sets. Turn dish upside down, stand on waxed (greaseproof) paper and leave to cool.

Coconut custard: Place coconut in a food processor or blender. Bring soy drink almost to the boil, pour over coconut and blend at high speed for 1 minute, scrape down and blend for another minute. Pour mixture through a strainer and squeeze coconut pulp well with the fingers to extract all the liquid to make coconut milk. Heat coconut milk with sugar until sugar dissolves. Beat eggs lightly, gradually stir in sweet coconut milk and add extra coconut if desired.

Pour mixture into caramel-coated soufflé dish, place in a large baking dish and pour 1/2 inch (1 cm) boiling water into the dish to create a 'hot-water bath'. Bake at 300°F (150°C) for 45 minutes or until firm. To test, insert a fine pointed knife and it should come out clean if ready.

Cool then chill in refrigerator for 3 hours before turning out onto a serving plate.

Serve accompanied by sliced oranges (red-fleshed ones look decorative) and kiwifruit.

CROISSANTS DE PROVENCE

MAKES 40

This scented almond petit four is delightful served with poached fruit or fruit compote. Use almonds with the skin on for the best results.

1 cup (5 oz/165 g) freshly blanched almonds

5/8 cup (5 oz/155 g) fine white (caster) sugar

1 tablespoon apricot jam

1 teaspoon orange flower water or rosewater

approx. 1 tablespoon egg white

flour for shaping

beaten egg for coating and glazing

1 1/3 cups (8 oz/250 g) finely chopped almonds for coating

1 tablespoon sugar dissolved in 2 tablespoons milk for glazing

Blanch almonds in boiling water and remove skin. Place half the almonds in a blender or food processor and mix until very fine, then place in a mixing bowl.

Blend remaining almonds likewise and add to bowl with sugar, apricot jam, orange flower water or rosewater and egg white, then mix to form a smooth, and not sticky, paste.

Roll mixture on a lightly floured board to a thick sausage shape, cut into quarters. Roll each quarter out until as thin as your middle finger, then cut into 10 equal portions. Roll each portion out neatly to the length and width of your middle finger.

Coat each length with egg and chopped almonds and twist into a neat crescent shape and place on a lined, greased baking tray and brush lightly with beaten egg.

Bake at 350°F (180°C) for 12–15 minutes. Cool on wire cooling trays.

Serve as a petit four with dessert and coffee.

KIWIFRUIT TART

SERVES 8–12

This delicious French tart can also be made with halved stoneless Angelina or dark red plums. Orange flower water is available at health food stores.

8 oz (250 g) pâte sucrée (page 229)

Filling:

2 lb (1 kg) kiwifruit, approx. 12 large or 18 small

1/4 cup ground almonds

4 tablespoons vanilla sugar

2 x 2 oz (60 g) eggs

5 tablespoons cream or orange soy drink

1 tablespoon orange flower water

Prepare the pastry and chill for at least 20-30 minutes. Roll pastry out thinly to a round and line a 12 inch (30 cm) flan tin. Trim and neaten edge, prick base and chill until filling is ready.

Filling: Peel kiwifruit with a vegetable peeler and cut into 1/4 inch (5 mm) slices. Beat all the remaining ingredients together.

To finish tart: Arrange kiwifruit, overlapping slices, in circles in the pastry case, starting at edge, working into middle. Pour egg mixture over and brush over any fruit that is not coated.

Bake at 425°F (220°C) for 25–30 minutes or until filling is firm and fruit (if plums) is cooked. Serve warm or cold sifted with confectioner's (icing) sugar if desired.

CUSTARD APPLE SOUFFLÉ

SERVES 4

3 tablespoons polyunsaturated margarine

1/3 cup (1 1/2 oz/45 g) all-purpose (plain) flour

1 large ripe custard apple

soy drink or milk

3 tablespoons vanilla sugar

1 tablespoon vanilla extract (essence)

4 large eggs, separated

1 egg white

Melt margarine in a saucepan, add flour and stir over a medium heat for 1–2 minutes. Remove from heat. Scoop out custard apple pulp and make up to 10 fl oz (300 ml) with soy drink or milk. Add fruit pulp mixture, vanilla sugar and extract to pan, return to heat and bring to the boil, stirring continuously. Remove from heat and mix in egg yolks one at a time. Whisk egg whites until firm. Add 3 tablespoons egg white foam to custard and fold in with a wire balloon-shaped whisk. Fold in remaining egg white very gently with a light cut-and-fold action. Pour mixture into a greased soufflé dish. Bake at 350°F (180°C) for 30-35 minutes until well-risen.

Serve using warm cutlery, and accompany it by rhubarb and strawberry coulis if desired.

Kiwifruit tart

CHERRY APPLE STRUDEL

SERVES 6

2 cups ripe cherries or 13 ½ oz (425 g) can stoneless black cherries

2 apples, peeled, cored and sliced

2 tablespoons butter or polyunsaturated margarine

1 tablespoon lemon juice

2 tablespoons toasted flaked almonds

8 oz (250 g) cottage cheese

8 sheets filo pastry

extra 2 tablespoons butter or margarine, melted

confectioner's (icing) sugar for sifting

Remove cherry stones with a cherry stoner. If using canned cherries, drain well. Gently fry apples in butter until soft but not mushy. Remove from heat, stir in lemon juice, three-quarters of almonds and all cherries. Mix cottage cheese in a food processor until smooth, stir into cherry mixture.

Spread 2 sheets of filo out on a clean work surface and brush with melted butter. Cover with 2 more sheets and continue brushing and layering until all filo is used. Spoon cherry mixture onto bottom third of pastry parallel to short side, then roll up neatly, Swiss roll style, from short side to other short side, forming a strudel. Place strudel on a baking tray, brush with melted butter and sprinkle remaining flaked almonds on top. Bake at 350°F (180°C) for 30 minutes or until cooked, crisp and golden.

Serve with cherry yogurt or Soy Cream (page 238).

CREAM OF MASCARPONE WITH BERRIES

SERVES 8

Mascarpone is a delicious Italian-style cream cheese which you can transform into this delightful light-textured dessert. It is sensational when accompanied by fresh berries, particularly raspberries. Perfect for a dinner party!

8 oz (250 g) mascarpone

2 eggs, separated

¼ cup (2 oz/60 g) fine white (caster) sugar

2 tablespoons concentrated orange juice

8 oz (250 g) raspberries, strawberries or boysenberries

Press mascarpone through a sieve, using a wooden spoon, into a mixing bowl. Add egg yolks, sugar and orange juice and beat until combined. Whisk egg whites until firm and gently cut and fold into the mascarpone mixture using a wire whisk.

Serve in individual small soufflé dishes. It may be covered and stored in the refrigerator at this stage. Serve accompanied by a bowl of raspberries, which should be spooned onto the cream at the table as they tend to sink!

PÂTE SUCRÉE

MAKES 8 OZ (250 G) PASTRY, SUFFICIENT TO LINE A SHALLOW 9-12 INCH (23-30 CM) FLAN TIN

This sweet French pastry is used for tarts and flans. It is best when rolled out thinly and baked 'blind' before filling.

1/2 cup (4 oz/125 g) unsalted butter or margarine, chilled

2 cups (8 oz/250 g) all-purpose (plain) flour

1/2 cup (2 oz/60 g) pure confectioner's (icing) sugar

2 egg yolks or 1 egg

1 teaspoon water (only if necessary)

Cut butter into cubes and place in a food processor. Sift flour and sugar together onto a sheet of waxed (greaseproof) paper.

Add flour mixture to butter and mix at top speed, until mixture resembles fine breadcrumbs. Should take about 20 seconds. Add egg and mix until dough comes together. If dough is too dry and will not come together, add water and mix to bind. Texture depends on room temperature and variety of wheat flour. Knead dough very lightly on a lightly floured marble slab or board just until smooth, then wrap in waxed (greaseproof) paper and chill in refrigerator for 30 minutes or until firm.

PECAN STREUSAL PEAR TART

SERVES 6

6 oz (185 g) pâte sucrée (above)

Filling:

3 ripe dessert pears

1 egg

2 tablespoons raw sugar

1/4 teaspoon ground ginger

1/8 teaspoon ground nutmeg

finely grated rind of 1 lemon

1 cup (8 fl oz/250 ml) light sour cream

Topping:

2 tablespoons wholewheat (wholemeal) flour

3 tablespoons dark brown sugar

3 tablespoons chopped pecans

1/4 teaspoon ground nutmeg

1/4 cup (2 oz/60 g) unsalted butter

Make pastry and chill according to directions. Roll pastry out and line a 9 inch (23 cm) flan tin. Trim and decorate edge and prick base. Chill until filling is ready.

Filling: Cut pears in half lengthwise, peel carefully and remove core neatly. Place pears in pastry case with narrow tops towards middle. Beat egg with sugar, spices, lemon rind and sour cream and pour over the pears.

Topping: Mix all ingredients together, rubbing in butter to resemble coarse crumbs. Sprinkle over tart.

Bake at 400°F (200°C) for 25 minutes or until filling is set and pastry is cooked. Cool slightly.

Serve tart warm sifted with confectioner's (icing) sugar accompanied by passionfruit puree.

CHOCOLATE WALNUT TART WITH RASPBERRY COULIS

SERVES 8

Very rich, but delicious if you have a sweet tooth.

6 oz (185 g) pâté sucrée (page 229)

Filling:

1/2 cup (4 oz/125 g) sugar

3 tablespoons water

pinch of cream of tartar

1/4 cup (2 oz/60 g) coarsely chopped walnuts

1/2 cup (4 fl oz/125 ml) honey

1 cup (8 fl oz/250 ml) cream

2 x 2 oz (60 g) eggs, lightly beaten

4 oz (125 g) fresh dates, seeded and chopped, or 4 oz (125 g) dessert dates, seeded, chopped and soaked in 3 tablespoons orange juice

Icing:

6 oz (185 g) cooking chocolate

1/2 cup (4 fl oz/125 ml) sour cream

8 oz (250 g) raspberries

Make pastry and chill well.

Filling: Place sugar, water and cream of tartar in a saucepan. Bring slowly to the boil over a low heat, stirring and washing down any sugar crystals clinging to sides of pan with a brush dipped in cold water, until sugar is dissolved. Increase heat to medium and cook syrup until it turns deep caramel. Add walnuts, honey and cream and cook over a high heat for 2–3 minutes or until slightly thickened. Reduce heat to low, stir in eggs and cook gently for 2 minutes.

To finish tart: Roll pastry out to a thin round and line a 9 inch (23 cm) flan tin. Bake 'blind' at 400°F (200°C) for 10 minutes, remove baking beans and paper (blind filling) and bake at 375°F (190°C) for a further 10–15 minutes or until cooked. Cool on a wire cooling tray.

Pour filling into pastry case and chill in refrigerator until filling is set. Spread chopped dates over top, then cover with chocolate icing and leave to set.

Icing: Melt chocolate in a microwave oven on Defrost setting for cycles of 2 minutes or in the top of a double-boiler over gently simmering water. Remove from heat and mix sour cream in until combined. Use while warm. Mix berries to a puree in a blender or food processor.

Serve tart with raspberry coulis.

Chocolate walnut tart with raspberry coulis

LIME BUTTERMILK TART

SERVES 8

A delicious and nutritious tart; its spicy crumb crust delightfully complements the tangy filling.

Crumb crust:

8 oz (250 g) wholewheat
(wholemeal) cookies

1 teaspoon ground cinnamon

1 teaspoon ground nutmeg

5 tablespoons (3 oz/90 g) unsalted
butter, melted

Filling:

1/2 cup (4 oz/125 g) unsalted
butter

1/2 cup (4 fl oz/125 ml) honey

2 eggs, separated

1/4 cup (1 oz/30 g) wholewheat
(wholemeal) flour

1 1/2 cups (12 fl oz/375 ml)
buttermilk

grated rind of 2 limes

2 tablespoons lime juice

Crumb crust: Crush cookies into crumbs. Place crumbs in a mixing bowl with spices and butter, mix until well combined. Press mixture over the base and three-quarters up the sides of a greased 8 inch (20 cm) cheesecake tin. Bake at 300°F (150°C) for 10 minutes.

Filling: Cream butter with honey. Beat in egg yolks one at a time. Stir in flour then slowly stir in buttermilk, lime rind and juice. Whisk egg whites until stiff and fold into buttermilk mixture.

Pour filling into crumb crust and bake at 325°F (160°C) for 45 minutes or until puffed, golden brown and firm. Test with a skewer if necessary.

Serve tart warm or cold with sliced carambola, blueberries and strawberries.

❖ THE SIMPLEST AND LEAST MESSY WAY TO MELT CHOCOLATE IS TO DO IT IN A MICROWAVE OVEN. BREAK THE CHOCOLATE INTO CHUNKY PIECES AND PLACE IT IN A MICROWAVE-SAFE BOWL. PLACE THE BOWL IN THE MICROWAVE OVEN FOR 2 MINUTE CYCLES ON THE DEFROST SETTING, STIRRING AFTER EVERY 2 MINUTES, UNTIL THE CHOCOLATE HAS MELTED TO A SMOOTH, GLOSSY CONSISTENCY.

RICH BREAD AND BUTTER PUDDING ♟◈

SERVES 6

This creamy, rich pudding is wonderful 'comfort food' in cold winter weather. If served turned out, the stripes add to its attractiveness.

3 tablespoons maple (golden) syrup

6 tablespoons raisins (or sultanas)

unsalted butter for spreading

12 slices wholegrain bread

6 slices white bread

4 eggs

2 egg yolks

1/4 cup (2 oz/60 g) fine white (caster) sugar

1 cup (8 fl oz/250 ml) milk

5 fl oz (150 ml) cream

1 teaspoon vanilla extract (essence)

1/2 teaspoon ground cinnamon

Place 2 teaspoons maple syrup in the bottom of six individual buttered soufflé dishes. Sprinkle 1 teaspoon raisins over syrup.

Butter slices of bread and cut into rounds to fit dishes, using a pastry cutter. Place three rounds of bread into each dish, starting and finishing with wholegrain bread and sprinkle remaining raisins between each layer.

Beat eggs with yolks, sugar, milk, cream, vanilla and cinnamon. Make some holes in the layered bread with a skewer and pour the egg custard over.

Bake at 350°F (180°C) for 30 minutes or until custard is firm.

Serve in soufflé dishes or turn out and serve whole or cut in wedges, with pureed, poached dried apricots.

CHOCOLATE SELF-SAUCE PUDDING

SERVES 6

1 cup (4 oz/125 g) self-raising wholewheat (wholemeal) flour

2 tablespoons cocoa

1/4 cup (1 oz/30 g) soy flour

1/4 cup (1 oz/30 g) ground almonds

1/2 cup (3 oz/90 g) brown sugar

1/4 cup (2 oz/60 g) margarine

3/4 cup (6 fl oz/185 ml) soy drink

2 teaspoons vanilla extract (essence)

Topping:

1 tablespoon cocoa

1 cup (6 oz/185 g) brown sugar

1 3/4 cups (14 fl oz/425 ml) boiling water

Place all dry ingredients into a mixing bowl and make a well in the middle. Add remaining ingredients and stir until well combined, as for mixing a batter. Pour into a large greased soufflé dish or round casserole.

Topping: Mix cocoa with sugar and sprinkle evenly on the top of the pudding mixture. Pour boiling water over gently.

Bake pudding at 350°F (180°C) for 45 minutes or until cooked. A delicious sauce will form at the bottom of the pudding.

Serve accompanied by natural yogurt.

MANDARIN MUESLI CHEESECAKE

Muesli is used in the crumb crust for this protein-rich dessert. Agar agar is a gelatin made from seaweed and is available at good health food stores.

Crumb crust:

2 cups muesli, non-toasted variety

1/2 cup wholewheat (wholemeal) cookie crumbs

1 tablespoon soy compound

1/4 cup (1 oz/30 g) ground hazelnuts

1 teaspoon ground cinnamon

1 teaspoon ground nutmeg

1/4 teaspoon ground cloves

5 oz (150 g) unsalted butter or polyunsaturated margarine, melted

Filling:

10 oz (310 g) can mandarins

2 eggs

3/4 cup (6 oz/185 g) raw sugar

1/6 oz (5 g) agar agar

12 oz (375 g) cream cheese

10 fl oz (300 ml) cream

passionfruit and pistachio nuts for decoration

Crumb crust: Mix all ingredients together until well combined. Press over the bottom and up the sides of a greased 9 inch (23 cm) springform tin. Chill in refrigerator until set.

Filling: Drain mandarins, reserve juice and make up to 1 cup (8 fl oz/250 ml) with water. Place 1 egg, 1 egg yolk and sugar in the top of a double-boiler and beat with a wire whisk over gently bubbling water until thick and creamy. Cool to blood heat (lukewarm).

Soak agar agar with reserved juice and water in a pan then simmer gently for 15 minutes or until dissolved. Cool to blood heat. Whisk agar agar into egg custard while both are at blood heat.

Sieve cream cheese into a mixing bowl, add egg custard mixture and mandarins and fold together. Whip two-thirds of cream and whisk egg white. Fold into cheese mixture, reserving a third of cream for decoration.

Pour filling into crumb crust and chill in refrigerator until set. Loosen crust carefully from side of tin with a palette knife before serving.

Serve decorated with remaining cream, whipped, passionfruit and chopped pistachio nuts.

Mandarin Muesli Cheesecake

ROMAN CHEESECAKE

SERVES 12

It's hard to surpass this Italian-inspired recipe for a baked cheesecake. Serve it accompanied by chilled grapes, ripe figs and tangy cape gooseberries to complement its richness.

Pastry:

1 cup (4 oz/125 g) wholewheat (wholemeal) flour

1 cup (4 oz/125 g) all-purpose (plain) flour

3/4 cup (6 oz/185 g) unsalted butter

3 egg yolks

1/4 cup (2 oz/60 g) fine white (caster) sugar

1 tablespoon concentrated orange juice

finely grated rind of 1 orange

Filling:

2 1/4 lb (1.25 kg) ricotta or cottage cheese

1/2 cup (4 oz/125 g) raw sugar

1 tablespoon cornstarch (cornflour)

4 egg yolks

1 teaspoon vanilla extract (essence)

finely grated rind of 1 orange

4 tablespoons raisins (or sultanas)

1 tablespoon chopped mixed peel

3 tablespoons ground almonds

1 egg white for glazing

slivered almonds for sprinkling

Pastry: Sift flours and place in a food processor. Add butter cut into small dice. Mix for 20 seconds or until mixture resembles breadcrumbs. Add egg yolks, sugar, orange juice and rind and mix until it forms a stiff dough, stopping and scraping bowl down after every 20 seconds to avoid toughening the dough. Turn out onto a lightly floured surface, pat into a round cake shape, wrap in waxed (greaseproof) paper and chill for 30 minutes before using.

Filling: Sieve ricotta into a large mixing bowl. Add all remaining ingredients and mix well.

To finish: Roll out three-quarters of pastry dough to a round and line a 9 inch (23 cm) springform tin and neaten top edge. Place filling into pastry case and spread smooth. Roll remaining pastry out thinly and cut into long narrow strips. Arrange strips on top of filling in a lattice pattern, trim ends neatly and brush with egg white. Sprinkle slivered almonds over the filling. Bake at 350°F (180°C) for 1 hour or until firm and golden. Cool in tin until firm.

Serve warm or cold.

APRICOT HAZELNUT ICE CREAM

SERVES 8

Home-made ice cream is delicious and easy to make if you have an electric ice cream machine or churn.

20 fl oz (600 ml) cream

1 vanilla bean

6 egg yolks

1/2 cup (4 oz/125 g) fine white (caster) sugar

1 lb (500 g) dried apricots, stewed and pureed

1/2 cup (2 oz/60 g) ground hazelnuts

Bring cream and vanilla bean to scalding point. Beat egg yolks and sugar together in a mixing bowl with a whisk, rotary beater, or electric mixer until pale yellow and thick enough to fall like a ribbon.

Remove vanilla pod from cream, pour cream onto egg yolk mixture, beating continuously. Place mixture in the top of a double-boiler and cook over simmering water, stirring continuously, until custard coats the back of a metal spoon. Strain into a bowl, then stir in apricot puree and nuts, and leave to cool. Chill for 30 minutes.

Pour cold mixture into a commercial ice cream machine and mix according to manufacturer's instructions until thick. Scrape thick ice cream down from sides of container and mix well with a plastic spatula. Store in a covered container in the freezer.

If you do not have an ice cream machine, pour mixture into shallow freezer containers and freeze until firm around the edge. Transfer to the bowl of a food processor or mixer and beat to a smooth texture. Return to freezer containers and freeze until totally firm.

Serve with petit fours such as Hazelnut and Chocolate Aristocrats (page 248).

SOY CREAM

SERVES 4

True vegans usually miss out on the luxury of creams and custards when they eat puddings and desserts. This sweet soy cream is a pleasant substitute.

1 cup (8 fl oz/250 ml) soy drink

2 tablespoons maple (golden) syrup

2 teaspoons vanilla extract (essence)

Place all ingredients in a glass screw-top jar, cover and shake well to mix. Store in the jar in the refrigerator.

Serve with hot puddings and sweet tarts.

APPLE AND BERRY CRUMBLE

SERVES 4–6

This crumble is always popular with children. You can save time by cooking the apples in a microwave oven. For the berries, use strawberries, raspberries, boysenberries or blueberries.

1 lb (500 g) cooking apples

2 tablespoons raw sugar

1 cup (8 fl oz/250 ml) canned or frozen berries

Crumble:

1 cup (4 oz/125 g) all-purpose wholewheat (plain wholemeal) flour

1/4 cup (2 oz/60 g) unsalted butter or polyunsaturated margarine

1 tablespoon cracked wheat

1 tablespoon wheatgerm

1 tablespoon pepitas

2 tablespoons raw sugar

Peel, core and slice half the apples into an oval or oblong pie dish, sprinkle sugar over and cover with remaining apples. Drain 1/4 cup juice from berries, pour over apples. Cover dish with clear plastic wrap and cook in a microwave oven on High setting for 5 minutes or until cooked. Stew the apples if you do not have a microwave oven. Carefully stir berries into cooked apples.

Crumble: Sift flour, add butter and rub in or mix in a food processor until mixture resembles breadcrumbs. Stir in remaining ingredients and sprinkle over the fruit.

Bake at 350°F (180°C) for 20 minutes or until crumble is browned and fruit is bubbling hot. Serve with Soy Cream (above) or custard sauce.

Apple and berry crumble

238

239

CHOCOLATE MACADAMIA ICE CREAM

SERVES 8

Eating this ice cream is like eating 'manna from the Gods' but you have to be an ovo-lacto-vegetarian to enjoy it. However, true vegans may replace the chocolate custard with 16 fl oz (500 ml) carob soy drink and 1/2 cup honey and the cream with 10 oz (300 g) silken tofu (mixed together in a food processor) and come up with a delicious Carob Macadamia Ice Cream.

2 cups (16 fl oz/500 ml) milk

1 cup (8 oz/250 g) fine white (caster) sugar

6 egg yolks

6 tablespoons cocoa

10 fl oz (300 ml) cream

2 oz (60 g) dark cooking chocolate, grated

1/2 cup (2 oz/60 g) ground toasted macadamia nuts

Bring milk and half the sugar to the boil, cool until lukewarm. Beat egg yolks and remaining sugar together with a rotary beater until mixture whitens and forms a ribbon when lifted. Stir in lukewarm milk. Pour mixture into the top of a double-boiler and stir over gently simmering water until mixture thickens to form a custard that will coat the back of a metal spoon. Place cocoa in a mixing bowl and whisk in hot custard, a tablespoon at a time at first, increasing gradually until smoothly combined.

Stir cream into chocolate custard, cover and chill in refrigerator for at least 1 hour.

Stir in chocolate and macadamia nuts, pour into an ice cream machine and churn for 20–30 minutes or until firm. Store in a sealed container in the freezer. If you do not have an ice cream machine, pour mixture into shallow freezer containers and freeze until firm around the edge. Working quickly, transfer to the bowl of a food processor or mixer and beat to a smooth texture. Return to freezer containers and freeze until totally firm. If ice cream becomes too hard to scoop out, place in a microwave oven on Defrost setting for a few seconds or leave to stand outside the refrigerator until it has softened slightly.

Serve with petit fours or as an accompaniment to a dessert.

GINGER TOFU ICE CREAM

SERVES 8–12

Lacto-vegetarians can enjoy this silky textured, ginger ice cream.

1 lb 3 oz (600 g) silken tofu

1 cup (4 oz/125 g) confectioner's (icing) sugar

20 fl oz (600 ml) thickened cream

4 tablespoons chopped crystallized ginger in syrup

1/2 teaspoon ground ginger

1/2 teaspoon ground nutmeg

1 tablespoon vanilla extract (essence)

Place all ingredients in a food processor and mix until blended. Chill for 30 minutes then pour into an electric ice cream machine and churn for 20 minutes or until firm. Store in freezer until required. If you do not have an electric ice cream machine, refer to Apricot Hazelnut Ice Cream (page 237) or Chocolate Macadamia Ice Cream (page 240) for alternative method.

Delicious served with tropical fruits such as pineapple or sapote.

STRAWBERRY SOY ICE CREAM

SERVES 8

Soy drink varieties, mixed with pureed fruit, produce some delicious ice creams. Look out for banana, chocolate, carob or vanilla soy drinks and combine with pureed bananas, berries, poached stone fruits or custard apple pulp.

8 oz (250 g) strawberries

1/2 cup (4 oz/125 g) fine white (caster) sugar

2 cups (16 fl oz/500 ml) vanilla soy drink

Mix strawberries to a puree in a food processor or blender. Add sugar and soy drink and mix until combined. Pour into an ice cream maker and churn for 20 minutes or until firm. If you do not have an electric ice cream machine, refer to Apricot Hazelnut Ice Cream (page 237) or Chocolate Macadamia Ice Cream (page 240) for alternative method. Store in freezer.

Serve with petit fours or with a dessert.

STRAWBERRY SORBET

SERVES 8

You can substitute the strawberries with any other fresh berry fruit or stewed stone fruit in this basic sorbet recipe. Serve as an accompanying palate cleanser with a rich dessert or as an accompaniment to poached or stewed fruit or compote; or make it a feature in itself, accompanied by crisp petit fours to add some texture.

1 lb (500 g) fresh strawberries
1 cup (8 fl oz/250 ml) water
1/2 cup (4 oz/125 g) sugar
juice of 1 1/2 lemons
mint leaves for decoration

Wash strawberries, reserve eight for decoration and hull the rest. Place half strawberries in a blender and blend until smooth. Repeat with remaining half of strawberries. Place together in a bowl.

Place water and sugar in a saucepan over a medium heat and stir until sugar dissolves. Increase heat and boil gently for about 5 minutes until mixture starts to become syrupy. Remove from heat and leave aside until cold.

When syrup is cold, stir in strawberry puree and lemon juice and pour mixture into an electric ice cream maker and mix until firm. Store in freezer.

If you do not have an ice cream machine, freeze mixture in shallow freezer containers until icicles form around edge, then fold in a stiffly whisked egg white and freeze until mixture has a 'mushy' consistency.

To serve, fill champagne glasses with sorbet, decorate each with a strawberry and fresh mint leaves.

Serve with petit fours.

Almond cookies with nectarines, lychees and rambutans

ALMOND COOKIES WITH NECTARINES, LYCHEES AND RAMBUTANS

SERVES APPROXIMATELY 10–15

1 cup (4 oz/125 g) rice flour/ground rice

1/2 cup (3 oz/90 g) raw sugar

2 cups (8 oz/250 g) ground almonds

3/4 cup (6 oz/185 g) unsalted butter

1 tablespoon iced water

30 whole blanched almonds

Sift rice flour into a bowl, stir in sugar and ground almonds. Add butter and work in with the hand, with a squeeze-and-knead action (as for Scottish shortbread) to form a stiff dough. The mixing can be done with a food processor but may have to be finished off by hand. Finally knead and squeeze in the iced water.

Roll tablespoons of mixture in clean, cool hands into balls. Place on greased baking trays 1 inch (2.5 mm) apart, flatten slightly and top each with an almond.

Bake at 350°F (180°C) for 12 minutes or until delicately browned. Cool on wire cooling trays.

Arrange wedges of nectarine in a fan shape, peeled lychees and half-peeled rambutans on two thirds of individual dessert plates. Place 2–3 almond cookies on each plate and serve.

NESSELRODE PUDDING

SERVES 8–12

This chestnut ice cream gâteau may be served as an iced Christmas pudding on the summery Christmas days of the southern hemisphere. It can look spectacular and doesn't need an ice cream churn!

$^{1}/_{3}$ cup (2 oz/60 g) currants

$^{1}/_{3}$ cup (2 oz/60 g) seedless raisins

4 tablespoons white rum or concentrated orange juice

4 egg yolks

$^{3}/_{4}$ cup (6 oz/185 g) fine white (caster) sugar

2 cups (16 fl oz/500 ml) thickened cream

8 oz (250 g) can crème de marrons (chestnut puree)

1 teaspoon vanilla extract (essence)

1 teaspoon almond oil

$^{4}/_{5}$ cup (7 fl oz/200 ml) thickened cream, whipped with 1 tablespoon confectioner's (icing) sugar for piping

marrons glacé for decoration

Soak currants and raisins in rum or orange juice for at least 15 minutes, drain and reserve rum and fruit separately.

Beat egg yolks with an electric mixer for about 1 minute, then beat in fine white sugar. Continue to beat until yolks are thick and fall slowly back into bowl in a ribbon when beater is lifted up.

Heat 1 cup (8 fl oz/250 ml) cream in a saucepan until small bubbles form around edge of pan; do not boil. Meanwhile, chill remaining cream.

Slowly beat hot cream into egg yolk mixture. Place in the top of a double-boiler and stir constantly over simmering water, until mixture thickens enough to coat the back of a metal spoon. Do not allow to come near boiling point or custard may curdle.

Remove from heat and stir in crème de marrons and vanilla. Chill for 30 minutes in refrigerator.

Whip $^{1}/_{2}$ cup (4 fl oz/125 ml) chilled cream until thick. Fold into custard mixture and freeze until nearly set, then stir in dried fruit and rum, and the remaining cream, stiffly whipped.

Place mixture into a charlotte tin or mold, previously brushed with almond oil, cover securely with foil and freeze for at least 6 hours or until set.

To remove, run a round-bladed knife around the edge and dip bottom of tin into hot water for 5 seconds, invert onto a flat serving plate and gently lift tin.

Decorate pudding with piped rosettes of whipped cream and marrons glacé.

The mixture may be set in ice cream containers if preferred and served spooned into individual dessert dishes.

Mango Hazelnut Meringue Gateau

SERVES 12

Serve this rich, delicious gâteau for a birthday treat.

5 x 2 oz (60g) egg whites

pinch of cream of tartar

1 cup (4 oz/125 g) confectioner's (icing) sugar, sifted

1/2 cup (4 oz/125 g) fine white (caster) sugar

1/2 teaspoon white vinegar

1 teaspoon vanilla extract (essence)

3/4 cup (4 oz/125 g) ground hazelnuts

4 oz (125g) dark cooking chocolate or carob

3 tablespoons unsalted butter or margarine

2 egg yolks

extra 3 egg whites

2 large mangoes

Line two large baking trays with waxed (greaseproof) paper, brush with melted butter and coat with all-purpose (plain) flour. Make three 7 inch (17 cm) circles on the trays as a guide to shape.

Whisk egg whites with cream of tartar until stiff. Add confectioner's sugar and fine white sugar slowly and continuously, whisking at top speed. Whisk in vinegar and vanilla. Gently fold in hazelnuts.

Divide meringue mixture between the prepared circles and spread evenly to fill the rounds, or alternatively pipe mixture on to fill circles.

Bake in the middle and bottom of a slow oven at 300°F (150°C) for 1–1 1/4 hours or until set. Cool on wire cooling trays.

Melt chocolate in a microwave oven on Defrost setting, stopping and stirring every 2 minutes, or melt in the top of a double-boiler, remove from heat, stir in chopped butter. Cool until like thick cream, then stir in egg yolks one by one. Whisk egg whites and fold into chocolate mixture. Peel and slice mango into neat slices for decoration.

To finish gâteau, place a layer of meringue on a flat serving plate, spread with a quarter of the chocolate mixture, then place next layer of meringue on and spread with a further quarter of chocolate mixture. Finally top with third layer of meringue. Spread remaining chocolate mixture carefully on top and sides of gâteau. Chill in refrigerator for 1 hour.

Decorate with mango slices before serving.

Mango hazelnut meringue gateau

HAZELNUT AND CHOCOLATE ARISTOCRATS

MAKES 32 COOKIES

These elegant nut cookies are dainty enough to serve as petit fours with poached fruit or ice cream. They may also be frozen raw, then baked quickly for unexpected visitors.

7 tablespoons (3 1/2 oz/100 g) unsalted butter or margarine

2 1/2 oz (75 g) fine white (caster) sugar

1/2 egg, lightly beaten

1 1/4 cups (5 oz/155 g) all-purpose (plain) flour, sifted

1/3 cup (1 2/3 oz/50 g) dark cooking chocolate, finely chopped

1/3 cup (1 2/3 oz/50 g) ground hazelnuts

beaten egg for glazing

coffee crystal sugar for decoration

Cream butter and sugar until light and fluffy, then beat in egg. Gently fold in flour, 1/4 cup at a time until mixture forms a dough.

Halve the dough, wrap one half in waxed (greaseproof) paper, then foil, and chill. Knead chocolate and hazelnuts into remaining dough and roll into two 5 inch (12 cm) cylinder or sausage shapes. Chill well.

On a lighly floured board, roll the reserved dough into a 6 x 5 inch (15 x 12 cm) rectangle and halve the rectangle lengthwise. Brush dough with beaten egg and place one of the cylinders in the middle of each half. Roll one of the rectangles around each cylinder forming to enclose cylinders completely, smoothing the seams and pressing the ends together firmly. Brush rolls with beaten egg, then roll in coffee crystals, coating well. Wrap in waxed paper and foil and chill for at least 2 hours. The mixture may be frozen at this stage, for up to 3 months.

Slice each roll into 16 rounds, arrange 1/2 inch (1 cm) apart on greased, lightly floured baking trays and bake at 400°F (200°C) for 10 minutes or until golden. Transfer cookies to cooling trays and allow to cool.

Serve as a petit four with Poached Peaches (page 216) or Apricot Hazelnut Ice Cream (page 237).

LUXURY ALMOND ORANGE CAKE ♀

SERVES 12

Enjoy with morning coffee or afternoon tea served with thick clotted cream and raspberries.

1 cup (8 oz/250 g) unsalted butter or polyunsaturated margarine

1 cup (8 oz/250 g) fine white (caster) sugar

6 large eggs, separated

grated rind of 2 oranges

1/2 teaspoon almond extract (essence)

1 1/2 cups (6 oz/185 g) ground almonds

1 1/2 cups (6 oz/185 g) self-raising wholewheat (wholemeal) flour

2/3 cup (6 fl oz/160 ml) fresh orange juice

Syrup:

1/2 cup (4 oz/125 g) fine white (caster) sugar

1 cup (8 fl oz/250 ml) fresh orange juice

Cream butter and sugar until light and fluffy. Add egg yolks 2 at a time, beating well after each addition. Stir in orange rind and almond extract. Add ground almonds and flour alternately with orange juice and stir in gently. Whisk egg whites until stiff and fold gently into the cake mixture.

Put into a lined and greased 9 inch (23 cm) cake tin and bake at 350°F (180°C) for 1 hour or until cooked. Test with a warm skewer. Stand cake tin on a cooling tray.

Syrup: Dissolve sugar in orange juice and pour over cake while still hot. Leave cake in tin to cool before turning out.

BANANA CAKE ♀ ⬢

SERVES 8–12

1/2 cup (4 oz/125 g) unsalted butter or polyunsaturated margarine

3/4 cup (6 oz/185 g) raw sugar

2 very ripe large bananas, peeled and quartered (approx. 1 cup)

2 x 2 oz (60 g) eggs

1/4 cup (2 fl oz/60 ml) natural yogurt

1/2 teaspoon double-acting baking powder (1 teaspoon baking powder)

1 cup (4 oz/125 g) self-raising flour

1 cup (4 oz/125 g) self-raising wholewheat (wholemeal) flour

1/4 cup (1 oz/30 g) milk powder

Place butter, sugar and bananas into the bowl of a food processor and process until mixture is creamed and bananas are pureed. Add eggs, one at a time, mixing after each addition. Add yogurt and sifted dry ingredients and mix just until evenly combined.

Pour mixture into a lined and greased 8 inch (20 cm) round cake tin and bake at 350°F (180°C) for 45-50 minutes or until cooked when tested with a fine, warm skewer. Cool on a wire cooling tray.

Serve topped with or accompanied by whipped cream and passionfruit puree.

PLUM CAKE

♟

SERVES 8-12

This is delicious. Try it accompanied with sliced nectarines or more fresh plums.

8 oz (250 g) Angelina plums or similar

1 1/2 cups (6 oz/185 g) self-raising wholewheat (wholemeal) flour

1 cup (8 oz/250 g) raw sugar

2 large eggs

1/2 cup (4 fl oz/125 ml) vegetable oil

1/2 cup (4 fl oz/125 ml) orange juice

Wash and dry plums, cut into chunky pieces and discard stones. Sieve flour into a mixing bowl, add sugar and make a 'well' in the middle. Place eggs, oil and orange juice in the well and mix with a fork to form a thick batter. Fold plums in gently. Place in a base-lined and greased 7 inch (18 cm) cake tin and bake at 180°F (350°C) for 40–45 minutes or until cooked. Test with a warm skewer. Cool on a wire cooling tray.

SUGAR PLUM SEMOLINA CAKE

♟

SERVES 12

Select dessert prunes to add moisture to this delicious, grainy-textured cake

1 cup (7 oz/200 g) pitted dessert prunes

1/2 cup (4 oz/125 g) unsalted butter or margarine

1/2 cup (4 oz/125 g) fine white (caster) sugar

2 x 2 oz (60 g) eggs

1 1/4 cups (5 oz/155 g) self-raising flour

2/3 cup (4 oz/125 g) semolina

1/3 cup (2 1/2 fl oz/80 ml) orange juice

Syrup:

1/2 cup (4 fl oz/125 ml) water

3 tablespoons fine white (caster) sugar

1 teaspoon orange flower water

Cover prunes with boiling water, leave for 10 minutes to plump up then drain well. Cream butter with sugar until light and fluffy. Add eggs, one at a time, beating well after each. Sift in flour, add semolina and orange juice and stir gently until combined.

Place two-thirds of mixture in a lined and greased 8 inch (20 cm) cake tin, spread smooth. Arrange prunes in a circle on top, then spread remaining mixture over smoothly.

Bake at 350°F (180°C) for 50 minutes or until cooked. Cool on a wire cooling tray.

Syrup: Place water and sugar in a saucepan and stir over heat until dissolved. Alternatively dissolve in a microwave oven on High setting for 1 minute. Stir in orange flower water. Stand cake on cooling tray over a large plate and pour hot syrup over warm cake. Transfer moist cake carefully to a serving plate before serving.

Sugar plum semolina cake

BAKLAVA

MAKES APPROXIMATELY 24

1 cup (8 oz/250 g) unsalted butter or polyunsaturated margarine

4 tablespoons vegetable oil

2 cups (8 oz/250 g) walnut pieces

2 cups (8 oz/250 g) blanched almonds

1 lb (500 g) filo pastry

Syrup:

1 1/2 cups (12 oz/375 g) sugar

1/2 cup (4 fl oz/125 ml) water

1 tablespoon lemon juice

2 tablespoons honey

Melt butter slowly in a saucepan without burning. Remove from heat and add vegetable oil. Mix walnuts in an electric blender or processor until coarsely ground, then place in a bowl. Mix almonds in blender until coarsely ground, then stir into the walnuts.

Unwrap filo, cover with a clean cloth, then cover this with another clean cloth wrung out in cold water, to prevent filo from drying out. Brush the bottom and sides of a shallow 8 x 12 in (20 x 30 cm) rectancular tin generously with the melted butter mixture.

Fold a sheet of filo pastry in half, place in the bottom of the tin, then fold the excess sides down neatly on to the bottom. Brush the filo with melted butter mixture, cover with another folded sheet of filo as before and brush with butter mixture as before. Sprinkle 3–4 tablespoons nuts over the buttered filo.

Continue layering 2 folded sheets of filo, brushing each with melted butter mixture and sprinkling with 4 tablespoons nuts until there are 34 layers of pastry. Place remaining folded sheet of pastry on top neatly and brush with remaining butter mixture.

Cut parallel lines across the pastry 1/2 inch (1 cm) deep and 2 inches (5 cm) apart, then cut across the lines to form diamonds.

Bake at 350°F (180°C) for 30 minutes, cover top with a sheet of waxed (greaseproof) paper and continue baking for a further 30 minutes until crisp and golden brown. Remove from oven and stand on a wire cooling tray.

Syrup: Place sugar, water and lemon juice in a saucepan and heat gently, stirring frequently until sugar is dissolved. Increase heat to high and boil syrup briskly for 5 minutes. Remove from heat and add honey. Cool. Pour cool syrup over warm Baklava when it comes out of the oven and leave to cool. When cold, cut Baklava into diamonds and serve with chilled grapes or sliced peaches and coffee.

BON VIVANT

SERVES 24

This is a delicious Jewish recipe, rich in nuts and chocolate.

First layer:

8 large eggs, separated

3/4 cup (6 oz/185 g) fine white (caster) sugar

8 oz (250 g) ground hazelnuts, or almonds, or walnuts

Second layer:

3/4 cup (6 oz/185 g) fine white (caster) sugar

8 oz (250 g) dark cooking chocolate

3/4 cup (6 oz/185 g) unsalted butter or polyunsaturated margarine

First layer: Whisk egg whites until stiff. Whisk in sugar gradually, whisking at top speed. Gently fold in ground hazelnuts.

Pour mixture into a large jelly roll (Swiss roll) tin, previously lined with waxed (greaseproof) paper and coated with cornstarch (cornflour), and spread smooth. Bake at 350°F (180°C) for 20 minutes. Cool until only lukewarm.

Second layer: Meanwhile, beat egg yolks with sugar until thick and white and a ribbon forms when the mixture is lifted. Melt chocolate in the top of a double-boiler over gently bubbling water (or in a microwave set on Defrost). Melt butter and mix into melted chocolate. Mix chocolate mixture into egg yolk mixture.

Spread over lukewarm meringue and return to oven and bake for a further 20–25 minutes, until cooked.

Cool, then cut into slices to serve. Serve with a dollop of whipped cream, decorated with chocolate leaves and accompanied by fresh berries if desired.

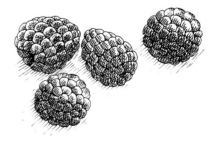

LEMON COCONUT CAKE

SERVES 8–12

Serve this moist cake accompanied by orange segments and blueberries and cream or natural yogurt.

1/2 cup (4 oz/125 g) unsalted butter or margarine

1 cup (8 oz/250 g) fine white (caster) sugar

4 large eggs

2 cups (6 oz/185 g) unsweetened (desiccated) coconut

1 cup (4 oz/125 g) self-raising flour, sifted

Syrup:

1 cup (8 oz/250 g) sugar

1/2 cup (4 fl oz/125 ml) water

finely grated rind and juice of 1 lemon

1 teaspoon rosewater, optional

Cream butter and sugar until light and fluffy. Add eggs one at a time and beat well after adding each one. Stir in coconut and flour gently until combined. Put mixture into a base-lined and greased 8 inch (20 cm) round cake tin and bake at 325°F (160°C) for 1 hour or until cooked.

Syrup: Bring all ingredients to the boil, stirring until sugar is dissolved. Pour syrup over cake as soon as it comes out of the oven. Leave cake to cool in tin before turning out.

CARROT AND POPPY SEED CAKE

SERVES 8–12

The poppy seeds give this carrot cake an enjoyable, interesting texture but you may prefer to omit them if making it for a children's birthday cake.

1 cup (8 oz/250 g) raw sugar or honey

3 x 2 oz (60 g) eggs

1/2 cup (4 fl oz/125 ml) macadamia nut or sunflower oil

1 teaspoon vanilla extract (essence)

1 cup (4 oz/125 g) self-raising wholewheat (wholemeal) flour

1 teaspoon ground cinnamon

1/4 cup poppy seeds, optional

2 cups grated carrot

1/2 cup (3 oz/90 g) raisins (sultanas)

Beat sugar and eggs together until thick and frothy. Add oil and vanilla. Sift flour and cinnamon into a mixing bowl. Stir in poppy seeds if used, carrot and raisins and make a well in the middle. Add egg mixture and fold in gently.

Place in a lined and greased 8 inch (20 cm) square cake tin or 9 inch (23 cm) round cake tin and bake at 350°F (180°C) for 45 minutes or until cooked. Test with a fine, warm skewer. Cool on a wire cooling tray.

Serve decorated with a lemon icing if desired.

Lemon coconut cake

Scottish Gingerbread

A delicious, moist gingerbread which improves with keeping, so you can make it in advance.

1/2 cup (4 oz/125 g) butter or polyunsaturated margarine

3/4 cup (6 fl oz/185 ml) molasses or treacle

1/4 cup (2 fl oz/60 ml) corn syrup or golden syrup

2/3 cup (4 oz/125 g) dark brown sugar

2 x 2 oz (60 g) eggs, beaten

1/2 cup (4 fl oz/125 ml) milk or soy drink

2 cups (8 oz/250 g) all-purpose (plain) flour

1 teaspoon baking soda (bicarbonate of soda)

1 teaspoon ground ginger

1 teaspoon ground cinnamon

1/2 teaspoon mixed spice

1/2 cup (3 oz/90 g) steel cut oats or coarse oatmeal

Melt butter, molasses, syrup and sugar in a saucepan over a gentle heat, stirring until sugar has dissolved. Cool slightly then stir in eggs and milk.

Sift flour, bicarbonate of soda, ginger, cinnamon and mixed spice into a mixing bowl, add oats and make a well in the middle. Add melted mixture and beat with a wooden spoon until batter is smooth. Pour mixture into a lined, greased 8 inch (20 cm) square cake tin and bake in the lower half of an oven at 350°F (180°C) for 1 hour or until cooked. Test with a warm skewer. Stand for 10 minutes in tin, then cool on a wire cooling tray. Delicious served in slices, topped with apricot jam, accompanied by sliced nashi (Asian pear).

Vegan Chocolate Cake

SERVES 8–12

1/4 cup (2 oz/60 g) margarine

1/4 cup (2 oz/60 g) raw sugar

1/4 cup (2 fl oz/60 ml) honey

1 cup (4 oz/125 g) self-raising flour

1/2 cup (2 oz/60 g) self-raising wholewheat (wholemeal) flour

1/2 teaspoon baking soda (bicarbonate of soda)

5 teaspoons cocoa

1/4 cup (1 oz/30 g) ground hazelnuts

1 teaspoon vanilla extract (essence)

1 tablespoon white vinegar

2/3 cup (5 fl oz/160 ml) soy drink

Cream margarine with sugar and honey until light and fluffy. Sift flours, baking soda and cocoa into mixture and stir in gently. Add hazelnuts, vanilla, vinegar and soy drink and mix in gently until evenly combined.

Place the mixture in a base-lined and greased 8 inch (20 cm) shallow cake tin and spread evenly. Bake at 300°F (150°C) for 20 minutes or until cooked.

Serve topped with chocolate icing accompanied by berries.

GERMAN APPLE CAKE

½ cup (4 oz/125 g) unsalted butter or polyunsaturated margarine

½ cup (4 oz/125 g) raw sugar

1 large egg

1 cup (8 fl oz/250 ml) milk or soy drink

grated rind of 1 lemon

1 cup (4 oz/125 g) self-raising wholewheat (wholemeal) flour

½ cup (2 oz/60 g) ground brown rice

3 tablespoons currants or cranberries

2 green apples

Topping:

¼ cup (2 oz/60 g) unsalted butter or polyunsaturated margarine

½ cup (2 oz/60 g) all-purpose wholewheat (plain wholemeal) flour

2 tablespoons soy grits

1 tablespoon raw sugar

1 teaspoon ground cinnamon

Cream butter and sugar, add egg and beat well. Stir in milk and lemon rind. Fold in flour and ground rice. Spread mixture into a base-lined and greased 8 inch (20 cm) shallow cake tin, sprinkle currants over. Cut apples into quarters, remove core and peel, and slice into thin wedges. Arrange apple slices overlapping in a circle on top of the cake mixture.

Topping: Rub butter into flour, stir in soy grits, sugar and cinnamon and sprinkle over apples.

Bake at 350°F (180°C) for 35–40 minutes or until cooked.

Serve sifted with confectioner's (icing) sugar, accompanied by mixed berries and natural yogurt.

❖ KEEP WHOLEWHEAT (WHOLEMEAL) FLOUR STORED IN THE REFRIGERATOR IF YOU DON'T 'TURN OVER' YOUR SUPPLY QUICKLY. IF YOU STORE IT AT ROOM TEMPERATURE, CHECK IT REGULARLY FOR WEEVILS, PARTICULARLY IN HOT, HUMID WEATHER.

ZUCCHINI AND ORANGE CAKE

SERVES 12

¹/₂ cup (4 oz/125 g) unsalted butter or margarine

¹/₂ cup (4 oz/125 g) raw sugar

3 x 2 oz (60 g) eggs, separated

1 teaspoon vanilla extract (essence)

1 cup grated zucchini (courgette), firmly packed

finely grated rind of 1 orange

1 cup (4 oz/125 g) self-raising wholewheat (wholemeal) flour, sifted

1-2 tablespoons sunflower kernels

Syrup:

¹/₂ cup (4 oz/125 g) vanilla or fine white (caster) sugar

¹/₂ cup (4 fl oz/125 ml) orange juice

Beat the butter and sugar together until light and fluffy. Add egg yolks, one at a time, and beat well after each addition. Stir in vanilla, zucchini and orange rind. Whisk egg whites until stiff. Gently fold flour into mixture in three batches, alternating with stiff egg white.

Place mixture in a base-lined and greased 8 inch (20 cm) round cake tin. Sprinkle with sunflower kernels. Bake at 350°F (180°C) for 40 minutes or until cooked. Test with a warm skewer.

Syrup: Dissolve sugar in orange juice. Pour over cake when it comes out of oven. Leave to cool in tin before removing.

Serve with orange segments and natural yogurt or crème fraîche.

APPLE PUREE FRUIT CAKE

SERVES 12–24

6 large green cooking apples

1 cup (8 oz/250 g) polyunsaturated margarine

2 cups (1 lb/500 g) raw sugar

3 cups (12 oz/375 g) all-purpose wholewheat (plain wholemeal) flour

1 tablespoon baking soda (bicarbonate of soda)

1 teaspoon ground cinnamon

1 teaspoon mixed spice

2 cups (12 oz/375 g) seedless raisins (or 1 cup of raisins and 1 of sultanas)

¹/₃ cup (2 oz/60 g) mixed peel

¹/₃ cup (2 oz/60 g) glacé cherries, chopped

¹/₂ cup (2 oz/60 g) hazelnuts, chopped

Peel, core and slice apples, stew with 1 tablespoon water, then mix to a purée when cool. Measure 2 ¹/₂ cups purée and place in a pan. Add margarine and sugar and heat gently, stirring until sugar is dissolved.

Sift flour, baking soda and spices into a mixing bowl, and make a 'well' in the middle. Pour apple mixture into well and stir until combined. Stir in raisins, mixed peel, cherries and nuts.

Place mixture in a lined, greased, 9 inch (23 cm) round cake tin and bake at 375°F (190°C) for 1 ¹/₂ hours, until cooked. Test with a warm skewer. Stand in tin for at least 10 minutes before turning out. Cool on a wire cooling tray.

Apple puree fruit cake (left); Zucchini and orange cake (top)

ALL-AMERICAN CHRISTMAS CAKE

SERVES 24

This Christmas cake recipe is a typically American dish, rich with a bounty of fruit and nuts. An added bonus is that you don't have to ice it!

8 oz (250 g) glace cherries, drained

4 oz (125 g) dessert dates, pitted

4 oz (125 g) dessert prunes, pitted

4 oz (125 g) glace pineapple

4 oz (125 g) dried apricots, chopped

8 oz (250 g) Brazil nuts

4 tablespoons rum or brandy or concentrated orange juice

1/2 cup (3 oz/90 g) dark brown sugar

2 eggs

2 tablespoons unsalted butter or polyunsaturated margarine

1/2 cup (2 oz/60 g) self-raising wholewheat (wholemeal) flour

Place all fruit and nuts in a bowl, add half rum and leave to stand. Beat sugar with eggs until thick and creamy. Add butter and beat well. Stir in sifted flour, fruit and nuts and mix until well combined. Place mixture into a lined and greased loaf tin. Bake at 325°F (160°C) for 1 1/2–2 hours or until cooked when tested with a warm skewer. Pour remaining rum over while cake is hot and leave to cool in tin. Wrap cake in foil and store in refrigerator. Cut with a serrated bread knife or an electric knife to serve.

WHOLEWHEAT MINCE PIES

MAKES 18–24

You can make these a couple of weeks before Christmas and freeze them to help you get organized for the festive feast.

Pastry:

2 cups (8 oz/250 g) wholewheat (wholemeal) flour

1/2 cup (1 1/2 oz/45 g) soy flour

2/3 cup (5 oz/155 g) unsalted butter or margarine

1/4 cup (1 oz/30 g) ground almonds

1/3 cup (3 oz/90 g) fine white (caster) sugar

2 egg yolks

lemon juice or cold water to mix

Filling:

1 cup (8 oz/250 g) fruit mincemeat

2 tablespoons concentrated orange juice or brandy

confectioner's (icing) sugar for sifting

Sift flours into the bowl of a food processor. Cut butter into small pieces, add to flour and mix for 20 seconds or until mixture resembles breadcrumbs. Add almonds, sugar, egg yolks and sufficient lemon juice and mix to form a stiff dough which leaves side of processor bowl cleanly. Transfer to a lightly floured marble slab or pastry board and knead very lightly until smooth underneath. Wrap in waxed (greaseproof) paper and chill for 30 minutes before rolling out.

Filling: Mix mincemeat with orange juice.

To finish: Roll pastry out on a lightly floured surface and cut out 18-24 rounds, large enough to line tartlet or pie tins. Line tins neatly with pastry then cut out 18–24 smaller rounds to cover pies. Place a heaped teaspoon of filling into pastry cases. Brush edges of pies with cold water and place pastry tops on, pressing carefully around edge to seal. Make two neat holes with a metal skewer in the top of each pie to allow steam to escape. Alternatively cut a star out of pastry tops before covering pies.

Bake at 425°F (220°C) for 15–20 minutes, until cooked and golden.

Serve warm, sifted with confectioner's sugar, accompanied by ice cream if desired.

261

SNACKS

The habit of 'grazing' is very much a part of the social life of teenagers and adults so this chapter on vegetarian snacks is very important. Whether they graze at home, order home-delivered or take-out (take-away) food, or eat out in a restaurant, vegetarians must remember to select nutritious whole foods, such as Lebanese felafel rolls, wholewheat (wholemeal) pizzas, wholewheat vegetable quiches and pies and wholewheat salad sandwiches. This chapter deals with snacks which you can prepare at home, and many of them are suitable to pack for a picnic or a packed lunch.

As the mother of a vegetarian who snacks a lot at home, my advice to other parents is to buy wisely and make sure you always have a supply of healthy wholesome breads and crispbreads, nut butters and spreads, crisp salad ingredients, carrots, celery and fresh and dried fruit for your children to be creative with. Dips such as Guacamole, Hummus Tahina, Baba Ghannooj and Frijole with corn chips are popular for snacking on, as are Stuffed Vine Leaves, Felafel (see Hors d'oeuvres chapter) and marinated olives. If you have the time and patience you will find it more economical to make these than to buy them. Make a different one each weekend when you can spare the time.

Some of these snacks such as Bruschetta with Red Pepper and Goat's Feta and Eggplant and Brie with Spicy Pepper Sauce, can be served as a delicious quickly prepared meal for a weekend lunch or light supper. Some such as Vine-Ripe Crostini are good for hot weather. Others such as the Winter Jaffle and Chili Bean Burgers are perfect for cold weather. Scrambled Tofu and Orange Pancakes, the fruity Soyshake and Smoothie, Tiger's Milk and Apricot Lhasi, are all delicious ideas for a quick vegetarian breakfast.

The majority of recipes in this chapter are selected to help you provide a nutritionally well balanced and delicious packed lunch. There are many ideas for complete protein sandwiches, pies, pastries, health bars, muffins and cookies. So snack on and enjoy good health!

Bagel nicoise, p.272

GUACAMOLE
AVOCADO DIP

This dip is delicious to graze on with vegetable crudités, but is also a traditional accompaniment to Mexican food such as tortillas and nachos.

2 large ripe avocados
1 tablespoon lemon juice
1 teaspoon grated onion
2 cloves garlic, crushed
dash of tabasco sauce
sea salt
1 tablespoon olive oil

Cut avocados in half, remove stone. Scoop flesh into a bowl and mash well or mix in a blender or food processor. Add lemon juice, onion, garlic and tabasco sauce and sea salt to taste. Mix all ingredients thoroughly. Stir in 1 tablespoon olive oil or more if you prefer. Serve as a dip with carrot and celery sticks, radishes, sprigs of raw cauliflower and taco chips.

HUMMUS TAHINA
CHICK PEA DIP

Hummus tahina is a dip or spread made from chick peas, high in vegetable protein. Canned chick peas may be used to save time. Tahini paste is made from sesame seeds and is available at health food stores.

3/4 cup (4 oz/125 g) yellow chick peas, soaked overnight in cold water
juice of 3 large lemons
2-3 cloves garlic, crushed
sea salt to taste
1/2 cup (4 fl oz/125 ml) tahini
1 tablespoon olive oil
paprika

Boil the soaked chick peas in fresh water for 1 1/2–2 hours, or until soft, or cook in a pressure cooker for 30 minutes. The cooking time depends on the freshness of the chick peas. Drain chick peas and put a few aside for garnishing. Reserve liquid.

Mix chick peas, half at a time, to a puree in an electric blender or food processor. Pour lemon juice into mixture gradually to keep it moist. Add remaining ingredients and blend to a creamy paste, adding some of the reserved water the chick peas were cooked in, if necessary.

Pour mixture into a serving bowl and sprinkle with olive oil and a pinch of paprika over the surface. Garnish with reserved chick peas.

Serve as a dip with warm, torn Lebanese bread as part of the first course of a Lebanese meal, or serve with vegetable crudités for a snack.

Baba Ghannooj
EGGPLANT DIP
SERVES 8

This dip may be served as an appetizer before a Lebanese meal, or kept in the refrigerator as a snack for hungry children home from school.

1 lb (500 g) eggplant (aubergine)

2 tablespoons tahini

3 tablespoons lemon juice

2 plump cloves garlic, crushed

1 teaspoon salt

freshly ground black pepper

2 teaspoons olive oil

2 tablespoons finely chopped onion

2 tablespoons finely chopped parsley

Prick eggplant in a few places, then place on a rack 4 inches (10 cm) under a hot broiler (grill) and turn regularly until the skin is charred on all sides, about 15 minutes. Wrap the charred eggplant in a clean, wet cloth, leave for 5 minutes, then unwrap and peel off the skin, using a vegetable peeler where required.

Cut eggplant in half lengthwise, chop finely, then mix to a smooth pulp in a food processor or blender. Add tahini paste, lemon juice and garlic and mix well. Season to taste with salt and pepper.

To serve, place in a shallow serving bowl and sprinkle the top with olive oil, finely chopped onion and parsley.

Serve chilled, accompanied by warm, torn Lebanese bread and Lebanese cucumber sticks for dipping.

Frijole
RED BEAN DIP
SERVES 6–8

This popular Mexican dip is quick and easy to prepare. You can serve it with corn chips for dipping or on top of jacket baked potatoes for a substantial and nourishing snack meal.

1 x 10 oz (310 g) can red kidney beans or pinto beans

1 tablespoon jalapeno chilies or red chili

1/2 cup (4 fl oz/125 ml) light sour cream

2 tablespoons chopped parsley

Mix beans to a coarse puree in a blender or food processor. Wearing rubber gloves, remove seeds from chilies, and slice them thinly. Add chili, sour cream and parsley and mix together.

Serve with vegetables and corn chips for dipping into the frijole.

WARM SUNFLOWER AND CAPER DIP ◈

SERVES 8–12

This recipe was inspired by the traditional Italian Bagna Cauda dip from Piedmont which is based on cream and anchovies. It's rich, so it's good to serve in cold weather.

2 cups (16 fl oz/500 ml) cream

1 tablespoon butter or margarine

2 tablespoons sunflower kernels

2 tablespoons drained, rinsed capers, coarsely chopped

1 teaspoon finely chopped garlic

Italian bread sticks and crisp refreshing vegetable crudités for dipping

Place cream in a saucepan, bring to the boil, then simmer, stirring frequently, until reduced to half volume, about 10-15 minutes.

Melt butter and fry sunflower kernels, capers and garlic until garlic is golden. Add cream and bring to simmering point. Blend in a food processor or blender until sunflower is crushed.

Serve dip warm with grissini (Italian bread sticks) and strips of cucumber, carrot, fennel or celery.

TASHA'S FOCCACIA ◈

SERVES 1

My teenage vegetarian daughter loves grazing on food both at home and in smart coffee shops. This is one of the snacks she loves best.

1 portion foccacia, approximately 6 x 4 inches (15 x 10 cm)

olive oil with crushed garlic

sun-dried tomato pâté

sliced avocado

wedges of brie or camembert cheese

lettuce leaves

canned artichoke hearts, sliced

scallions (spring onions)

snow pea (mange-tout) sprouts

yellow tear-drop tomatoes and extra snow pea (mange-tout) sprouts for garnish

Slice foccacia in half through middle and brush olive oil with crushed garlic on inside surface. Place under a hot broiler (grill) until lightly toasted. Spread toasted surfaces with sun-dried tomato pâté, then layer bottom slice with avocado, brie or camembert, lettuce, artichoke, scallions and snow pea sprouts. Place top layer on filling at a jaunty angle and serve garnished with yellow tomatoes and extra snow pea sprouts. Serve with a knife and fork and enjoy.

Tasha's foccacia

RICE CRACKERS WITH ARTICHOKE PÂTÉ

SERVES 4

12 rice crackers

artichoke pâté for spreading

12 wedges vine-ripened tomato, marinated in lime or ruby grapefruit juice

zucchini (courgette) in oil for topping

Spread rice crackers with artichoke pâté. Top each one with a wedge of tomato and some drained zucchini in oil.

WINTER JAFFLE

SERVES 2

Sauerkraut is one of the few natural sources of vitamin B12 in a vegetarian diet and this is an unusual yet surprisingly tasty way to serve it.

4 slices multi-grain wholewheat (wholemeal) bread

margarine for spreading

sliced low-fat or soy cheese

sliced cooked beet (beetroot)

4 tablespoons sauerkraut, rinsed and well drained

Spread the bread with margarine and turn 2 slices over, margarine side down. Top this bread with thin slices of cheese, then cover with slices of beet, finally top each with 2 tablespoons sauerkraut. Cover the filling with remaining bread, margarine side uppermost.

Carefully place sandwiches in a preheated electric sandwich toaster, seal and cook until bread is golden brown on both sides. Serve toasted sandwiches hot garnished with sprigs of parsley.

PIZZA SNACK

SERVES 1

2 teaspoons tomato paste

1 teaspoon tahini

1 small wholewheat (wholemeal) pita bread, approx. 6 inch (15 cm) diameter

1 medium tomato, thinly sliced

1/4 cup (1 oz/30 g) tasty or cheddar cheese, grated

1 tablespoon thinly sliced scallions (spring onions)

1 tablespoon sliced sun-dried red pepper (capsicum)

Mix tomato paste with tahini and spread over the pita, spreading to the edge. Place tomato slices, overlapping on the spread. Mix cheese with scallions and sprinkle over the tomato. Scatter sun-dried red pepper on top. Cook under a hot broiler (grill) until cheese is melted and golden brown. Serve at once and enjoy.

SPICED POPCORN MIX

MAKES 4 CUPS (32 FL OZ/1 L)

This is fun to serve at a children's party. Your teenagers will also love it for snacking or grazing.

1 tablespoon sesame oil

1 tablespoon butter or margarine

1/4 cup (1 2/3 oz/50 g) popping corn

1/4 teaspoon curry powder

1/4 teaspoon ground cumin

1/2 teaspoon ground turmeric

1 tablespoon sunflower oil

1/4 cup (1 oz/30 g) raw skinless peanuts

1/4 cup pepitas

1/4 cup sunflower kernels

1/3 cup (2 oz/50 g) raisins

1/4 cup (1 oz/30 g) slivered almonds

1/2 cup (1 oz/30 g) shredded coconut, toasted

Heat sesame oil and butter in a heavy-based pan, add corn, cover and cook on a high heat, shaking pan occasionally, for 3 minutes or until all corn has popped.

Place spices and oil in a mixing bowl, add all remaining ingredients including popped corn and toss together. Store in an air-tight container. Serve in a bowl.

RICE CAKES WITH GINGER DATE CHEESE SPREAD

SERVES 1

Make this for a light lunch or snack.

1/4 cup ginger date and nut spread
1/4 cup cottage cheese
2 rice cakes
1 peach or nectarine

Mix ginger date and nut spread with cottage cheese and spread over the rice cakes. Cut peach around circumference from top to bottom. Cut fruit into wedges and remove from stone. Arrange fruit on top of spread and serve.

EGGPLANT AND BRIE WITH SPICY PEPPER SAUCE

SERVES 2

Combine an Italian-style vegetable and a French-style cheese with cilantro (coriander) from the East and chili from the southwest of the USA, and the result is a delicious East meets West snack.

4 round slices eggplant
(aubergine), 1/2 inch (1.5 cm) thick
1 tablespoon olive oil
4 oz (125 g) round of brie cheese

Sauce:

1 large red pepper (capsicum),
deseeded
1 teaspoon minced chili
1/2 cup cilantro (coriander) leaves
1 vine-ripened tomato, skinned
and chopped

Score both sides of eggplant slices, place on a foil-covered baking tray and brush with olive oil. Broil (grill) under a red hot broiler (grill) until golden. Cut cheese in half through circumference, place on top of 2 golden rounds of eggplant, cover with remaining eggplant, golden side down, making two 'sandwiches'. Score tops of eggplant, brush with oil and broil until golden. Turn over carefully using an egg slice, score tops of eggplant again, brush with remaining oil and broil until golden.

Sauce: Cut red pepper into strips and place under a hot broiler until skin blisters. Wrap in a damp cloth for 5 minutes, then peel off skin. Puree pepper with chili and cilantro, add tomato and puree again until combined.

Serve broiled eggplant and brie on individual plates with the sauce, accompanied by salad greens.

Eggplant and brie with spicy pepper sauce

270

BAGEL NIÇOISE

SERVES 1

1 bagel
olive oil with crushed garlic
black olive pâté
eggplant (aubergine) in oil, drained
sliced hard-boiled egg
sliced dill pickled cucumber
small romaine (cos) lettuce leaves

Slice bagel in half through middle, brush olive oil with crushed garlic on cut surface. Warm in oven or microwave oven. Spread both surfaces with olive pâté. Cover bottom half with layers of eggplant in oil, hard-boiled egg, pickled cucumber and romaine lettuce. Place top of bagel over filling and serve with some cherry tomatoes on the side if desired.

TASTY CROISSANT SNACK

SERVES 1

1 croissant
1/4 cup (1 oz/30 g) low-fat tasty or cheddar cheese, sliced
1 scallion (spring onion), thinly sliced
1 tablespoon zucchini (courgette) in oil, well drained
2-3 slices sun-dried red pepper (capsicum) in oil, well drained

Slice croissant open and fill with layered cheese, scallion, zucchini and red pepper. Place on a baking tray and heat in the oven at 300°F (150°C) for 10–15 minutes. Enjoy while warm.

PLOUGHMAN'S LUNCH MUFFIN

SERVES 1

1 multi-grain wholewheat (wholemeal) muffin
1/2 cup (2 oz/60 g) cheddar cheese, grated
pinch of mustard powder
6 drops tabasco sauce
2 teaspoons milk
salt and pepper
2 brown pickled onions

Split muffin in half and toast outer sides first, then turn over and lightly toast inner surfaces. Mix cheese with mustard, tabasco, milk and salt and pepper to taste. Divide mixture between toasted muffin and spread to the edge. Cut pickled onions in half from top to bottom and place 2 halves on top of cheese mixture. Place under a hot broiler (grill) and broil until cheese mixture has melted and is bubbling hot. Serve while warm accompanied by some mustard and cress.

BRUSCHETTA WITH RED PEPPER AND GOAT'S FETA 🏷

SERVES 2

This attractive, tasty snack brings the sunny Mediterranean into your kitchen. Serve for a light lunch or quick supper. Some delicatessens marinate the goat's milk feta cheese to give it a richer taste. Look out for wholewheat French bread!

4 thick slices French loaf, cut diagonally, approx. 1 inch (2.5 cm) thick

olive oil

2 cloves garlic, crushed

1 red pepper (capsicum), deseeded

4 tablespoons sun-dried tomatoes

4 oz (125 g) goat's milk feta cheese

black olives for garnish

salad greens for serving, optional

Brush both sides of the bread generously with olive oil mixed with garlic. Place on a baking tray and bake at 350°F (180°C) for 10 minutes.

Cut peppers into long flat strips, brush with oil and place under a red hot boiler (grill) and cook until soft but not burned. Place red pepper on the bread slices, arrange sun-dried tomatoes on top. Slice feta cheese thinly, place over tomatoes, then return bruschetta under the hot broiler until cheese melts.

Serve immediately, garnished with black olives and accompanied with salad greens if desired.

GRILLED TOFU CLUB SANDWICH

SERVES 1

The famous foodie Ken Hom says you can always judge the quality of food in international hotels by ordering a Club Sandwich from room service. Wonder how he would judge this one!

2 oz (60 g) firm tofu, sliced 1/2 inch (1.5 cm) thick

1 teaspoon soy sauce or tamari

1 teaspoon lemon juice

2 slices wholegrain bread

tofu mayonnaise (page 209)

crisp lettuce leaves

sliced vine-ripened tomato

alfalfa sprouts

1 tablespoon tahini

Broil (grill) the tofu until golden, cut into finger-size strips, drizzle with soy sauce and lemon juice and allow to absorb seasoning.

Spread one slice of bread with mayonnaise, place tofu on bread, top with lettuce, tomato and alfalfa sprouts. Spread other slice of bread with tahini and place on top of sandwich.

Serve garnished with sprigs of watercress or snow pea sprouts.

VINE-RIPE CROSTINI

MAKES APPROXIMATELY 24

This is a simple-to-prepare snack suitable for a finger-food party.

1 wholewheat (wholemeal)
French loaf

olive oil for brushing

olive pâté for spreading

8 oz (250 g) cottage or ricotta
cheese

vine-ripened tomatoes, sliced and
marinated in sunflower dressing
(page 205)

black olives and basil leaves
for garnish

Cut French loaf into thin slices, place on a baking tray and brush with olive oil. Bake at 350°F (180°C) for 5-8 minutes until crisp, then leave to cool. Spread olive pâté thinly to the edge of the crostinis. Spread some cottage cheese on top, leaving a border of pâté showing. Top with a slice of marinated tomato and serve garnished with olives and basil.

FRIJOLES REFRITOS
MEXICAN REFRIED BEANS

SERVES 4

This does not look appealing but it is very nourishing, providing the necessary complete protein for teenagers, who love it served on hamburger buns or tortillas, topped with a poached egg or covered with corn chips and melted cheese and accompanied by Guacamole (page 264) and/or light sour cream.

1 onion, chopped

2 cloves garlic, crushed

1 tomato, coarsely chopped

1 teaspoon minced red chili

14 oz (440 g) can red kidney beans

1/2 cup (4 fl oz/125 ml) water

1/4 teaspoon freshly ground black
pepper

1/4 cup (2 oz/60 g)
polyunsaturated margarine

Place half onion, half garlic and half tomato in a heavy-based pan, add chili, beans, water and pepper. Bring to the boil then simmer, half covered, for 30 minutes or until water is reduced and absorbed.

In a frying pan, gently fry remaining onion and garlic in half margarine for 5 minutes until soft. Add remaining tomato and fry, stirring, for 2 minutes. Add 3 tablespoons bean mixture and mash with a fork. Stir in 2 teaspoons of remaining margarine. Continue adding bean mixture and margarine in this method until it is all mixed together. Mixture should be stiff so simmer longer if too runny.

Vine-ripe crostini

SCRAMBLED TOFU

SERVES 2

This looks and tastes like the classic scrambled egg. True vegans can replace the eggs by doubling the quantity of tofu and gently frying 1 small chopped onion and 1 small grated carrot in 1 tablespoon nut oil first, which binds the mixture and enhances its appearance and taste.

1 tablespoon butter or margarine

6 oz (185 g) firm tofu, crumbled

2 eggs, beaten

2 teaspoons salt-reduced tamari or soy sauce

Melt butter in a heavy-based, preferably ceramic-lined saucepan. Add tofu and gently fry, mashing well, until golden. Add eggs and stir continuously over a low heat, with a wooden spoon, until mixture coagulates and thickens to a creamy texture. Stir in tamari and serve immediately on toasted wholegrain bread for a complete protein snack.

TOFU AND MUSHROOM OMELET

SERVES 1

An omelet is a good snack meal for busy people because you can make it very quickly. The addition of tofu, tahini and mushrooms makes this omelet particularly appetizing to vegetarians.

1 small leek, thinly sliced

2 mushrooms, chopped

1 tablespoon polyunsaturated margarine

2 large eggs

2 oz (60 g) tofu, crumbled

1 tablespoon tahini

2 teaspoons tamari or soy sauce

Gently fry leek and mushrooms in margarine in an omelet pan. Beat eggs and mix in remaining ingredients. Add egg mixture to pan over a medium-high heat and, using a fork, stir egg in from around edge of pan to the middle, as it sets. Leave a thin layer of egg to set around edge, then loosen carefully with a palette knife and fold over in half, away from the handle. Cook folded omelet a few seconds to set into shape, then loosen and tip over and out onto a dinner plate. Serve with a green salad if desired.

SWEETCORN WITH UMEBOSHI PLUM SAUCE ⬧

SERVES 2

The umeboshi plum is a salted pickled Japanese plum. You can buy umeboshi plum paste at leading health food stores or you can puree the plums to make this tangy sauce. The Japanese eat umeboshi plums as a digestive aid.

2 tablespoons umeboshi plum paste or 3 umeboshi plums, pureed

2 teaspoons finely chopped peanuts

3 tablespoons light sour cream

2 sweetcorn on the cob

Mix umeboshi plum paste or puree with nuts and sour cream.

Remove husks and silk from sweetcorn and cook by boiling, steaming or in a microwave oven.

Serve sweetcorn topped with the sauce.

CRUNCHY JACKET POTATOES

SERVES 2

Choose from either of these fillings. The first is lacto-vegetarian, the second is vegan.

2 medium-large, oval-shaped, red-skinned potatoes

Filling 1:

2 teaspoons butter

4 tablespoons grated tasty or cheddar cheese

1 tablespoon soy drink

salt and pepper

paprika for sprinkling

Filling 2:

2 teaspoons polyunsaturated margarine

1 tablespoon soy drink

2 teaspoons snipped chives

1 tablespoon chopped peanuts

salt and pepper

2 teapoons millet

Wash potatoes well. Prick potatoes with a fork then place directly on the rack in an oven and bake at 400°F (200°C) for 1 hour or until cooked. Test with a skewer. Cut a slice from the top of the potatoes and scoop cooked flesh out into a bowl.

Filling 1: Add butter, half cheese and soy drink, mash well and season to taste with salt and pepper. Pile mixture back into potato cases and top with remaining cheese.

Filling 2: Add margarine, soy drink and chives, mash well. Add peanuts and season to taste with salt and pepper. Pile mixture back into potato cases and top with millet.

Return stuffed potatoes to oven and bake at 350°F (180°C) for 15 minutes until heated through and golden brown. Sprinkle paprika pepper over Filling 1.

Serve for a satisfying winter snack, accompanied by Sauerkraut Salad (page 201).

CHILI BEAN BURGERS

SERVES 2

This is very popular with teenagers, particularly in cold weather. It's simple and quick to prepare and provides all necessary amino acids required for growth. Eat with a knife and fork if not already out on the ski slopes!

1/4 cup finely chopped red pepper (capsicum)

1 teaspoon butter or margarine

8 oz (260 g) can baked beans in tomato sauce, vegetarian

1 tablespoon tomato paste

1 tablespoon sweet chili sauce

2 hamburger buns or wholewheat (wholemeal) bread rolls

2 tablespoons sour cream or natural yogurt

Gently fry pepper in butter, or cook in a microwave on High for 1 minute. Stir in baked beans, tomato paste and sweet chili sauce and heat until boiling, stirring occasionally.

Split hamburger buns or bread rolls and toast until golden. Spoon chili beans onto bottom half of buns, top with sour cream and cover with top half of bun at a jaunty angle.

WHOLEMEAL AND RYE DAMPER

SERVES 8

This is a nourishing bread traditionally made in Australia which is good served with soup in the wintertime.

2 cups (8 oz/250 g) self-raising wholewheat (wholemeal) flour

1 cup (4 oz/125 g) rye flour

1/4 cup (1 oz/25 g) soy compound

1/2 teaspoon double-acting baking powder (1 teaspoon of baking powder)

1/2 teaspoon salt

1/3 cup (3 oz/90 g) butter or polyunsaturated margarine

1 cup (8 fl oz/250 ml) water

2 teaspoons wheatgerm for sprinkling

Sift flours, soy compound, baking powder and salt into a mixing bowl. Cut butter in with a round-bladed knife then rub in until mixture resembles breadcrumbs. Add water and stir with the knife until mixture forms a soft dough. Turn out onto a floured surface and knead very lightly and quickly into a 6 inch (15 cm) round. Place on a floured baking tray, sprinkle with wheatgerm and cut a cross over the middle, 1/2 inch (1 cm) deep.

Bake at 400°F (200°C) for 10 minutes, reduce to 350°F (180°C) and bake for a further 15-25 minutes until cooked. Remove from oven and wrap in a clean cloth. Serve warm.

Vegetarian sandwiches, p.280

279

VEGETARIAN SANDWICHES

SERVES 1

It is important to make the vegetarian packed lunch tempting as well as nutritionally well balanced. Fortunately there are lots of nourishing products available today to help achieve this goal. Look for wholegrain breads using rye and wholewheat flours, interesting nut butters and soy cheese with appetizing seasonings as a starting point, add some salad ingredients, and you have a complete protein sandwich.

2 slices bread, black rye, sweet and sour rye, schinkenbrot or wholegrain with sunflower seeds

Filling 1:
cashew nut butter
soy cheese with black pepper
sliced cucumber
sliced avocado
alfalfa sprouts

Filling 2:
almond nut butter
soy cheese with chives
sliced radish
sliced avocado
snow pea (mange-tout) sprouts

Filling 3:
macadamia nut butter
soy cheese with onion and garlic
grated carrot
sliced celery
lentil sprouts

Make sandwich with the bread and filling of your choice, layering as listed. Try sprinkling 1 teaspoon French dressing over the sprouts or spreading the top slice of bread with mayonnaise in place of nut butter. Wrap sandwich up securely for a packed lunch.

FLAT BREAD ROLLS

Flat breads are ideal for sandwiches if you are on a yeast-free diet. Wholewheat flat bread or lavash, which goes back to biblical times, is the most popular. Barley, oat and rye flat breads are also available in leading health food stores. Any one of these fillings makes a tasty healthy snack or packed lunch when rolled up in a sheet of flat bread.

Filling 1:

1/2 cup soy cheese with chili, mashed

1 tablespoon snipped chives

1 tablespoon chopped sun-dried tomatoes

sliced cucumber

sliced mushrooms

Filling 2:

1 2/3 oz (50 g) smoked cheese, grated

1 tablespoon cranberry sauce

1 small stalk celery, sliced

4 cherry tomatoes, quartered

snow pea (mange-tout) sprouts or sprigs of landcress or watercress

Filling 3:

1/2 cup cottage cheese

1 tablespoon sliced scallions (spring onions)

1 tablespoon toasted chopped nuts

1 ring pineapple, chopped

1/4 avocado, sliced

bean sprouts

Mix the first 3 ingredients of the filling together. Place along the middle of a sheet of flat bread and sprinkle the remaining ingredients on top. Sprinkle with salt and pepper if desired. Fold the flat bread over in half, then roll up tightly and serve, or wrap up tightly and pack for a school lunch.

Following page: Spicy berry muffins (left), p.290; Banana honey health bars (front), p.292; Energy bars(right), p.289

Vegetarian Pita Pocket

SERVES 1

Use bought felafel and hummus from a Lebanese take-away or food store for convenience, or make up a batch if you have time.

2 small wholewheat (wholemeal) pita pocket breads

1/4 cup hummus (chick pea dip, page 264)

1/4 cup cottage cheese

4 small felafel (page 49)

diced cucumber

quartered cherry tomatoes

bean sprouts

Make a slit carefully around half the edge of the pita breads. Mix the hummus with the cottage cheese. Slice the felafel. Divide the hummus mixture between the pita breads spooning in carefully. Place the felafel on top, then top with cucumber, tomatoes and bean sprouts. Roll up carefully and serve warm or cold or wrap up carefully for a packed lunch.

Peanut Butter Wholegrain Sandwich

SERVES 1

This sandwich is very popular with young children.

2 slices wholegrain bread

2 teaspoons peanut butter

2 teaspoons tahini

yeast extract for spreading

1 slice cheese

grated carrot

Select multi-grain wholewheat bread if possible. Mix peanut butter with tahini. Spread one slice of bread with yeast extract, spread half peanut butter mixture on top. Cover with cheese and grated carrot. Spread remaining peanut butter mixture on second slice of bread and place on top of sandwich. Cut into quarters and serve or wrap securely for a packed lunch.

LITTLE CHEESE AND VEGETABLE PIES ⛪

MAKES 6–8

Shape these in small, half-moon pies, as the English do with Cornish pasties. These are good for a substantial and nourishing packed lunch, or make them for a picnic.

1 onion, finely chopped

1 tablespoon olive oil

1 cup finely shredded curly or Chinese cabbage

1 cup thinly sliced beans

1 cup grated pumpkin

1 cup grated cheddar cheese

1 teaspoon wholegrain mustard

salt and pepper

1 quantity Wholewheat Wheatgerm Pastry (page 288)

soy drink for glazing

mustard seeds for sprinkling, optional

Gently fry onion in oil until soft. Add cabbage, beans and pumpkin and stir-fry for 3 minutes or until cabbage wilts. Remove from heat, stir in cheese and mustard and salt and pepper to taste.

Roll out pastry thinly and cut out 6 or 8 rounds using a saucer and small sharp pointed knife. Turn rounds over, divide filling evenly between them and brush edges with soy drink. Bring opposite edges up to join over the top of the filling and seal edges. Roll edges over, starting from one end to seal like a Cornish pasty; alternatively pinch a frill along the sealed edges. Place on a baking tray, brush with soy drink and sprinkle with extra mustard seeds if desired. Bake at 400°F (200°C) for 10 minutes, then at 350 F (180°C) for 15-20 minutes until cooked. Eat warm or cold accompanied by a mug of soup.

CURRIED MUSHROOM TRICORNS

MAKES 20

10 sheets filo pastry

1/4 cup (2 oz/60 g) butter or polyunsaturated margarine

Filling:

1 1/2 tablespoons butter or polyunsaturated margarine

1/4 cup thinly sliced scallions (spring onions)

8 oz (250 g) mushrooms, chopped

extra 1 tablespoon butter or margarine

2 tablespoons all-purpose (plain) flour

1 teaspoon curry powder or paste

freshly ground black pepper

1/2 cup (4 fl oz/125 ml) reduced-fat milk or soy drink

parsley sprigs for garnish

Unwrap filo pastry and layer 10 sheets between waxed (greaseproof) paper covered with a clean, cold damp cloth. Melt butter.

Filling: Heat butter in a frying pan and fry scallions and mushrooms over a medium-high heat, stirring occasionally, until mushrooms are soft. Reduce heat, add extra butter and heat until melted. Stir in flour, curry powder and pepper over a medium heat for 1–2 minutes. Stir in milk, then stir continuously until mixture comes to the boil and thickens. Leave to cool.

To finish tricorns: Brush 1 sheet of filo pastry with melted butter, cut in half lengthwise with kitchen scissors. Fold each half in half lengthwise and brush with more butter. Place 1 tablespoon mushroom filling in a lower corner of each strip, then fold filo over the filling to form a triangle. Continue folding the strip of filo over the filling, keeping the triangle shape, until all pastry is wrapped around filling. Continue shaping triangles in this method and place on a greased baking tray. Brush with melted butter and bake at 375°F (190°C) for 20–25 minutes or until puffed and golden.

Serve warm as a snack or for a party dish, garnished with parsley.

Curried mushroom tricorns

VEGETABLE LENTIL PIES

MAKES 16

Good for a packed school lunch or picnic.

1/4 cup sliced shallots

1 clove garlic, crushed

2 teaspoons olive oil

1 cup well-drained, cooked lentils

1 cup grated carrot

1 cup grated zucchini (courgette)

1/2 cup frozen peas or corn, thawed

1 tablespoon toasted sesame seeds

1 tablespoon lemon juice

salt and pepper

1 quantity Wholewheat Wheatgerm Pastry (below)

soy drink for glazing

Gently fry shallots and garlic in oil until soft. Remove from heat, add lentils, vegetables, sesame seeds, lemon juice and salt and pepper to taste.

Roll out pastry and cut out rounds 4 1/2 inch (11 cm) in diameter. Turn rounds over, divide vegetable mixture equally between them and brush edges with soy drink. Fold circles in half, seal edge firmly and roll over or press with a fork to seal, like a turnover.

Place on a baking tray, brush with soy drink and bake at 425 F (220°C) for 15 minutes or until cooked and golden. Eat warm or cold with celery and cucumber sticks and cherry tomatoes. These freeze well.

WHOLEWHEAT WHEATGERM PASTRY

This nourishing delicious pastry is good for home-made small pies, tarts and fruit pies.

2 cups (8 oz/250 g) all-purpose wholewheat (plain wholemeal) flour

2 cups (4 oz/125 g) wheatgerm

3/4 cup (6 oz/185 g) butter or margarine

iced water to mix

Place flour and wheatgerm in the bowl of a food processor. Cut butter into small cubes, add to flour and mix for 20 seconds or until mixture resembles breadcrumbs. Add enough water to bind mixture together, mixing in bursts of 20 seconds to avoid overmixing. Dough should leave sides of processor bowl cleanly when sufficient water has been added.

Knead pastry very lightly on a floured surface, just until smooth underneath. Pat dough into a round cake, wrap in waxed (greaseproof) paper and chill for at least 30 minutes before using. This pastry freezes well.

ENERGY BARS

MAKES 16–20

Make these for the packed lunch bag. Rich in iron and B vitamins as well as a source of complex carbohydrate and complete protein, these are good for athletes and for people who snack on the run.

3 cups (12 oz/375 g) wholewheat (wholemeal) flour

1/4 cup (2/3 oz/20 g) soy flour

1/2 cup (2 1/2 oz/75 g) soy grits

1 cup (3 1/3 oz/100 g) dried soy compound

1 teaspoon double-acting baking powder (2 teaspoons baking powder)

1 cup (6 oz/185 g) brown sugar

1 1/2 cups (6 oz/185 g) dried apricots

1 1/4 cups (6 oz/185 g) seedless raisins

1 cup pepitas or sunflower kernels

1/4 cup (3 oz/90 g) molasses or treacle

3/4 cup (6 fl oz/185 ml) polyunsaturated oil

1 cup (8 fl oz/250 ml) water

Place all dry ingredients in a large mixing bowl and make a 'well' in the middle. Add remaining ingredients and mix well to combine. Pour mixture into a lined and greased shallow tin 12 in x 8 in (30 cm x 20 cm) and bake at 350°F (180°C) for 30–40 minutes, until cooked. Cool in tin then cut into bars. Store in an air-tight container.

DATE SLICE

MAKES 16–20

Serve with wedges of persimmon or apple dipped in lemon juice for a snack, or serve with ice cream or Egg Custard Sauce (page 222) for pudding.

1 1/2 cups (6 oz/185 g) self-raising wholewheat (wholemeal) flour

1/2 cup wheat-based cereal flakes

1 cup (8 oz/250 g) raw sugar

1 1/2 cups (8 oz/250 g) dates

1/2 cup (4 oz/125 g) unsalted butter or margarine, melted

1 egg, beaten

1 teaspoon vanilla extract (essence)

Place flour, cereal flakes and sugar into a mixing bowl. Chop dates, remove any seeds and stir into bowl. Add all remaining ingredients and mix until evenly combined.

Put mixture into a lined, greased shallow tin 12 in x 8 in (30 cm x 20 cm) and spread evenly. Bake at 350°F (180°C) for 25–30 minutes, or until cooked. Cut into slices in tin. Cool until firm then remove and store in an air-tight container.

CHEESE AND CARROT MUFFINS

MAKES 12

1 1/4 cups (5 oz/150 g) wholewheat (wholemeal) flour

1/2 cup (1 1/2 oz/45 g) soy flour

1/2 teaspoon salt

2 teaspoons double-acting baking powder (1 tablespoon baking powder)

1/4 cup (1 oz/30 g) bran, oat, barley or rice

1 onion, finely chopped

3 tablespoons polyunsaturated oil

1 carrot, grated

3 tablespoons chopped parsley

1/2 cup (4 oz/125 g) cottage cheese

1 egg, beaten

1 cup (8 fl oz/250 ml) soy drink or milk

3 teaspoons grated parmesan cheese or 3 tablespoons grated low-fat cheddar cheese

1 tablespoon chopped peanuts

Sift flours, salt and baking powder into a mixing bowl. Stir in bran and make a 'well' in the middle. Fry onion in oil and combine with remaining ingredients. Add to mixing bowl and stir very lightly with a fork for fifteen stirs until combined. Don't worry if not completely mixed. Spoon into 12 greased muffin tins, sprinkle cheese and peanuts on top and bake at 375°F (190°C) for 25–30 minutes until cooked.

SPICY BERRY MUFFINS

MAKES 12

2 cups (8 oz/250 g) wholewheat (wholemeal) flour

1/4 cup (2/3 oz/20 g) soy flour

2 teaspoons double-acting baking powder (1 tablespoon baking powder)

1/2 teaspoon ground cinnamon

1/2 teaspoon ground nutmeg

1 cup blueberries

1 cup small strawberries, quartered

1 egg, beaten

1 cup (8 fl oz/250 ml) buttermilk or milk

4 tablespoons vegetable oil or melted margarine

1/2 cup (4 oz/125 g) honey or raw sugar

Sift all dry ingredients into a mixing bowl. Reserve 36 blueberries, stir remainder with strawberries into dry ingredients and make a 'well' in the middle. Combine all remaining ingredients, pour into middle of bowl and, using a fork, stir lightly fifteen times until combined. Don't worry if flour is not completely mixed in. Spoon mixture into 12 greased muffin tins and top each one with 3 reserved blueberries. Bake at 375°F (190°C) for 25 minutes or until cooked.

Cheese and carrot muffins

BANANA HONEY HEALTH BARS

MAKES 20

This is a delicious moist health bar to make for packed lunches or to snack on at home with some tofu or soy ice cream.

1 cup (4 oz/125 g) all-purpose (plain) rye flour

1 cup (4 oz/125 g) all-purpose (plain) buckwheat flour

1 cup (6 oz/185 g) cornmeal

1/2 cup (1 1/2 oz/45 g) rolled oats

1 teaspoon double-acting baking powder (2 teaspoons baking powder)

1 cup (5 oz/150 g) sun-dried bananas, sliced

1 cup (2 1/2 oz/75 g) shredded coconut

1 cup (6 oz/185 g) brown sugar

1 cup (3 1/3 oz/100 g) soy compound

1 cup (5 oz/150 g) pepitas

1/2 cup (4 fl oz/125 ml) honey

1 cup (8 fl oz/250 ml) polyunsaturated oil

1 cup (8 fl oz/250 ml) water

Place all dry ingredients into a large mixing bowl, mix together and make a 'well' in the middle. Add honey, oil and water and mix until combined. Spread into a lined, greased shallow cake tin, 12 in x 8 in (30 cm x 20 cm) and bake at 375°F (180°C) for 30 minutes. Cool on a wire cooling tray and cut into bars when cold.

OAT BRAN COOKIES

1 cup (3 1/3 oz/100 g) oat bran

1 cup (4 oz/125 g) all-purpose wholewheat (plain wholemeal) flour

1 cup (8 oz/250 g) raw sugar

1/2 cup (1 1/2 oz/45 g) unsweetened (desiccated) coconut

1/2 cup (2 1/2 oz/75 g) sunflower kernels

1/4 cup (1 oz/25 g) wheatgerm

6 oz (175 g) polyunsaturated margarine

2 tablespoons maple syrup (golden syrup)

1/2 teaspoon baking soda (bicarbonate of soda)

2 tablespoons crunchy peanut butter

Place all dry ingredients, except baking soda, into a mixing bowl. Stir to mix and make a 'well' in the middle. Melt margarine with maple syrup, add baking soda and quickly pour into middle of dry ingredients. Add peanut butter and mix well.

Place heaped teaspoons of mixture on greased baking trays, allowing room for spreading, and bake at 300°F (150°C) for 15 minutes until golden brown. Leave a few minutes until firm, then loosen with a palette knife and cool on a wire cooling tray. Store in an air-tight container.

CARROT ROCK CAKES

This is a healthy home-made cake for children to enjoy, best eaten within two days of making.

2 cups (8 oz/250 g) self-raising wholewheat (wholemeal) flour
3 tablespoons soy compound
1/4 teaspoon mixed spice
1/3 cup (3 oz/90 g) polyunsaturated margarine
1 cup grated carrot
1/2 cup (4 oz/125 g) raw sugar
2 tablespoons raisins (or sultanas)
1 cup (8 fl oz/250 ml) water

Sieve flour, soy compound and spice into a mixing bowl. Rub margarine in with the fingertips, or use a food processor. Add remaining ingredients and mix together with a round-bladed knife to form a stiff consistency.

Using 2 teaspoons, place rocky heaps of mixture onto a greased baking tray. Bake at 400°F (200°C) for 10–12 minutes. Cool on a wire cooling tray. Store in an air-tight container.

PUMPKIN SCONES/BISCUITS

MAKES 16–24

How does a scone turn into a biscuit? By being located in the southern states of the USA. Whatever you call them, these pumpkin creations are delicious.

4 cups (1 lb/500 g) self-raising flour
1 cup (3 1/2oz/100 g) soy compound
1 teaspoon salt
1/2 cup (4 oz/125 g) unsalted butter or margarine
2 tablespoons raw sugar
1 cup (8 fl oz/250 ml) mashed butternut pumpkin, well drained
1 1/4 cups (10 fl oz/300 ml) water

Sift flour, soy compound and salt into a large mixing bowl. Add butter and rub in lightly with the fingertips until mixture resembles breadcrumbs. Add sugar, pumpkin and water and mix in with a round-bladed knife until mixture forms a soft dough. Turn out onto a lightly floured board, pat down very lightly to an even thickness then cut out rounds with a scone cutter.

Place on a floured baking tray and bake at 500°F (260°C) for 15–20 minutes until well-risen, golden and cooked.

Serve warm, split and spread with butter and jam or honey. For a less sweet-tasting pumpkin scone, replace sugar with 2 tablespoons chopped parsley and sprinkle grated cheese on top before baking. The latter are delicious with soup.

ORANGE PANCAKES

MAKES 12–16

Try these for a weekend brunch accompanied by seasonal fresh fruit.

1 cup (4 oz/125 g) self-raising flour

2 tablespoons raw sugar

finely grated rind of 2 oranges

2 tablespoons raisins (or sultanas)

4 tablespoons cottage or ricotta cheese

1 large egg

1/4 cup (2 fl oz/60 ml) soy drink

1/4 cup (2 fl oz/60 ml) fresh orange juice

butter or polyunsaturated margarine for frying

raw sugar or maple syrup and orange wedges for serving, optional

Sift flour into a mixing bowl, add sugar, orange rind and raisins and make a 'well' in the middle. Sieve cheese into the bowl, then add egg, soy drink and orange juice. Mix with a wooden spoon to form a thick batter.

Heat just sufficient butter in a frying pan to cover the base, and drop mixture in from the point of a large cooking spoon or old-fashioned tablespoon to form neat rounds. When bubbles appear on the top of the mixture, turn over and cook on other side until puffed and golden and cooked in the middle. Place on a cloth over a cooling tray and wrap up to keep warm until all mixture is cooked.

Serve on individual plates, sprinkled with raw sugar or maple syrup accompanied by orange wedges to squeeze over pancakes.

MANGO BUTTERMILK SMOOTHIE

SERVES 1

You can replace the mango with a large ripe peach or nectarine if mangoes are too expensive or out of season.

1 ripe mango

1 cup (8 fl oz/250 ml) buttermilk

1-2 teaspoons maple syrup or honey

ground nutmeg and wheatgerm for sprinkling, optional

Peel mango and slice fruit off stone into a blender or food processor. Mix mango to a puree, then add buttermilk and mix until thick and frothy. Add maple syrup to taste. Pour into a tall glass and serve, sprinkled with freshly ground nutmeg and wheatgerm if desired.

Mango buttermilk smoothie (left); Banana and berry soy shake (right), p.296

BANANA AND BERRY SOY SHAKE

SERVES 1

This is a nourishing, easy-to-digest liquid snack. Try serving it to teenagers who decline breakfast. You can add extra vanilla to taste.

1 ripe banana

4 large or 8 small ripe strawberries

1 cup (8 fl oz/250 ml) vanilla soy drink

Peel banana, slice thickly into a blender or food processor. Wash and hull strawberries, add to banana and mix to a puree. Add vanilla soy drink and mix until thick and frothy. Pour into a tall glass and serve.

TIGER'S MILK

SERVES 1

Start your day off with this breakfast in a glass, which is good for a tonic diet, as it is rich in B vitamins, iron and calcium. Follow with muesli or wholewheat toast to provide complex carbohydrate for energy.

1/2 cup (4 fl oz/125 ml) freshly squeezed orange juice

1 teaspoon wheatgerm

1 teaspon brewer's yeast

1 teaspoon honey

1 small banana, peeled and sliced

1/2 cup (4 fl oz/125 ml) natural yogurt

Place all ingredients in a blender and mix until well combined. Serve in a tall glass and consume as soon as possible after preparation.

APRICOT LHASI

SERVES 1

This is a good liquid breakfast for those who have to eat and run and it is also a lovely drink to serve with a curry meal.

1/2 cup (4 fl oz/125 ml) apricot nectar

1/2 cup (4 fl oz/125 ml) natural yogurt

pinch of ground nutmeg

honey or maple syrup to taste

ice cubes for serving

Mix apricot nectar, yogurt and nutmeg all together in a blender or food processor. Add honey to taste. Serve poured over ice cubes.

GLOSSARY

Agar Agar
Also called Bengal isinglass, Ceylon moss, Japanese moss, Kanten. A gelatinous product derived from seaweed, used as a setting agent. Available as a powder and as threads. Keeps indefinitely at room temperature. Soak the powder in hot water and stir until dissolved. Soak the threads in cold water until swollen then dissolve in boiling liquid.

Amino Acids
There are 20 different amino acids that the body uses to make the protein it needs. Nine of the amino acids are called essential amino acids because they must be provided by the food we eat. The remaining eleven amino acids can be manufactured by the body. They are combined in different ways to make a 'complete protein'.

Animal Protein
Animal protein is derived from animal sources, such as meat, fish, poultry, eggs, cheese, and milk. It should not be the sole ingredient of a meal because a variety of foods is necessary to provide a good balance of nutrients.

Apple Cider Vinegar
Made from cider apples, apple cider vinegar is not as strong as wine vinegar and can substitute rice vinegar.

Blood Oranges
The blood orange variety has an orange skin with attractive pink fruit inside. It is an excellent source of Vitamin E.

Bocconcini Cheese
Young fresh unripened mozzarella. It is a ball of stretched curd cheese, as large as a big tomato, soft, moist and white. Sold from large jars of natural whey to keep it moist. Originally made from buffalo's milk, it is now made from cow's milk. Use in salad and pizzas.

Buttermilk
Original buttermilk is the liquid that remains after butter is churned from cream. Buttermilk is now made by adding cultures to skim milk. Has a mildly acidic, creamy taste with a thick consistency. Good for digestive problems.

Capers
Capers are the unopened flower buds of the caper bush which is native to the dry barren area of the Mediterranean. The capric acid content of the buds gives them an aromatic taste, which is enhanced by pickling in wine vinegar.

Carob
A caffeine-free chocolate substitute, also called St John's bread. Made from the large pods of a leguminous tree which grows in the Middle East. The pods have a slightly sweet, chocolate taste and are eaten as a snack or used to make a syrup called *dibs*. Available as powder and in blocks.

Chinese Rice Wine Vinegar
A clear, pale yellow, slightly viscous, mild vinegar made from fermented rice.

Complex Carbohydrates
Mixtures of various sugars which are not broken down by enzymes in the small gut. Wholegrain cereals are a rich source. Help lessen the risk of constipation.

Copha
A brand name of a solidified coconut produc. Can be melted and used in confectionery and Asian cookery.

Crème de Marron
A purée made from cooked chestnuts. It is available plain or sweetened and is usually processed and canned.

Crème Fraîche
This originated in France and translates as 'fresh cream' but in cookery the term refers to a mixture of 2 parts fresh cream and 1 part sour cream. A good substitute for yogurt.

Daikon
A Japanese variety of radish. Long, white skinned, and cylindrical in shape. Use it grated, thinly sliced, pickled, and for garnishing food.

Dietary Fiber
Found in grains, cereals, legumes, vegetables, fruit, and nuts. Increases the rate at which food passes through the gut.

Dijon Mustard
A pale yellow, sharp spicy mustard made from ground brown and black mustard seeds and white wine.

Feta Cheese
Also spelled fetta. A white uncooked, soft cheese 'pickled' by maturing in brine, which gives it a salty taste. Traditionally made from ewe's milk and goat's milk. Now made sometimes using goat's milk but more generally from cow's milk. Use in cooking or crumble into salads.

Filo Pastry
Also spelled phyllo. A tissue-thin pastry made from flour, a little oil, salt and water, used for Middle Eastern pastries. Use with care and keep moist while layering. Cover with a dry cloth then top with a damp cloth to prevent drying out. It is usually layered with melted butter or margarine.

Food Chain
The transfer of food energy from the source in plants through various organisms with repetitious eating, e.g. from grains to cattle to meat or from grass to cattle to milk.

Fromage Blanc
A mixture of cottage cheese and natural yogurt, used as a substitute for cream to enrich sauces.

Ghee
Clarified butter or clean butter fat with the milk solids and salt removed. It stands a higher temperature than butter so is used for frying ingredients for a curry and deep frying battered foods and doughs. Popular in Indian cookery.

Goat's Cheese
Also called chevres and zieger. Made from goat's milk. Pure chalk-white and soft textured with a piquant taste. Sold in a herb and oil marinade. Over 400 varieties and shapes from soft and creamy to feta.

Hijiki
An edible seaweed which is a rich source of calcium, iron, and iodine. It is dried and sold in the form of long thin black strings. Soak in water for 15 minutes before use. Add to soup, casseroles, stir-fries, and salads.

Insoluble Fiber
Fiber varies considerably in chemical structure and physical properties. Cellulose from wholegrain cereals and lignins from vegetables are insoluble and affect the excretion of waste products.

Kumara
The New Zealand variety of red-skinned, yellow-fleshed sweet potato. It can be used like potato.

Lacto-Ovo-Vegetarian
A vegetarian who supplements a vegan diet with dairy products and eggs.

Lacto-Vegetarian
A vegetarian who supplements a vegan diet with dairy products.

Lemon Grass
Also called citronella and serai. Grows abundantly in Southeast Asia and is important in Thai cuisine. The grass grows in thick, tall, green layered stalks with a white-yellow or rust-red base. Only the bottom 3 inches (7.5 cm) are used for cooking, the rest may be infused to make tea. Also available preserved in jars or dried.

Marron Glacé
Cooked chestnuts which are glacéed in sugar syrup whole and sold as confectionery.

Mascarpone
A fresh, unripened, smooth textured, triple cream cheese. Made from cream and sometimes lemon juice so is high in fat content. Has a rich, sweet taste with a slight acidic aftertaste. Used mainly in dessert dishes. Sold in tubs.

Mirin
A sweet rice wine, pale yellow and like sherry, used in sauces and stir-fries. Developed in Japan, by brewing rice.

Miso
Also called soy bean paste. A thick paste made from fermented soy beans mixed with a grain and used as a condiment in savory dishes. Light or white miso is made with soy beans and rice; red miso with soy beans and barley; dark miso with soy beans and Japanese koji beans.

Monounsaturated Fats and Oil
These help reduce blood cholesterol levels. Olive oil is a good source of monounsaturated fats and oils.

Mushroom Cups
This is the second size in the growing stage of the cultivated champignon or common variety of mushroom. The baby button is allowed to grow slightly bigger and open up underneath to reveal fresh pink gills before it is harvested for consumption.

Mushroom Flats
This is the last stage in the growing of the champignon mushroom. It is allowed to grow to a large flat round shape as big as a coffee cup saucer before harvesting.

Nori
An edible seaweed. Ranges from dark green to dull purple. A rich source of calcium, iron, and iodine in the Asian diet. Sold in packs of flat sheets and used for sushi rolls or shredded and added to soups, noodles, and rice dishes.

Orange Flower Water
An extraction from orange blossoms by steam distillation, produced in the Middle East. A clear liquid, sometimes with a light orange shade. Used in Turkish delight, sorbet, syrup, and pastries.

Ovo-Vegetarian
A vegetarian who supplements a vegan diet with eggs.

Oyster Mushrooms
Also called Abalone mushroom, Chinese mushroom, and Hiratake. A pale silvery mushroom with stems at one side due to a clustered growing pattern. It tastes like oysters! They may be sliced and used in stir-fries.

Palm Sugar
A crumbly red-brown sugar extracted from a tropical palm tree, known as a sugar or sao palm. Tastes like molasses or treacle. Sold in compressed blocks or cone shapes.

Plant Protein
Plant protein is available in and provided by legumes, grains, nuts, vegetables, and fruits.

Polyunsaturated Fats and Oils
Polyunsaturated fats and oils include sunflower, safflower, corn and soybean oils, and margarines made from these oils. They help reduce blood cholesterol levels.

Protein
Protein is an important nutrient that is necessary in the body for tissue growth and development, maintenance and repair of damaged cells, such as skin, muscle and bone. Protein also participates in a number of regulatory functions such as the composition of the blood and the production of enzymes.

Quark
A clear white, variation of skim milk unsalted cottage cheese which has cream blended into it, making it 10% fat. A low-fat alternative to cream cheese.

Quick-cooking Barley
The barley grain is hulled and steamed then dried before it is marketed for human consumption. This process allows

the barley grain to cook much quicker and is usually indicated on the packaging.

Ricotta Cheese
A high moisture fresh, soft delicate textured, white cheese made from the whey of milk. Traditionally made in Italy from sheep's milk or cow's milk. It is characterized by the basketweave pattern on the cheese and is popular in cheesecakes, other desserts, and savory dishes.

Rose Water
An essence distilled from fragrant rose petals. Used in sweet dishes, milk dishes, and Turkish delight.

Ruby Grapefruit
Also called Texan pink grapefruit. A variety of pink fleshed grapefruit with a yellow skin which is tinged with pink. A little sweeter than yellow fleshed grapefruit.

Smoked Cheese
Smoked cheeses are orange-brown with a shiny caramel shaded rind and often shaped like a large sausage. They have a smoky taste.

Soluble Fiber
Fiber varies considerably in chemical structure and physical properties, eg pectin from fruit and guar gum from certain beans are soluble and are linked with the reduction of blood cholesterol and the rate of glucose absorption.

Sorbet
A frozen water ice made from water and fruit juice or fruit purée. Home-made sorbet made without the use of an ice cream churn also have a whisked egg white folded into the mixture.

Sorrel
Also called Dock and French sorrel. A green vegetable, sometimes classified as a herb. Resembles spinach in appearance. Turns yellow-green when cooked and has a slightly sour lemony taste. Easy to grow from seed. Popular in soup, sauces and salads.

Soy Cheese
A soft textured cheese made from soy beans.

Soy Compound
The term used to describe dehydrated soy drink. It can be used as a substitute for dried milk powder in vegan recipes.

Soy Drink
Also known as soy milk, it is available in many interesting varieties. See Introduction.

Soy Grits
Soy beans crushed and broken into small particles. Useful to add to muesli and home-baked breads, cookies, and crumble toppings.

Sun-dried Bananas
Peeled bananas which are dried in the sun and are ideal for snacks and baked goods.

Sun-dried Red Peppers
Red bell peppers (capsicum) which are dried in the sun and preserved in oil.

Sun-dried Tomatoes
Ripe tomatoes dried in the sun and preserved in oil.

Tabasco Sauce
A thin pungently hot red sauce made from the red chili peppers from the Tabasco region of Mexico. Also contains vinegar and salt. Use with caution, drop by drop!

Tahini
Also called sesame paste. A fawn, oily paste made from toasted, ground sesame seeds. It has a nutty taste. Used in Asian and Middle Eastern cooking, dips, and sauces. It can be used to substitute peanut butter in sandwiches.

Tamari
A sauce made from soy beans. Looks like a thick soy sauce. Used as a seasoning and as a substitute for salt in Asian cooking. Served with sushi. Useful in a gluten free diet.

Tamarind Sauce
A brown fruity sauce. The tamarind is a brown pulpy fruit enclosed inbrown rectangular pod with a thin shell.

Tempeh
A yellow-brown cake of compressed soy beans injected with a culture which creates fermentation. Has a crumbly texture and a definite acrid taste. Good in curries or marinated and added to stir-fries.

Tofu
Also called bean curd. A creamy white, compressed spongy cake made from soy beans. See Introduction.

Umeboshi Plums
A pickled, salted sour plum popular in Japanese cuisine. Sold in vacuum-sealed plastic bags. Beneficial to digestion.

Vegan
A vegetarian who obtains protein from plant sources only and does not eat dairy produce or eggs.

Vegetable Crudités
Small crisp pieces of raw or blanched vegetables used for snacking on and for dipping into dips.

Vegetable Protein
Vegetable protein is derived from plant sources such as vegetables, legumes, grains, and nuts.

Warrigal Greens
Also called Botany Bay spinach. A green vegetable native to Australia; similar to spinach.

Yeast Extract
A sticky dark brown paste made by treating fresh brewer's yeast with acid. A good source of the B group of vitamins. Used to season soups and casseroles in a vegetarian diet.

Index

ACKNOWLEDGMENTS

I would like to thank Ann Bollard and Lee Gold for their willing hard work and cheerful enthusiasm in assisting with the testing of these vegetarian recipes. Another big thank you goes to Fiona Janes for her care and calmness in coping with an enormous typing task. Thank you also to Carolyn Kelly for advice and thorough checking of nutritional information. Thank you to good supportive friends Sybil and Joan for helping me with the detailed proof reading. I must also include Mary Harris, who put a lot of artistic energy as well as hard work into the food styling of the lovely photographs, and Andrew Elton, who added his technical and creative talents in taking the superb shots. Thank you all and well done team! Thanks also to Redlemans Fabrics, Woollahra.

Finally a big thank you to my daughter Natasha who started this whole project off by becoming a vegetarian, and was an enormous motivating spirit of inspiration and encouragement, as well as a patient and willing chief taster.